5 (0/c)
26. SEP. 1985
-4. APR. 1989
C11-94
03. MAR 95
O11 . 6.8.9
19 OCT 198
JUL 95
2 (0/c2)
KRON WA
28.7.87
1987
5/06
06
GW00393183

YOUNG, ANDREW 1885-1971
THE POETICAL WORKS OF ANDREW
YOUNG.
821.912 YOU 01-518753
30130 135276136

THE POETICAL WORKS OF ANDREW YOUNG

The POETICAL WORKS *of* ANDREW YOUNG

Edited and with an Introduction and Notes by

EDWARD LOWBURY

and

ALISON YOUNG

Wood engravings by Joan Hassall

SECKER & WARBURG
LONDON

First published in England 1985 by
Martin Secker & Warburg Limited
54 Poland Street, London W1V 3DP

Poems copyright ©the Estate of the late Andrew Young 1985
Introduction and Notes copyright ©Edward Lowbury and Alison Young

British Library Cataloguing in Publication Data

Young, Andrew, *1885–1971*
The poetical works of Andrew Young.
I. Title II. Lowbury, Edward
III. Young, Alison
821′.912 PR6047.O46

ISBN 0-436-26884-1
ISBN 0-436-26885-X Pbk

SUBSIDISED BY THE
Arts Council
OF GREAT BRITAIN

ESSEX COUNTY LIBRARY

Printed in Great Britain by
Redwood Burn Ltd, Trowbridge

821.912 EW73781

CONTENTS

SECTION 2: SELECTED EARLIER POEMS (1910–1931)

SECTION 3: UNPUBLISHED AND OTHER MISCELLANEOUS SHORT POEMS

SECTION 4: LONGER POEMS AND VERSE PLAYS

INTRODUCTION

Andrew Young is an exceptional figure among poets of the twentieth century. He was nearly fifty before his highly individual style reached its full development, but the poems of that rather belated maturity brought him an acclaim which has continued undiminished for fifty years, through changes of fashion that dislodged many seemingly established reputations. His work has appealed strongly both to general readers and to literary specialists, including the avant-garde.

Young's late maturation brought with it some practical problems. In 1936, replying to a request from Rupert Hart-Davis for some of his early books of poems, he wrote:

> 'When I tell you that only last month I rescued a copy of *The New Shepherd* from a friend's library and proudly carried it home and put it in the domestic boiler, you will understand with how very bad grace I give you these books. So there is no need for you to write and thank me for them.'

The New Shepherd was the last of a series of eight volumes published in small editions between 1910 and 1931 which, by 1936, Young considered immature and regarded as an unpublished 'quarry' – his own word – from which he could extract passages and a few whole poems for use in his new books. The first of the new books was *Winter Harvest* (1933); it was his first book from a major publisher, the Nonesuch Press, and the first in which his name appeared as Andrew Young, not A. J. Young as in earlier volumes. He was cultivating a new persona, trying to make a clean break with his literary past. So it is not surprising that only the contents of the books from *Winter Harvest* onwards were admitted to *Collected Poems* (1950), which Young himself edited. That collection contained what he came to regard as his 'canon' of short poems, and also the play *Nicodemus* (1937); it had attractive wood-engravings by Joan Hassall, and the poems were arranged in an order related to the seasons but unrelated to time of composition or earlier publication.

Young was an avid reviser and a judicious re-user of his early poems, many of which were altered, slightly or radically, and issued as new poems in the books of his canon. The editor of a new collected edition is thus faced with some unusual problems of choice and chronology. *Collected Poems* (1960), edited by Leonard Clark, contained the whole of the 1950 edition, to which the editor added some previously uncollected poems and some from the early books. This collection was arranged in approximately chronological order. In 1974, three years after the poet's death, appeared *Complete Poems*, edited again by Leonard Clark, who was Young's literary executor until 1979. It consisted of a reprint of *Collected Poems* (1960), to which were added *Out of the World and Back* (1958) and a section containing most of the remaining short poems from early books and manuscripts.

We have adopted a somewhat different plan in preparing this edition. Of the poems that appeared in *Complete Poems* (1974) but not in Young's 'canon' we have included a selection showing, we think, sufficient merit to be placed beside the mature poems as examples of his earlier manner. We include also three substantial works reprinted after sixty years, and a few previously unpublished short poems. Though inferior to the mature work, Young's early writings throw light on the stages of his development.

Section 1, sub-titled *Collected Short Poems 1933–1947*, is a reprint of the short poems of the canon, reverting to the order in which Young had arranged them in their original volumes. That arrangement is often very apt, as when *Twilight*, a retrospective, self-appraising poem, is placed at the end of his last book of short poems, *The Green Man*, as a sort of epilogue. The text we have used is that of *Collected Poems* (1950), the most recent collected edition compiled by the poet himself. The sources of revised and reprinted poems are given in the Notes.

The short poems of the early books are of uneven quality, and those which Young salvaged were usually revised to fit the specifications of his mature style. The poems we have chosen and placed in Section 2 (*Selected Earlier Poems 1910–1931*) seem to us to have stood up reasonably well to critical scrutiny, fifty or more years after they were written. They include earlier versions of a few poems that appear in Section 1 where the two versions are sufficiently different to be regarded as separate poems. To have included all the early poems would, in our opinion, have diluted and seriously diminished the poetic impact of this collection; Andrew Young would certainly have been dismayed to see all his early indiscretions resuscitated. For those making an academic study of Young's work, most of the early short poems can be found in the edition of 1974 (which was criticised by some for including too much of the immature writing). We have placed the selection of earlier short poems after the mature ones, so that a reader's first impression on opening the book will be that of Young's fully developed personal style.

Several poems from manuscript books in the handwriting of Janet Young, the poet's wife, were printed in *The Bird-Cage* (1926). From the remainder, which Young discarded but which appeared in *Complete Poems* (1974), we have selected three for inclusion in Section 3 (*Unpublished and Other Miscellaneous Short Poems*). Also in this section are six poems from Young's letters and typescripts which are published here for the first time, and five previously uncollected poems. The subject of one of the unpublished poems, *The Bleeding Nun*, may surprise readers unfamiliar with Young's interest in ghosts and the macabre. Two 'prose poems', as Young called them, from *The New Poly-Olbion* (1967), the last book published during his life, are included as examples in this genre: they are highly condensed versions of essays he had previously published in *A Prospect of Britain* (1956).

Section 4 (*Longer Poems and Verse Plays*) contains two outstanding works of Young's maturity, the play *Nicodemus: A Mystery* (1937), and the mystical poem *Out of the World and Back* (1958). The latter work is subtitled 'Two Poems' (*Into Hades* and *A Traveller in Time*), but the two are halves of a single creative adventure. This section also contains two early verse plays, *The Adversary* and *Rizpah*, published together in 1923 and reprinted here for the first time, and *Memorial Verses* (1918), a long elegy for a friend, Cecil Barclay Simpson, killed in France. The quality of *Memorial Verses* is uneven, but the poem contains some very impressive writing in a manner Young later abandoned. It seemed to us necessary to reprint it unabridged as it has not previously appeared in a collected edition and could not be cut down without serious damage to its content. *Memorial Verses*, incidentally, show Young as a First World War poet, a role in which he is almost entirely unknown. Also included in this section are excerpts from an unpublished play for children, *The Sirens*, written during 1939 and 1940. Two immature early plays, *Saul and the Asses* and *Jephthah*, are not printed here, but a chorus from *Jephthah*, which was published by Young in his book *Boaz and Ruth* (1920), is included in Section 2. The items in Section 4 show the pattern of Young's development in chronological sequence over a period of forty years, and the book ends, as it begins, with work of his maturity.

A glance at Andrew Young's life, particularly the early life, reveals a number of unusual features, some of which may have contributed to the late emergence of his poetic maturity: *Winter Harvest* did not appear until he was forty-eight. He was born at Elgin on April 29th, 1885, the youngest of four children, one of whom died in infancy; a plaque commemorating his birth at the Highland Railway Station, where his father was stationmaster, has recently been unveiled. His sister Margaret used to say there was a family relationship with Carolina, Lady Nairne, who wrote 'Charlie is my Darling' and other popular Jacobite songs, though Young would say only that he 'came from a long line of illiterate shepherds'. He spent his childhood in Edinburgh, where his father rose to become secretary to a well-known insurance company. He went to the Royal High School and was fond of recalling that he, like Sir Walter Scott, had played truant, and that he did so 'on principle'. During his illicit wanderings in the country he discovered an interest in wild flowers and a capacity for mystical experience. Another interest which developed at an early age was in problems of crime and detection, real and fictional. At the University of Edinburgh he studied for an arts degree, hoping to take up the law and become a barrister. He took his degree in 1907. A university prize enabled him – with additional help from his father – to spend some time in Paris, studying works of art and church architecture. This was the time of his friendship with the Beardsleyan artist and poet W. W. Peploe, who published poems in English and French, and with his brother, the more famous artist S. J. Peploe; both brothers were much at home in France. In Paris Young became, as he put it forty years later in *Into Hades*, 'a St John the Baptist in the Latin Quarter', arming himself against temptations of the flesh with mystical intuitions and Platonic idealism. He seems to have been fascinated by John the Baptist, for he attended five performances of Richard Strauss's *Salome* when it was first shown in Paris.

In 1907 his elder brother David, who had gone two years before to work in Singapore as a doctor, disappeared without trace, having (as a recent study of Singapore newspapers reveals) been involved in some irregularities on the stock market. The police had a warrant for his arrest in this connection, and 'other serious matters' were under investigation. He was sacked by his senior medical partner, apparently because of his involvement when a pharmacist was convicted for illegal supply of morphine to a patient. Andrew seems to have suffered amnesia about events in the year of his brother's disappearance; he believed he had spent five years at the University when in fact he had spent four. This amnesia, and his surprising inability to remember what David looked like, suggest that he experienced, at this time, a severe mental trauma. In his memory he demoted David from his position as first-born, believing, in later life, that his sister Margaret was born first. He hardly ever mentioned David. In the long poem *Out of the World and Back* his guide in the afterlife is his dead brother – not David, as one might expect, but William, who died at the age of eight months, before Andrew was born. If, as we may assume, Andrew knew something of David's misdeeds, the innocent William must have seemed to him a more appropriate guide.

It was probably as a direct consequence of the tragedy of David that Andrew acceded to the wishes of his father – a pillar of the Presbyterian Church – and entered a theological college (New College, Edinburgh) in 1908; he gave up the idea of becoming a barrister. At New College he created quite a stir with his first book of poems, *Songs of Night*, which his father paid sixteen pounds to have published. A fellow student sharing his interest in poetry was John Baillie, who became a well-known theologian and a lifelong friend. In 1914 Young was appointed Minister in the village of Temple, Midlothian, fulfilling in the pulpit some of his potentialities for the bar. In the same year he married Janet Green, who had been one of the most brilliant students of her year at the University of Glasgow, graduating with first-class honours in French, German and English. When Young met her she was a lecturer in English at a teachers' training college in Glasgow. Her gentle, sympathetic personality, her taste and her judgment helped and supported Young for more than fifty years.

During the First World War he served as Superintendent at an army rest-camp near Boulogne. The death of his best friend, Cecil Barclay Simpson, at the front, and the hardship and suffering that he saw affected him deeply; he became strongly drawn towards pacifism. In 1920 he moved south with his wife and five-year-old son Anthony to be Minister of the Presbyterian Church at Hove, where in 1922 his daughter Alison was born. At the Sussex Poetry Society and in London he met a number of poets, including John Freeman and Viola Meynell, who became his close friends. He was also in touch with the bookseller and publisher J. G. Wilson, whom he had met before the war in Glasgow; Wilson, who was now in London at Bumpus's bookshop, brought out seven books by Young between 1920 and 1931. Viola Meynell helped to bring his work to the notice of a wider circle of readers by enthusiastic reviews of *The Bird-Cage, The Cuckoo Clock* and *The New Shepherd*, and by introducing him to her brother, Francis Meynell, Director of the Nonesuch Press, who launched Young's next book of poems. That book, *Winter Harvest*, had good reviews and sold out very quickly. Viola Meynell also introduced Young to Rupert Hart-Davis, then a director of Jonathan Cape, his publisher from 1935 until 1950. *Nicodemus* (1937), a play for performance in church or cathedral, was written in the wake of Eliot's *Murder in the Cathedral* at the time when religious drama was enjoying some popularity. It had considerable success, with over fifty performances, and was broadcast in this country and in Sweden.

In 1939, after much mental conflict and while his father (aged ninety-three) was still alive, Young took a step he had been contemplating for years and applied for admission to the Anglican Ministry. He became Vicar in the small country parish of Stonegate, Sussex, a position he held for eighteen years. Here, as in Hove, he was a popular preacher, although frequent references to death in his sermons worried a few people. While at Stonegate he published his last book of short poems, and the long mystical poem *Into Hades* (1952), which appeared much revised with its sequel in *Out of the World and Back* (1958); these long poems, reflecting his obsession with death, had been Young's main preoccupation for many years. Through life he had an unquestioning faith in personal survival after death, and it seemed sometimes that the eternal world had greater reality for him than the temporal. It is perhaps symbolic that the only flowers he allowed in his house were everlastings. But he had a passion for discovering rare wild flowers in their natural habitats, and travelled all over the British Isles in search of them; these travels, and his extensive reading, provided material for the lively and popular prose books, *A Prospect of Flowers* (1945), *A Retrospect of Flowers* (1950) and *A Prospect of Britain* (1956). He received several honours, including an Hon. LL.D (1951) from the University of Edinburgh and the Queen's Gold Medal for Poetry (1952). In 1957 Rupert Hart-Davis, who now had his own publishing house, with Young as one of his authors, brought out *Andrew Young: Prospect of a Poet*, a book of tributes edited by Leonard Clark. The contributors included

Young's two closest friends of the Stonegate years, John Arlott, with whom he shared an interest in poetry, crime and sport, and the poet Christopher Hassall.

Young retired from his ministry at Stonegate in 1959, and moved with his wife to the village of Yapton, near Chichester; he was already a canon of Chichester Cathedral. His circle of literary friends there included Leslie Norris, Christopher Fry and Ted Walker. Further prose books – *The Poet and the Landscape* (1962) and *The New Poly-Olbion* (1967) – appeared in these later years, and *The Poetic Jesus* (1972) was published shortly after his death on November 25th, 1971.

Andrew Young had a strong personality, with a teasing wit and humour that emerges in many of his poems as it did in his life. It is this quality that gives some of his death-haunted writing an almost light-hearted air. In spite of his preoccupation with death he was not a morose person, and the image that he projects in his poetry is not morbid. Those who knew him will recall his fine but distinctive appearance, strongly built, with a head that someone likened to that of a benign Roman emperor, the profile aquiline, the eyes bright blue. His daughter, when small, used to think that a white plaster cast of the mask of Dante which hung in his study was her father's face. Though courteous, especially to strangers, he wasted few words in chatter, and would often sound cross or querulous; then suddenly – with a shrug of the shoulders and a broad smile or mocking chuckle – he would dispel the gloom. In spite of his lack of small talk and almost pathological reserve, he was loved and admired by his parishioners and friends. Those who knew him came to see, through his protective armour of silence, a compassionate warmth within.

As a student Andrew Young came under the spell of Swinburne and the art and poetry of the Aesthetic and Decadent movements. These influences are shown in *Songs of Night*, which is full of an atmosphere of sin, wine, blood, roses and wounds, with a mixture of religious and sensual imagery. The voice of Swinburne is apparent in the dancing rhythms and in the virtual equation of pleasure with pain in, for example:

> Art thou drunk with the strong
> Glad wine-cup's song,
> Or with bitter delight of luxurious pain?

There are few hints in the book of Young's future style, though his strong visual imagination and descriptive powers are already apparent in such lines as the following (from *Landscape*):

> A grey hawk at a dizzy height
> Thrills with its sharp suspended flight,
> And like a soft, insidious kiss
> The snakes within the heather hiss.

Memorial Verses develop this descriptive vein further, with overtones of Dante and Shelley as well as Swinburne.

From 1920 onwards Young's books showed his emancipation from Swinburne and the Decadents, and his gradual adoption of a style of writing that could be described as 'Georgian'. But it was at this time that his personal voice started to emerge, at first in individual images, as in *Autumn* (*The Death of Eli*, 1921):

> where the catkins swung their tails
> Like caterpillars on the trees

and later in whole poems, like *The Stars* (*Thirty-One Poems*, 1922) and *Snow* (*The Bird-Cage*, 1926), both of which were reprinted without alteration in books of the canon. His writing showed affinities with that of Robert Frost and Edward Thomas, two poets whose work appealed to Young more than that of most contemporaries except Hardy, whose poetry he read and re-read; Hardy's preoccupation with death struck a responsive chord with Young.

The poems of his maturity express a narrower range of experiences and emotions than those which inspired many of his earlier poems: in particular, human figures become scarce, and appear more often as figures in a landscape, or even as ghosts, than as individuals. He was on safer ground, both as a person and as a poet, when accompanied by plants, animals and mountains, than in human company. But this restricted scope, more true to his own character, gave strength to the poetry. He now cultivated a greater terseness of utterance and an avoidance of 'dead words' which was also consistent with his character and speech. He sharpened the clarity and precision of his language, achieving a simplicity that was often deceptive, for in most of these splendid poems there are subtle and startling insights, conceits, flashes of wit and paradoxes; as when, seeing the wind blow clothes which a shepherd's wife had hung out to dry, he observes:

She little knows
That ghosts are trying on her children's clothes

or when, marvelling at God's contemplation of His created world, he promises that he

will learn to shirk
No idleness that I may share your work.

Sometimes there is a reminder of Nature's cruelties, as in the ironic note on the cuckoo (a bird that haunted many of his poems):

The cuckoos in a few well-chosen words
Tell they give Easter eggs to the small birds.

Young's obsession with death was undoubtedly linked with an avidity for the afterlife, and in *Out of the World and Back* he stole a march on time, taking himself on a strange mental journey that began with his own funeral. The poem opens with the unexpected line, 'One midnight in the Paris Underground', but the blank verse gradually assumes a disembodied air, with interrogatives on almost every page that seem to emphasize the dreamlike sense of timeless wandering. There are numerous references to the temporal world, which he can see and remember but with which he cannot communicate. The language is often like that of the short poems, with similar images and paradoxes:

Morning was late that day,
Delayed by thick fog. Trees, their tops out of sight,
Scattered irregular rain: dew-hoary cobwebs
Drooped with false geometry.

Sometimes the paradoxes remind one of those of the great mystics – St John of the Cross, Richard Rolle and others – whom he admired. *Out of the World and Back*, Young's final poetic offering, was described, in an extensive *Times Literary Supplement* review, as 'the only impressive long poem which has appeared in the English language since Mr Eliot's *Four Quartets*'.

In 1985, the centenary of his birth, it is natural to wonder how Young's work will be regarded in fifty or a hundred years' time. Richard Church had no doubt of its survival: *Immortal Verse* was the title of a review in which he wrote, 'I have enjoyed it for forty years as I have enjoyed the poetry of W. H. Davies, De la Mare, Hardy and Graves, because I understand it, feel its music run along my nerves, kindling me to a passionate delight.' C. S. Lewis saw Young as 'a modern Marvell and a modern marvel'. In describing Young's work as 'poetry of diamond lucidity' Wilfrid Gibson was, perhaps, forgetting or disregarding inner storms, complexities and tensions that prompted Clifford Dyment to observe, 'He does not write about the countryside because it is a nice subject for his pen; he writes because it is an ugly subject, harsh and cruel and beautiful by turns, thus mirroring the infinite moods of men.' Another admirer, Geoffrey Grigson, recognized 'a slow turmoil' in the early as well as in the late poems: 'he is, in fact, most uncomfortably aware of negation, farce, blankness, pain, end and hopelessness.' Such awareness places Young in a different category from that of the 'simple nature poet' that he is often assumed to be, and gives his work an extra dimension. The complexity of Young's character is discussed, with many quotations from his letters, by the Editors in a biographical and critical book on Andrew Young which they are preparing.

Dr Roger Sell of the University of Åbo, Finland, has already published a long and perceptive monograph on Young's work (see footnote p. 315) – an instance of the seriousness with which it is now being taken by scholars. He points out that the best of it belongs to the English tradition in general and to twentieth-century poetry in particular, and adds, 'In the long perspective of history Young may well turn out to be central in certain ways that, say, Eliot, Pound and Auden were not.' Though his fame does not rank with theirs, Andrew Young's poems have perhaps given pleasure to a wider range of people, and have always had a special appeal for the young, not least for children. As he once said to a distinguished elderly poet whose pontifications had irritated him, 'at least young people *read* me'. Fifty years later his poems still appeal to those who were young then, as they do to the young of our own time.

ACKNOWLEDGMENTS

The Editors wish to thank the following for access to manuscripts of previously unpublished poems and letters: Henry W. and Albert A. Berg Collection, The New York Public Library: Astor, Lenox and Tilden Foundations; Mr S. M. Simpson of The National Library of Scotland; Mr John Arlott, Mr Robin Haines, Sir Rupert Hart-Davis and Mr R. Lancelyn Green. They also thank Rev. John Yates for drawing their attention to a poem on the dust-cover of *The Bird-Cage*; Dr Roger Sell, Sir Rupert Hart-Davis, Professor J. G. Davies and Dr B. S. Benedikz for valuable suggestions and information; Mr Nigel Nicolson for permission to quote in the *Notes* two lines by Victoria Sackville-West; and the Literary Trustees of Walter de la Mare and The Society of Authors for permission to quote, also in the *Notes*, two lines by Walter de la Mare. They are particularly grateful to Miss Joan Hassall for generously allowing the reproduction of wood engravings illustrating some of the poems.

Section 1

Collected Short Poems (1933–1947)

Winter Harvest (1933)

Killed by a Hawk

I stir them with my stick,
   These trembling feathers left behind
To show a hawk was sick,
   No more to fly except on the loose wind.

How beautiful they are
   Scattered by death yet speaking of
Quick flight and precious care
   Of those great gems, the nest-eggs, warm with love.

Feathers without a bird!
   As though the bird had flown away
From its own feathers, fired
   By strange desire for some immortal spray.

In December

I watch the dung-cart stumble by
   Leading the harvest to the fields,
That from cow-byre and stall and sty
   The farmstead in the winter yields.

Like shocks in a reaped field of rye
  The small black heaps of lively dung
Sprinkled in the grass-meadow lie
  Licking the air with smoky tongue.

This is Earth's food that man piles up
  And with his fork will thrust on her,
And Earth will lie and slowly sup
  With her moist mouth through half the year.

The Green Woodpecker

Whether that popinjay
  Screamed now at me or at his mate
I could not rightly say,
  Not knowing was it love or was it hate.

I hoped it was not love
  But hate that roused that gaudy bird;
For earth I love enough
  To crave of her at least an angry word.

Winter Morning

All is so still;
The hill a picture of a hill
With silver kine that glimmer
Now whiter and now dimmer
Through the fog's monochrome,
Painted by Cotman or Old Crome.

Pale in the sky
The winter sun shows a round eye,
That darkens and still brightens;
And all the landscape lightens
Till on the melting meadows
The trees are seen with hard white shadows.

Though in the balk
Ice doubles every lump of chalk
And the frost creeps across
The matted leaves in silver moss,
Here where the grass is dank
The sun weeps on this brightening bank.

The Old Tree

The wood shakes in the breeze
  Lifting its antlered heads;
Green leaf nor brown one sees
  But the rain's glassy beads.

One tree-trunk in the wood
  No tangled head uprears,
A stump of soft touchwood
  Dead to all hopes and fears.

Even the round-faced owl
  That shakes out his long hooting
With the moon cheek-a-jowl
  Could claw there no safe footing.

Riddled by worms' small shot,
  Empty of all desire,
It smoulders in its rot,
  A pillar of damp fire.

The Dead Bird

Ah, that was but the wind
Your soft down stirred,
O bird, lying with sidelong head;
These open eyes are blind,
I cannot frighten you away;
You are so very dead
I almost say
'You are not a dead *bird*.'

Loch Luichart

Slioch and Sgurr Mor
Hang in the air in a white chastity
Of cloud and February snow
That less to earth they seem to owe
Than to the pale blue cloud-drift or
The deep blue sky.

Though high and far they stand,
Their shadows over leagues of forest come,
Here, to a purer beauty thinned
In this true mirror, now the wind,
That held it with a shaking hand,
Droops still and dumb.

As I push from the shore
And drift (beneath that buzzard) I climb now
These silver hills for miles and miles,
Breaking hard rock to gentle smiles
With the slow motion of my prow
And dripping oar.

The Forest of Dean

'Now here you could not lose your way,
Although you lost it', seemed to say
Each path that ran to left or right
Through narrowing distance out of sight.

'Not here, not here', whistled a thrush
And 'Never, never', sighed a thorn-bush;
Primroses looked me in the face
With, 'O too lovely is this place'.

A larch-bough waved a loose green beard
And 'Never, never', still I heard;
'Wayfarer, seek no more your track,
It lies each side and front and back'.

March Hares

I made myself as a tree,
No withered leaf twirling on me;
No, not a bird that stirred my boughs,
As looking out from wizard brows
I watched those lithe and lovely forms
That raised the leaves in storms.

I watched them leap and run,
Their bodies hollowed in the sun
To thin transparency,
That I could clearly see
The shallow colour of their blood
Joyous in love's full flood.

I was content enough,
Watching that serious game of love,
That happy hunting in the wood
Where the pursuer was the more pursued,
To stand in breathless hush
With no more life myself than tree or bush.

The Beech

Strength leaves the hand I lay on this beech-bole
So great-girthed, old and high;
Its sprawling arms like iron serpents roll
Between me and the sky.

One elbow on the sloping earth it leans,
That steeply falls beneath,
As though resting a century it means
To take a moment's breath.

Its long thin buds in glistering varnish dipt
Are swinging up and down,
While one young beech that winter left unstript
Still wears its withered crown.

At least gust of the wind the great tree heaves
From heavy twigs to groin;
The wind sighs as it rakes among dead leaves
For some lost key or coin.

And my blood shivers as away it sweeps
   Rustling the leaves that cling
Too late to that young withered beech that keeps
   Its autumn in the spring.

On the Pilgrims' Road

That I had hit the Road
   I partly knew
From a great Roman snail
   And sombre yew;
But that my steps went from
   And not towards
The shrine of good St Thomas,
   I thought of afterwards.

So I adored today
   No, not his ghost,
But the saints in Westwell window,
   And her the most
Who knelt there with no head
   But was so very
Adorable a saint
   In dress of crushed strawberry.

In Romsey Abbey

'Lady, the angel-heads
   That cusp your canopy
Are looking the other way;
   Why should not I
Stoop down and kiss your lips
   Or even your brow?
The little hound at your feet
   Would not bark Bow-wow.'

'Stranger, from the earth
    They dug me to sleep thus
In this organ-shaken church
    Like Eutychus;
Look! Time's clumsy fingers
    Broke my neck-bone;
I think that your lips too
    Would turn to stone.'

The Sheaf

I'd often seen before
That sheaf of corn hung from the bough –
Strange in a wood a sheaf of corn
Though by the winds half torn
And thrashed by rain to empty straw.
And then today I saw
A small pink twitching snout
And eyes like black beads sewn in fur
Peep from a hole in doubt,
And heard on dry leaves go tat-tat
The stiff tail of the other rat.
And now as the short day grows dim
And here and there farms in the dark
Turn to a spark,
I on my stumbling way think how
With indistinguishable limb
And tight tail round each other's head
They'll make tonight one ball in bed,
Those long-tailed lovers who have come
To share the pheasants' harvest-home.

The Star

A white mist swathed the valley;
    Each huge uncertain tree
Came looming through the darkness
    An island in a sea;

But when I climbed to Hawkley
The stars held all the night,
Spangles and glittering ouches
And clouds of hollow light.

I thought they were blest spirits
Borne upward on a wind
And the white mist the cerements
That they had left behind;
And you, your body sleeping,
In their bright numbers moved
And with raised face I questioned,
Which is my well-beloved?

The Lane

Years and years and man's thoughtful foot,
Drip and guttering rains and mute
Shrinkage of snows, and shaggy-hoofed
Horse have sunk this lane tree-roofed
Now patched with blossoming elder,
Wayfaring-tree and guelder;
Lane that eases the sharp-scarped hill
Winding the slope with leisurely will.

Foot of Briton, formal Roman,
Saxon and Dane and Sussex yeoman
Have delved it deep as river-bed,
Till I walk wading to my head
In air so close and hot
And by the wind forgot,
It seems to me that in this place
The earth is breathing on my face.

Here I loiter a lost hour,
Listen to bird, look on a flower.
What will be left when I am gone?
A trodden root, a loosened stone

And by the blackthorn caught
Some gossamery thought
Of thankfulness to those dead bones
That knit hills closer than loose stones.

In Moonlight

We sat where boughs waved on the ground
But made no sound;
'They cannot shake me off,'
Shrieked the black dwarf,
Impudent elf,
That was the shadow of myself.

I said to him, 'We must go now';
But from his bough
He laughed, securely perched,
'Then you rise first';
It seemed to me
He spoke in wicked courtesy.

We rose and 'Take my hand,' he whined,
Though like the wind
Each waving bough he leapt;
And as we stept
Down the steep track
He seemed to grow more hunched and black.

Palmistry

I lifted from the ground my grass-pressed hand
And pondered, as its strange new lines I scanned,
What is foretold? What hope, what fear,
What strife, what passion is prefigured here?

The Roman Wall

Though moss and lichen crawl
  These square-set stones still keep their serried ranks
Guarding the ancient wall,
  That whitlow-grass with lively silver pranks.

Time they could not keep back
  More than the wind that from the snow-streaked north
Taking the air for track
  Flows lightly over to the south shires forth.

Each stone might be a cist
  Where memory sleeps in dust and nothing tells
More than the silent mist
  That smokes along the heather-blackened fells.

Twitching its ears as pink
  As blushing scallops loved by Romans once
A lamb leaps to its drink
  And, as the quavering cry breaks on the stones,

Time like a leaf down-drops
  And pacing by the stars and thorn-trees' sough
A Roman sentry stops
  And hears the water lapping on Crag Lough.

The Spider

A single white dewdrop
That hung free on the air sang, Stop!
From twig to twig a speckled spider,
Legged like a hermit-crab, had tied her
Invisible web with WELCOME
For sign, and HOME SWEET HOME.

That spider would not stir,
Villain of her Greek theatre,
Till as I heedlessly brushed past her
She fled fast from her web's disaster
And from a twig-fork watched it swing,
Wind tangling string with string.

Now she weaves in the dark
With no light lent by a star's spark
From busy belly more than head
Geometric pattern of thin thread,
A web for wingy midge and fly,
With deadly symmetry.

The Rain

Fair mornings make false vows!
  When to that wood I came
I stood beneath fast-dripping boughs
  And watched the green leaves wink
  Spilling their heavy drink;
Some flowers to sleeping buds returned,
Some, lit by rain, with clear flames burned;
'Cuckoo' – again, again
  A cuckoo called his name
Behind the waving veil of dismal rain.

The rain bit yellow root
  And shone on the blue flints
And dangled like a silver fruit
  From blackened twigs and boughs;
  I watched those running rows
Splash on the sodden earth and wet
The empty snail-shells marked 'To let',
And whitened worms that lay
  Like stalks of hyacinths,
The last end of a children's holiday.

I heard a dead man cough
   Not twenty yards away –
(A wool-wet sheep, likely enough,
   As I thought afterwards);
   But O those shrieking birds!
   And how the flowers seemed to outstare
Some hidden sun in that dim air,
As sadly the rain soaked
   To where the dead man lay
Whose cough a sudden fall of earth had choked.

The Stars

The stars rushed forth tonight
Fast on the faltering light;
So thick those stars did lie
No room was left for sky;
And to my upturned stare
A snow-storm filled the air.

Stars lay like yellow pollen
That from a flower has fallen;
And single stars I saw
Crossing themselves in awe;
Some stars in sudden fear
Fell like a falling tear.

What is the eye of man,
This little star that can
See all those stars at once,
Multitudinous suns,
Making of them a wind
That blows across the mind?

If eye can nothing see
But what is part of me,
I ask and ask again
With a persuasive pain,
What thing, O God, am I,
This mote and mystery?

The Wood

Summer's green tide rises in flood
Foaming with elder-blossom in the wood,
And insects hawk, gold-striped and blue,
On motion-hidden wings the air looks through,
And 'Buzz, buzz, buzz',
Gaily hums Sir Pandarus,
As blue ground-ivy blossom
Bends with the weight of a bee in its bosom.

Heavy with leaves the boughs lean over
The path where midges in a loose ball hover,
And daisies and slow-footed moss
And thin grass creep across,
Till scarcely on the narrow path
The sparrow finds a dusty bath,
And caterpillars from the leaves
Arch their green backs on my coat-sleeves.

Bright as a bird the small sun flits
Through shaking leaves that tear the sky in bits;
But let the leaf-lit boughs draw closer,
I in the dark will feel no loser
With myself for companion.
Grow, leafy boughs; darken, O sun,
For here two robins mate
That winter held apart in a cold hate.

The Shadow

Dark ghost
That from tree-trunk to tree-trunk tost,
Flows with me still,
When on the shoulder of the hill
The late sunrise
Tangles its rainbows on my eyes –

Although
Each time I wave to you below
I see you stand
And wave back with a distant hand,
I ask, Can you be mine,
O shade gigantic and divine?

An Old Road

None ever walks this road
That used to lie open and broad
And ran along the oakshaw edge;
The road itself is now become the hedge.

Whatever brambles say
I often try to force a way,
Wading in withered leaves that spread
Over dead lovers' tracks a sighing bed.

Is it the thought of one
That I must meet when most alone
That makes me probe a place like this,
Where gossamer now gives the only kiss?

I shall see no one there
Though I had eyes to see the air,
But at the waving of a bough
Shall think I see the way she went but now.

The Round Barrow

A lark as small as a flint arrow
Rises and falls over this ancient barrow
And seems to mock with its light tones
The silent man of bones;

Some prince that earth drew back again
From his long strife with wind and mist and rain,
Baring for him this broad round breast
In token of her rest.

But as I think how Death sat once
And with sly fingers picked those princely bones,
I feel my bones are verily
The stark and final I.

I climbed the hill housed in warm flesh,
But now as one escaped from its false mesh
Through the wan mist I journey on,
A clanking skeleton.

A Barrow on the Quantocks

Each night I pass the dead man's mound
I keep on turning round;
I almost stumble on the track
With looking back.

Although that mound of ling and stones
May hide his brittle bones,
I do not think that there he sleeps
Or wakes and peeps.

He is too intimately near
To see or touch or hear;
I only feel my blood is crossed
By his chill ghost.

It may be that all things are made
Of substance and of shade
And such a hill as I walk here
He walks elsewhere.

I know not which the substance is,
This hill of mine or his,
Nor which of us is the true ghost
In shadows lost.

The Rat

Strange that you let me come so near
  And send no questing senses out
From eye's dull jelly, shell-pink ear,
  Fierce-whiskered snout.

But clay has hardened in these claws
  And gypsy-like I read too late
In lines scored on your naked paws
  A starry fate.

Even that snake, your tail, hangs dead,
  And as I leave you stiff and still
A death-like quietness has spread
  Across the hill.

The Feather

Briar, spindle and thorn tangled together
  Made dark the narrow track,
And from some hoarse-voiced rook the fallen feather
  That lay silent and black.

Gold lees left in the pink cup of dog-roses
  Nor the red campion
That the June cuckoo when his voice he loses
  Cast his white spittle on,

Nothing could lighten that track's narrow gloom,
  Except on ground or bark
Some honied light straggling through branches from
  The sun that made it dark.

The Men

I sat to listen to each sound
Of leaf on twig or ground
And finch that cracked a seed
Torn from a limp and tarnished weed
And rapid flirt of wings
As bluetits flew and used as swings
The bines of old man's beard,
When suddenly I heard
Those men come crashing through the wood
And voices as they stood,
And dog that yelped and whined
At each shrill scent his nose could find;
And knowing that it meant small good
To some of us who owned that wood,
Badger, stoat, rabbit, rook and jay
And smoky dove that clattered away,
Although no ill to me at least,
I too crept off like any stealthy beast.

Penelope

The leaves hang on the boughs
Filemot, ochreous,
Or fall and strangely greet
Green blades of winter wheat.
The long buds of the beech
Point where they cannot reach.

A sad Telemachus,
I stand under the boughs;
Patient Penelope,
Her heart across the sea,
Another year unweaves
Her web of wasted leaves.

Is bud and leaf and flower
All we are waiting for?
But we shall wait again
When these are gone, and then
When they are gone and gone
Penelope alone.

A Man with a Horse

I wondered at the mighty horse
  So meekly since the day began
Toiling to make himself a corse,
  And then I wondered at the man.

Mist

Rain, do not fall
Nor rob this mist at all,
That is my only cell and abbey wall.

Wind, wait to blow
And let the thick mist grow,
That fills the rose-cup with a whiter glow.

Mist, deepen still
And the low valley fill;
You hide but taller trees, a higher hill.

Still, mist, draw close;
These gain by what they lose,
The taller trees and hill, the whiter rose.

All else begone,
And leave me here alone
To tread this mist where earth and sky are one.

The Burnt Leaves

They have been burning leaves,
Dead leaves the little shrew upheaves
Poking in winter for his trifling food,
And large black pools lie in the wood
As though the sky had rained down ink;
It all means nothing as I think
That more and more are left behind
To rise and rustle in the wind,
That paws them as a cat plays with a mouse,
And June will bring green leafy boughs;
Yet often as I watched them run
I thought of you, O blue-eyed one,
Or thought about my thoughts of you,
Fitful and feeble too:
For as these ran a little way and stopped
When the wind rose and dropped,
So I would think of you a little, yet
So soon forget.

The Evening Star

I saw a star shine in bare trees
That stood in their dark effigies;
With voice so clear and close it sang
That like a bird it seemed to hang
Rising and falling with the wind,
Twigs on its rosy breast outlined.

An obvious moon high on the night
And haloed by a rainbow light
Sounded as loud as silver bell
And trees in flight before it fell,
Their shadows straggling on the road
Where glacier of soft moonlight flowed.

But moon nor star-untidy sky
Could catch my eye as that star's eye;
For still I looked on that same star,
That fitful, fiery Lucifer,
Watching with mind as quiet as moss
Its light nailed to a burning cross.

Late Autumn

The boy called to his team
  And with blue-glancing share
Turned up the rape and turnip
  With yellow charlock to spare.

The long lean thistles stood
  Like beggars ragged and blind,
Half their white silken locks
  Blown away on the wind.

But I thought not once of winter
Or summer that was past
Till I saw that slant-legged robin
With autumn on his chest.

On White Down

In a high wood,
Wind chilling my premonitory blood,
I play at death
Closing my eyes and holding back my breath.

Ah glad surprise
To wake from death, and breathe, and open eyes
To see again
This mist-capped hill that is so bright with rain.

But from a bough
A blackbird mocks, 'Blind eyes are not enough;
You act the ghost
With sight and breathing that you never lost.'

O bird, be still;
When I would walk on an immortal hill
You drag me back
As though I had not left this dim hill-track.

Illic Jacet

This was his little house;
Its moth-bright eye
Looks through the orchard-boughs
At the starry sky.

I never crossed his door
    But still preferred
To hunt some orchid or
    Watch for a bird.

We went one day to church,
    His friends and he;
We left him in the lurch,
    As it seemed to me.

But still from his grave he says,
    'You know the house;
You must one of these days
    Drop in on us.'

The Farmer's Gun

The wood is full of rooks
That by their faded looks
No more on thievery will thrive,
As when they were alive,
Nor fill the air with the hoarse noise
That most of all is England's pleasant voice.

How ugly is this work of man,
Seen in the bald brain-pan,
Voracious bill,
Torn wing, uprooted quill
And host of tiny glistening flies
That lend false lustre to these empty eyes.

More delicate is nature's way
Whereby all creatures know their day,
And hearing Death call 'Come,
Here is a bone or crumb',
Bury themselves before they die
And leave no trace of foul mortality.

The Yellow-Hammers

All up the grassy many-tracked sheep-walk,
  Low sun on my right hand, hedge on my left
  Blotted by a late leaf, else leaf-bereft,
I drove my golden flock.

Yellow-hammers, gold-headed, russet-backed,
  They fled in jerky flight before my feet,
  Or pecked in the green ranks of winter-wheat,
While I my footsteps slacked.

Myself, the road, the hedge, these flying things,
  Who led, who followed as we climbed the hill?
  Loud as their repeated trembling trill-trill
Was the swift flirt of wings.

So tame I would have touched them with my hand,
  But they were gone, darting with rise and fall;
  I followed, till at the hedge-end they all
Dispersed over the land.

There, where the hillside scattered the sheep-walk,
  Deserted by the birds I stood to muse
  How I but now had served so sweet a use,
Driving my golden flock.

Loch Brandy

All day I heard the water talk
From dripping rock to rock
And water in bright snowflakes scatter
On boulders of the black Whitewater;
But louder now than these
The silent scream of the loose tumbling screes.

Grey wave on grey stone hits
And grey moth flits
Moth after moth, but oh,
What floats into that silver glow,
What golden moth
That rises with a strange majestic sloth?

O heart, why tremble with desire
As on the water shakes that bridge of fire?
The gold moth floats away, too soon
To narrow to a hard white moon
That scarce will light the path
Stumbling to where the cold mist wreathes the strath.

After the Funeral

Standing beneath the jewelled trees
That waved with slow mournful unease;
I lifted up my eyes to them –
The stars caught in the trees' dark stratagem.

But when I asked which is the wonder,
All stars above the earth and under
And in the vast hollow of space
Or the stern look on that defeated face;

I said, 'Not even the Milky Way
Shines like the golden streak of clay –
All, all of her that I could save –
My foot has gathered from her open grave'.

The Last Leaf

I saw how rows of white raindrops
  From bare boughs shone,
And how the storm had stript the leaves
  Forgetting none
Save one left high on a top twig
  Swinging alone;
Then that too bursting into song
  Fled and was gone.

The Flood

The winter flood is out, dully glazing the weald,
The Adur, a drowned river, lies in its bed concealed;
Fishes flowing through fences explore paddock and field.

Bushes, waist-deep in water, stand sprinkled here and there;
A solitary gate, as though hung in mid-air,
Waits idly open, leading from nowhere to nowhere.

These bushes at nightfall will have strange fish for guests,
That wagtail, tit and warbler darkened with their nests;
Where flood strays now, light-headed lapwings lifted crests.

But soon comes spring again; the hazel-boughs will angle
With bait of yellow catkins that in the loose winds dangle
And starry scarlet blossoms their blind buds bespangle;

Dog's-mercury from the earth unfold seed-clasping fists
And green-leaved honeysuckle roll in tumbling twists
And dreams of spring shake all the seeds that sleep in cists.

O blue-eyed one, too well I know you will not awake,
Who waked or lay awake so often for my sake,
Nor would I ask our last leavetaking to retake.

If lesser love of flower or bird waken my song,
It is that greater love, too full to flow along,
Falls like that Adur back, flood-like, silent and strong.

The Pines

The eye might fancy that those pines,
With snow-struck stems in pallid lines,
Were lit by the sunlight at noon,
Or shadow-broken gleam of the moon;
But snowflakes rustle down the air,
Circling and rising here and there
As though uncertain where to fall,
Filling the wood with a deep pall,
The wood that hastens darkness to hide all.

The hurricane of snow last night
Felled one; its roots, surprised by light,
Clutch at the air in wild embrace;
Peace like an echo fills the place
Save for the quiet labour of snow,
That falling flake on flake below
The torn limbs and the red wounds stanches,
And with a sheet the dead trunk blanches,
And lays white delicate wreaths among the branches.

The Signpost

Snowflakes dance on the night;
   A single star
Glows with a wide blue light
   On Lochnagar.

Through snow-fields trails the Dee;
  At the wind's breath
An ermine-clad spruce-tree
  Spits snow beneath.

White-armed at the roadside
  Wails a signpost,
'Tonight the world has died
  And left its ghost.'

The White Blackbird (1935)

The Dark Wood

O wood, now you are dark with summer
Your birds grow dumber
And ink-stained leaves of sycamore
Slide slowly down and hit your floor;
But there are other signs I mark,
In ivy with the sunlight wet
And dried rains streaming down your bark,
A withered limb, a broken shoulder,
Signs that since first we met
Even you, O wood, have grown a little older.

The Bird

The blackbird darted through the boughs
Trailing his whistle in a shrill dispute
'Why do you loiter near our house?'
But I was mute,
Though as he perched with sidelong head
I might have said,
'I never notice nests or lovers
In hedges or in covers;
I have enough to do
In my own way to be unnoticed too.'

Young Oats

These oats in autumn sown,
That stood through all the winter's dearth
In so small ranks of green
That flints like pigmies' bones lay bare
And greater stones were seen
To change to hares and rise and run,
Today to such a height are grown
That drawn up by the sun,
That Indian conjuror,
The field is levitated from the earth.

The Ruined Chapel

From meadows with the sheep so shorn
They, not their lambs, seem newly born
Through the graveyard I pass,
Where only blue plume-thistle waves
And headstones lie so deep in grass
They follow dead men to their graves,
And as I enter by no door
This chapel where the slow moss crawls
I wonder that so small a floor
Can have the sky for roof, mountains for walls.

The Stockdoves

They rose up in a twinkling cloud
And wheeled about and bowed
To settle on the trees
Perching like small clay images.

Then with a noise of sudden rain
They clattered off again
And over Ballard Down
They circled like a flying town.

Though one could sooner blast a rock
Than scatter that dense flock
That through the winter weather
Some iron rule has held together,

Yet in another month from now
Love like a spark will blow
Those birds the country over
To drop in trees, lover by lover.

The Loddon

Through hoof-marked meadows that lie sodden
From winter's overflow, the Loddon
Winds by the winding pollard hedge, –
Stunt willow-trunks that line the edge,
Whose roots like buried eels are sunk,
A grove of saplings on each trunk.

Its water with a white-frothed mouth
Chewing and gnawing the uncouth
Loose sticks and straws that in disorder
Lie littered on its leaping border,
As breath of wind roughens its hide,
This way or that way makes its tide.

This way or that – But O let come
May-blossom that in buds lies dumb,
This water that laps bush and tree
Shall long have drifted to the sea;
I almost feel that I too go
Caught in its secret lapsing flow.

Stay, Spring

Stay, spring, for by this ruthless haste
You turn all good to waste;
Look, how the blackthorn now
Changes to trifling dust upon the bough.

Where blossom from the wild pear shakes
Too rare a china breaks,
And though the cuckoos shout
They will forget their name ere June is out.

That thrush too, that with beadlike eye
Watches each passer-by,
Is warming at her breast
A brood that when they fly rob their own nest.

So late begun, so early ended!
Lest I should be offended
Take warning, spring, and stay
Or I might never turn to look your way.

The White Blackbird

Gulls that in meadows stand,
The sea their native land,
Are not so white as you
Flitting from bough to bough,
You who are white as sin
To your black kith and kin.

The Copse

Here in the Horseshoe Copse
The may in such a snow-storm drops
That every stick and stone
Becomes a tree with blossom of its own.

And though loose sun-spots sway
The night so lasts through all the day
That no bird great or small
Sings in these trees but is a nightingale.

Time might be anything,
Morning or night, winter or spring;
One who in this copse strays
Must walk through many months of night and days.

Sea Wormwood

It grew about my feet
Like frost unmelted in the summer heat;
I plucked it and such oozes
Flowed from its broken bruises
That as I turned inland
Its loosened scent was hanging from my hand.

And so I thought the people
Stayed from pea-picking by the road to Steeple,
No, not to watch the stranger
Who landed from Goldhanger,
But breathe the odorous oil
That flowing from his hand sweetened their toil.

The Swans

How lovely are these swans,
That float like high proud galleons
Cool in the summer heat,
And waving leaf-like feet
Divide with narrow breasts of snow
In a smooth surge
This water that is mostly sky;
So lovely that I know
Death cannot kill such birds,
It could but wound them, mortally.

The Slow Race

I followed each detour
Of the slow meadow-winding Stour,
That looked on cloud, tree, hill,
And mostly flowed by standing still.

Fearing to go too quick
I stopped at times to throw a stick
Or see how in the copse
The last snow was the first snowdrops.

The river also tarried
So much of sky and earth it carried,
Or even changed its mind
To flow back with a flaw of wind.

And when we reached the weir
That combed the water's silver hair,
I knew I lost the race –
I could not keep so slow a pace.

The Sunbeams

The tired road climbed the hill
Through trees with light-spots never still,
Gold mouths that drew apart and singled
And ran again and met and mingled,
Two, three or five or seven,
No other way than souls that love in heaven.

Sunny and swift and cool
They danced there like Bethesda's pool;
Ah, if in those pale kissing suns
My halting feet could bathe but once
No slender stick would crack,
My footstep falling on its brittle back.

Eryngo

I came on that blue-headed plant
  That lovers ate to waken love,
Eryngo; but I felt no want,
  A lovesick swain, to eat thereof.

The Dead Crab

A rosy shield upon its back,
That not the hardest storm could crack,
From whose sharp edge projected out
Black pinpoint eyes staring about;
Beneath, the well-knit cote-armure
That gave to its weak belly power;
The clustered legs with plated joints
That ended in stiletto points;
The claws like mouths it held outside: –
I cannot think this creature died
By storm or fish or sea-fowl harmed
Walking the sea so heavily armed;
Or does it make for death to be
Oneself a living armoury?

An Evening Walk

I never saw a lovelier sky;
The faces of the passers-by
Shine with gold light as they step west
As though by secret joy possessed,
Some rapture that is not of earth
But in that heavenly climate has its birth.

I know it is the sunlight paints
The faces of these travelling saints,
But shall I hold in cold misprision
The calm and beauty of that vision
Upturned a moment from the sorrow
That makes today today, tomorrow tomorrow?

Fenland

Where sky is all around
And creeps in dykes along the ground,
I see trees stand outlined
Too distant to be tossed with wind.

And farther still than these
Stand but the tops of other trees,
As on the ocean's rim
Vessels half-sunk in water swim.

Where there is so much sky
And earth so level to my eye,
Trees and trees farther hide
Far down the steep world's mountain-side.

The Tree

Tree, lend me this root,
That I may sit here at your foot
And watch these hawking flies that wheel
And perch on the air's hand
And red-thighed bees
That fan the dust with their wings' breeze.
Do you not feel me on your heel,
My bone against your bone?
Or are you in such slumber sunk,
Woodpeckers knocking at your trunk
Find you are not at home?
To winds you are not dumb;
Then tell me, if you understand:
When your thick timber has been hewn,
Its boards in floors and fences sewn,
And you no more a tree,
Where will your dryad be?

The Track

Trodden by man and horse
Tracks change their course
As rivers change their bed;
And this that I now tread,
Where the lean roots obtrude,
Was not the first track through the wood.

There older traces flow,
Where ghosts may go
But no one else save I;
And as in turn I try
Each faint and fainter track,
Through what long ages I fall back.

Thistledown

Silver against blue sky
These ghosts of day float by,
Fitful, irregular,
Each one a silk-haired star,
Till from the wind's aid freed
They settle on their seed.

Not by the famished light
Of a moon-ridden night
But by clear sunny hours
Gaily these ghosts of flowers
With rise and swirl and fall
Dance to their burial.

To the River Dove

Swift under hollow shelf
Or spreading out to rest yourself
You flow between high ridge and ridge
To brim the heavy eyebrows of the bridge.

No, Dove, it is not mine
To stroke you with a fly and line,
A legless trunk wading your water;
I leave your fish to heron, pike and otter,

And him who haunts that inn
With 'Isaac Walton' for its sign,
Living there still as he lived once,
A wind-blown picture now, with creaking bones.

The Cuckoo

This year the leaves were late and thin,
And my eye wandering softly in
Saw perched upon a topmost twig,
Small bird to have a voice so big,
A cuckoo with long tail behind,
Twig and bird aswing on the wind,
That rose and flew with outspread tail
Guiding his flight like steering sail.

I waited, listened; came again
Across the distance of the rain
'Cuckoo' so faint and far away
It sounded out of yesterday,
Making me start with sudden fear
Lest spring that had seemed new and near
Was gone already. A sparrow hopped
In white plum-tree and blossom dropped.

Gossip

The wind shaking the gate
Impatiently as though in haste and late
Shook and shook it making it rattle,
And all the other tittle-tattle
It rushed to tell, –
Of how mahogany chestnuts fell
And how the gamekeeper
Had crackling paper here and there and there
To frighten pheasants back into the wood,
And how the flapping scarecrow stood
And guarding seeds from harm
Saluted with a broken arm,
And how the thin-voiced lamb
Still in the autumn sucked his dam,
A late and casual love-begot,
All that I heard and proudly thought
That I, a man, whom most things hate,
Shared country gossip with the wind and gate.

Mole-hills on the Downs

Here earth in her abundance spills
Hills on her hills,
Till every hill is overgrown
With small hills of its own;
Some old with moss and scorpion-grass,
Some new and bare and brown,
And one where I can watch the earth
Like a volcano at its birth
Still rise by falling down;
And as by these small hills I pass
And take them in my stride
I swell with pride,
Till the great hills to which I lift my eyes
Restore my size.

In Teesdale

No, not tonight,
Not by this fading light,
Not by those high fells where the forces
Fall from the mist like the white tails of horses.

From that dark slack
Where peat-hags gape too black
I turn to where the lighted farm
Holds out through the open door a golden arm.

No, not tonight,
Tomorrow by daylight;
Tonight I fear the fabulous horses
Whose white tails flash down the steep water-courses.

In the Fallow Field

I went down on my hands and knees
Looking for trees,
Twin leaves that, sprung from seeds,
Were now too big
For stems much thinner than a twig.
These soon with chamomile and clover
And other fallow weeds
Would be turned over;
And I was thinking how
It was a pity someone should not know
That a great forest fell before the plough.

A Windy Day

This wind brings all dead things to life,
Branches that lash the air like whips
And dead leaves rolling in a hurry
Or peering in a rabbits' bury
Or trying to push down a tree;
Gates that fly open to the wind
And close again behind,
And fields that are a flowing sea
And make the cattle look like ships;
Straws glistening and stiff
Lying on air as on a shelf
And pond that leaps to leave itself;
And feathers too that rise and float,
Each feather changed into a bird,
And line-hung sheets that crack and strain;
Even the sun-greened coat,
That through so many winds has served,
The scarecrow struggles to put on again.

Wood and Hill

Nowhere is one alone
And in the closest covert least,
But to small eye of bird or beast
He will be known;
Today it was for me
A squirrel that embraced a tree
Turning a small head round;
A hare too that ran up the hill,
To his short forelegs level ground,
And with tall ears stood still.
But it was birds I could not see
And larks that tried to stand on air
That made of wood and hill a market-square.

By the Tyne

What foolish birds were they
That built these nests exposed to day,
A score on every tree
So darkly clear between the river and me?

Not birds that haunt these woods,
But heavy, hurrying winter floods
With their foam-hissing billows
Left these wild driftwood nests on the lean willows.

The Comet

Why do I idly stand
And digging with my finger-tips
Tear the tree-trunk in strips?
Because such touchwood soft and damp
I once would stuff in a clay lamp
And blow on it with fiery face
To coax a sparkling light
And through the darkness race,
That lit lamp in my hand
A comet streaming through the autumn night.

The Knotted Ash

Is this a lover's vow?
Who else should tie it and for what,
This olive-coloured sapling in a knot,
Till now spring's sap must stoop
And bend back in a gouty loop
Rising from root to sooty-budded bough?

They may be tired of love,
Who found it not enough
To twine the glances of their eyes
Like kissing brimstone butterflies;
But death itself can not untwist
This piteous tree-contortionist.

The Fear

How often I turn round
To face the beast that bound by bound
Leaps on me from behind,
Only to see a bough that heaves
With sudden gust of wind
Or blackbird raking withered leaves.

A dog may find me out
Or badger toss a white-lined snout;
And one day as I softly trod
Looking for nothing stranger than
A fox or stoat I met a man
And even that seemed not too odd.

And yet in any place I go
I watch and listen as all creatures do
For what I cannot see or hear,
For something warns me everywhere
That even in my land of birth
I trespass on the earth.

A Heap of Faggots

Faggots of ash, elm, oak
That dark loose snowflakes touch and soak,
An unlit fire they lie
With cold inhospitality.

Nothing will light them now,
Sticks that with only lichen glow
And crumble to touchwood
Soft and unfit for fire's food.

And with wren, finch and tit
And all the silent birds that sit
In this snow-travelled wood
I warm myself at my own blood.

The Secret Wood

Where there is nothing more to see
Than this old earth-bound tree
That years ago dry sawdust bled
But sprouts each spring a leaf or two
As though it tried not to be dead,
Or that down-hanging broken bough
That keeps its withered leaves till now,
Like a dead man that cannot move
Or take his own clothes off,
What is it that I seek or who,
Fearing from passer-by
Intrusion of a foot or eye?
I only know
Though all men of earth's beauty speak
Beauty here I do not seek
More than I sought it on my mother's cheek.

Ploughing in Mist

Pulling the shoulder-sack
Closer about his neck and back,
He called out to his team
That stamped off dragging the weigh-beam;

And as he gripped the stilts and steered
They plunged in mist and disappeared,
Fading so fast away
They seemed on a long journey gone,
Not to return that day;
But while I waited on
The jingle of loose links I caught,
And suddenly on the hill-rise,
Pale phantoms of the mist at first,
Man and his horses burst
As though before my eyes
Creation had been wrought.

On Middleton Edge

If this life-saving rock should fail
Yielding too much to my embrace
And rock and I to death should race,
The rock would stay there in the dale
While I, breaking my fall,
Would still go on
Farther than any wandering star has gone.

Autumn

A new Teiresias and unreproved,
Not stricken by the goddess that I loved,
Today I looked and saw the earth undress
With intimate and godlike carelessness.

The Stones

Though the thick glacier,
That filled the mountains' rocky jaws
And lifted these great rocks like straws
And dropped them here,
Has shrunk to this small ale-brown burn,
Where trout like shadows dart and turn,
The stones in awkward stance
Still wait some starry circumstance
To bring the ice once more
And bear them to a distant shore.

The Eagle

He hangs between his wings outspread
  Level and still
And bends a narrow golden head,
  Scanning the ground to kill.

Yet as he sails and smoothly swings
  Round the hillside,
He looks as though from his own wings
  He hung down crucified.

Black Rock of Kiltearn

They named it Aultgraat – Ugly Burn,
This water through the crevice hurled
Scouring the entrails of the world –
Not ugly in the rising smoke
That clothes it with a rainbowed cloak.

But slip a foot on frost-spiked stone
Above this rock-lipped Phlegethon
And you shall have
The Black Rock of Kiltearn
For tombstone, grave
And trumpet of your resurrection.

Last Snow

Although the snow still lingers
Heaped on the ivy's blunt webbed fingers
And painting tree-trunks on one side,
Here in this sunlit ride
The fresh unchristened things appear,
Leaf, spathe and stem,
With crumbs of earth clinging to them
To show the way they came
But no flower yet to tell their name,
And one green spear
Stabbing a dead leaf from below
Kills winter at a blow.

The Paps of Jura

Before I crossed the sound
  I saw how from the sea
These breasts rise soft and round,
  Not two but three;

Now, climbing, I clasp rocks
  Storm-shattered and sharp-edged,
Grey ptarmigan their flocks,
  With starved moss wedged;

And mist like hair hangs over
  One barren breast and me,
Who climb, a desperate lover,
  With hand and knee.

The Fallen Tree

The shade once swept about your boughs
Quietly obsequious
To the time-keeping sun;
Now, fallen tree, you with that shade are one.

From chalky earth as white as surf
Beneath the uptorn turf
Roots hang in empty space
Like snakes about the pale Medusa's face.

And as I perch on a forked branch,
More used to squirrel's haunch,
I think how dead you are,
More dead than upright post or fence or chair.

The Fairy Ring

Here the horse-mushrooms make a fairy ring,
  Some standing upright and some overthrown,
A small Stonehenge, where heavy black snails cling
  And bite away, like Time, the tender stone.

New Poems
(in *Collected Poems, 1936*)

Cuckoo in May

Cuckoo that like a cuckoo-clock
Calls out the hours so fast,
Days, months and years go slipping past,
O for a while be dumb
Lest in a moment I become
Old as that man I stopped to watch
And chat with in my morning walk,
His back as rounded as a hoop,
Who did not need to stoop
To pull out weeds in his potato-patch.

Autumn Seeds

Although a thoughtful bee still travels
And midge-ball ravels and unravels,
Yet strewn along the pathway lie
Like small open sarcophagi
The hazel-nuts broken in two
And cobwebs catch the seed-pearl dew.

Now summer's flowers are winter's weeds,
I think of all the sleeping seeds;
Winds were their robins and by night
Frosts glue their leafy cover tight;
Snow may shake down its dizzy feathers,
They will sleep safely through all weathers.

The Ventriloquists

The birds sang in the rain
  That rhythmically waving its grey veil
From smoking hilltop flowed to misty plain,
  Where one white house shone sharply as a sail;

But not so bright as these,
  The anemones that held the wood snow-bound,
The water-drops waiting to fall from trees,
  The rusty catkins crawling on the ground.

March buds give little shelter;
  Better seek shelter in the open rain
Than where tree-gathered showers fall helter-skelter,
  I meditated; but 'Turn, turn again',

The birds shrieked through their song;
  So rooted to the leaf-soft earth I stood,
Letting my restless eye wander among
  The thick sky-scrawling branches of the wood.

But no bird could I see
  In criss-cross of thin twigs or sudden twists
Where branching tree interrupted branching tree;
  Yet everywhere those hidden ventriloquists

Were singing in the wood,
  Flinging their cheating voices here and there;
But seeing nothing though I walked or stood
  I thought the singing grew out of the air.

Walking in Beech Leaves

I tread on many autumns here
  But with no pride,
For at the leaf-fall of each year
  I also died.

This is last autumn, crisp and brown,
  That my knees feel;
But through how many years sinks down
  My sullen heel.

The Echoing Cliff

White gulls that sit and float,
Each on his shadow like a boat,
Sandpipers, oystercatchers
And herons, those grey stilted watchers,
From loch and corran rise,
And as they scream and squawk abuse
Echo from wooded cliff replies
So clearly that the dark pine boughs,
Where goldcrests flit
And owls in drowsy wisdom sit,
Are filled with sea-birds and their cries.

The Nest

Four blue stones in this thrush's nest
I leave, content to make the best
Of turquoise, lapis lazuli
Or for that matter of the whole blue sky.

The Chalk-Cliff

Blasted and bored and undermined
  By quarrying seas
Reared the erect chalk-cliff with black flints lined.
  (Flints drop like nuts from trees
When the frost bites
The chalk on winter nights.)

Save for frail shade of jackdaw's flight
  No night was there,
But blue-skyed summer and a cliff so white
  It stood like frozen air;
Foot slipped on damp
Chalk where the limpets camp.

With only purple of sea-stock
  And jackdaw's shade
To mitigate that blazing height of chalk
  I stood like a soul strayed
In paradise
Hiding my blinded eyes.

The Chalk-Quarry

A solitary yew,
  Fern-haired and ruddy-thewed,
That light with no sharp needle can prick through,
  Itself makes a small forest in the wood.

The strong sun darkening still
  That yew's *memento mori*
Fills with a fiercer light out on the hill
  The open sepulchre of the old chalk-quarry.

Snow

Ridged thickly on black bough
  And foaming on twig-fork in swollen lumps
At flirt of bird-wing or wind's sough
  Plump snow tumbled on snow softly with sudden dumps.

Where early steps had made
  A wavering track through the white-blotted road
Breaking its brightness with blue shade,
  Snow creaked beneath my feet with snow heavily shod.

I reached a snow-thatched rick
  Where men sawed bedding off for horse and cow;
There varnished straws were lying thick
  Paving with streaky gold the trodden silver snow.

Such light filled me with awe
  And nothing marred my paradisal thought,
That robin least of all I saw
  Lying too fast asleep, his song choked in his throat.

The Elm-Beetle

So long I sat and conned
That naked bole
With the strange hieroglyphics scored
That those small priests,
The beetle-grubs, had bored,
Telling of gods and kings and beasts
And the long journey of the soul
Through magic-opened gates
To where the throned Osiris waits,

That when at last I woke
I stepped from an Egyptian tomb
To see the wood's sun-spotted gloom,
And rising cottage smoke
That leaned upon the wind and broke,
Roller-striped fields, and smooth cow-shadowed pond.

South Downs

No water cries among these hills,
  The mist hides and enlarges,
Though rain in every road-rut spills
  Where leaves have sunk their barges.

No freshet in a hollow brake
  Utters its shy cold fears,
Only the chiming sheep-bells make
  One Sabbath of the years.

August

The cows stood in a thundercloud of flies,
  As lagging through the field with trailing feet
I kicked up scores of skipper butterflies
  That hopped a little way, lazy with heat.

The wood I found was in deep shelter sunk,
  Though bryony leaves shone with a glossy sweat
And creeping over ground and up tree-trunk
  The ivy in the sun gleamed bright and wet.

Songs brief as Chinese poems the birds sung
And insects of all sheens, blue, brown and yellow,
Darted and twisted in their flight and hung
On air that groaned like hoarse sweet violoncello.

No leaf stirred in the wood-discouraged wind,
But foliage hung on trees like heavy wigs;
The sun, come from the sky, was close behind
The fire-fringed leaves and in among the twigs.

February

So thick a mist darkened the day
Not two trees distant flew my friend, the jay,
To keep love's angry tryst
Somewhere in the damp mist,
And as I brushed each bush
Rain-buds fell in a rush,
One might have said it rained,
While green buds on the barer boughs remained.

But where with looped and twisted twine
Wild clematis, bryony and woodbine
And such reptilian growth
Hung in decaying sloth,
I stood still thinking how
Two months or three from now
The green buds would not tarry
More than those flashing drops of February.

The Missel-Thrush

That missel-thrush
Scorns to alight on a low bush,
And as he flies
And tree-top after tree-top tries,
His shadow flits
And harmlessly on tree-trunk hits.

Shutting his wings
He sways and sings and sways and sings,
And from his bough
As in deep water he looks through
He sees me there
Crawl at the bottom of the air.

The Scarecrow

He strides across the grassy corn
That has not grown since it was born,
A piece of sacking on a pole,
A ghost, but nothing like a soul.

Why must this dead man haunt the spring
With arms anxiously beckoning?
Is spring not hard enough to bear
For one at autumn of his year?

The Mountain

The burn ran blacker for the snow
And ice-floe on ice-floe
Jangled in heavy lurches
Beneath the claret-coloured birches.

Dark grouse rose becking from the ground
And deer turned sharp heads round,
The antlers on their brows
Like stunted trees with withered boughs.

I climbed to where the mountain sloped
And long wan bubbles groped
Under the ice's cover,
A bridge that groaned as I crossed over.

I reached the mist, brighter than day,
That showed a specious way
By narrow crumbling shelves,
Where rocks grew larger than themselves.

But when I saw the mountain's spire
Looming through that damp fire,
I left it still unwon
And climbed down to the setting sun.

Man and Cows

I stood aside to let the cows
Swing past me with their wrinkled brows,
Bowing their heads as they went by
As to a woodland deity
To whom they turned mute eyes
To save them from the plaguing god of flies.

And I too cursed Beelzebub,
Watching them stop to rub
A bulging side or bony haunch
Against a trunk or pointing branch
And lift a tufted tail
To thresh the air with its soft flail.

They stumbled heavily down the slope,
As Hathor led them or the hope
Of the lush meadow-grass,
While I remained, thinking it was
Strange that we both were held divine,
In Egypt these, man once in Palestine.

Speak to the Earth (1939)

Glow-Worms

As though the dark had called
To chrysolite and emerald,
Earth brings out jewel by jewel,
Love stoking their bright fires, itself the fuel.

To flying beetles, 'Come,
Find here your children and your home,'
They sing with a green light,
Each glow-worm her own Venus in the night.

Autumn Mist

So thick a mist hung over all,
Rain had no room to fall;
It seemed a sea without a shore;
The cobwebs drooped heavy and hoar
As though with wool they had been knit;
Too obvious mark for fly to hit!

And though the sun was somewhere else
The gloom had brightness of its own
That shone on bracken, grass and stone
And mole-mound with its broken shells
That told where squirrel lately sat,
Cracked hazel-nuts and ate the fat.

And sullen haws in the hedgerows
Burned in the damp with clearer fire;
And brighter still than those
The scarlet hips hung on the briar
Like coffins of the dead dog-rose;
All were as bright as though for earth
Death were a gayer thing than birth.

A Dead Mole

Strong-shouldered mole,
That so much lived below the ground,
Dug, fought and loved, hunted and fed,
For you to raise a mound
Was as for us to make a hole;
What wonder now that being dead
Your body lies here stout and square
Buried within the blue vault of the air?

Snow Harvest

The moon that now and then last night
Glanced between clouds in flight
Saw the white harvest that spread over
The stubble fields and even roots and clover.

It climbed the hedges, overflowed
And trespassed on the road,
Weighed down fruit-trees and when winds woke
From white-thatched roofs rose in a silver smoke.

How busy is the world today!
Sun reaps, rills bear away
The lovely harvest of the snow
While bushes weep loud tears to see it go.

The Gramophone

We listened to your birds tonight
By the firelight,
The nightingales that trilled to us
From moonlit boughs.

Though golden snowflakes from the gloom
Looked in the room,
Those birds' clear voices lingered on
Your gramophone.

'Goodnight' we said and as I go
High-heeled with snow
I almost hope to hear one now
From a bare bough.

Culbin Sands

Here lay a fair fat land;
   But now its townships, kirks, graveyards
Beneath bald hills of sand
   Lie buried deep as Babylonian shards.

But gales may blow again;
  And like a sand-glass turned about
The hills in a dry rain
  Will flow away and the old land look out;

And where now hedgehog delves
  And conies hollow their long caves
Houses will build themselves
  And tombstones rewrite names on dead men's graves.

The Shepherd's Hut

Now when I could not find the road
Unless beside it also flowed
This cobbled beck that through the night,
Breaking on stones, makes its own light,

Where blackness in the starlit sky
Is all I know a mountain by,
A shepherd little thinks how far
His lamp is shining like a star.

Suilven

It rose dark as a stack of peat
With mountains at its feet,
Till a bright flush of evening swept
And on to its high shoulders leapt
And Suilven, a great ruby, shone;
And though that evening light is dead,
The mountain in my mind burns on,
As though I were the foul toad, said
To bear a precious jewel in his head.

Nightfall on Sedgemoor

The darkness like a guillotine
   Descends on the flat earth;
The flocks look white across the rhine
   All but one lamb, a negro from its birth.

The pollards hold up in the gloom
   Knobbed heads with long stiff hair
That the wind tries to make a broom
   To sweep the moon's faint feather from the air.

What makes the darkness fall so soon
   Is not the short March day
Nor the white sheep nor brightening moon,
   But long June evenings when I came this way.

Essex Salt-Marsh

Now the tide's task is done,
Marsh runnels turn and chuckling run
Or come to a standstill,
The level ground for them a breathless hill.

And as they run or faint
Through mud that takes the sunset's paint,
The gullies they have worn
Shine as with purple grapes and golden corn.

A Brimstone Butterfly

The autumn sun that rose at seven
Has risen again at noon,
Where the hill makes a later heaven,
And fringing with bright rainbow hair
The boughs that lace the sky
Has wakened half a year too soon
This brimstone butterfly,
That fluttering every way at once
Searches in vain the moss and stones, –
Itself the only primrose there.

A Prehistoric Camp

It was the time of year
  Pale lambs leap with thick leggings on
Over small hills that are not there,
  That I climbed Eggardon.

The hedgerows still were bare,
  None ever knew so late a year;
Birds built their nests in the open air,
  Love conquering their fear.

But there on the hill-crest,
  Where only larks or stars look down,
Earthworks exposed a vaster nest,
  Its race of men long flown.

The Archaeologist

Although men may dig up
A broken Bacchus with a vine-wreathed cup
Or helmeted chryselephantine goddess;
Though Aphrodite divine and godless,
Helped by a rope, rise from the sea,
None is immortal but Persephone.

See, by an English lane
Cold Hades lets her rise again.
In celandines that in a blaze
Spread like gold starfish their flat rays
Revisiting our earth and sky
Death's wife reveals her immortality.

She glitters with a light
That sharpens, as is said, the swallow's sight;
I am not like that twittering bird;
Too clear a memory my eyes has blurred;
Not this side heaven I'll see again
As once I saw it a gold English lane.

Cuckoos

When coltsfoot withers and begins to wear
Long silver locks instead of golden hair,
And fat red catkins from black poplars fall
And on the ground like caterpillars crawl,
And bracken lifts up slender arms and wrists
And stretches them, unfolding sleepy fists,
The cuckoos in a few well-chosen words
Tell they give Easter eggs to the small birds.

The Swallows

All day – when early morning shone
With every dewdrop its own dawn
And when cockchafers were abroad
Hurtling like missiles that had lost their road –

The swallows twisting here and there
Round unseen corners of the air
Upstream and down so quickly passed
I wondered that their shadows flew as fast.

They steeplechased over the bridge
And dropped down to a drowning midge
Sharing the river with the fish,
Although the air itself was their chief dish.

Blue-winged snowballs! until they turned
And then with ruddy breasts they burned;
All in one instant everywhere,
Jugglers with their own bodies in the air.

Wiltshire Downs

The cuckoo's double note
Loosened like bubbles from a drowning throat
Floats through the air
In mockery of pipit, lark and stare.

The stable-boys thud by
Their horses slinging divots at the sky
And with bright hooves
Printing the sodden turf with lucky grooves.

As still as a windhover
A shepherd in his flapping coat leans over
His tall sheep-crook
And shearlings, tegs and yoes cons like a book.

And one tree-crowned long barrow
Stretched like a sow that has brought forth her farrow
Hides a king's bones
Lying like broken sticks among the stones.

Beaulieu River

Largest of Forest snakes, by heath and scrog
It stretches in its blue sky-borrowed coat,
For while its tail trails in a cotton bog
It grips with foaming mouth the Solent's throat.

Children Gathering Violets

Children, small Herods, slay these Innocents
With blue untidy faces and sweet scents;
But violets gone or even autumn here
Spring in the children lasts through all the year.

Mountain View

Can those small hills lying below
Be mountains that some hours ago
I gazed at from beneath?
Can such intense blue be the sea's
Or that long cloud the Hebrides?
Perhaps I prayed enough
By crawling up on hands and knees
The sharp loose screes,
Sweat dripping on the lichen's scurf,
And now in answer to my prayer
A vision is laid bare;
Or on that ledge, holding my breath,
I may have even slipped past Death.

Morning in the Combe

The low sun halves the combe,
One side in sunlight, one in gloom,
And where they meet together
I walk from winter into summer weather.

There hard mud kept the cast
Of hoof and claw and foot that passed,
While here I stumble over
Moist earth that draws me backward like a lover.

Climbing in Glencoe

The sun became a small round moon
And the scared rocks grew pale and weak
As mist surged up the col, and soon
So thickly everywhere it tossed
That though I reached the peak
With height and depth both lost

It might as well have been a plain;
Yet when, groping my way again,
On to the scree I stept
It went with me, and as I swept
Down its loose rumbling course
Balanced I rode it like a circus horse.

Reflections on the River

Rose-petals fall without a touch
As though it were too much
I should be standing by,
And poplars in no wind at all
Keep swaying left and right
With the slow motion of their height
Beneath a small white cloud that soon
Will pluck light from the dark and be the moon.

But where roach rise and bite the Ouse
Round ripples spread out like the first
Drops of a storm about to burst
And in the water toss the boughs
And crack the garden wall;
And as I gaze down in the sky
I see the whole vault shake
As though the heavens were seized with an earthquake.

Drought in the Fens

How often from the shade of trees
I thought of that rich man, Dives,
And how no diamond drop was given
To his or earth's cracked lips from heaven.

Green apples fell and lay around
As though they grew upon the ground,
And ditches, shrunk to muddy roads,
Starved limbless fish and man-legged toads.

So when the sand-walled flats I crossed
Hardened by heat as by a frost,
How strange it was that there could be
Still so much water in the sea.

The Cuillin Hills

Each step a cataract of stones
So that I rise and sink at once,
Slowly up to the ridge I creep;
And as through drifting smoke
Of mist grey-black as a hoodie-crow
The ghostly boulders come and go
And two hoarse ravens croak
That hopped with flapping wings by a dead sheep,
All is so hideous that I know
It would not kill me though I fell
A thousand feet below;
On you, Black Cuillin, I am now in hell.

Passing the Graveyard

I see you did not try to save
The bouquet of white flowers I gave;
So fast they wither on your grave.

Why does it hurt the heart to think
Of that most bitter abrupt brink
Where the low-shouldered coffins sink?

These living bodies that we wear
So change by every seventh year
That in a new dress we appear;

Limbs, spongy brain and slogging heart,
No part remains the selfsame part;
Like streams they stay and still depart.

You slipped slow bodies in the past;
Then why should we be so aghast
You flung off the whole flesh at last?

Let him who loves you think instead
That like a woman who has wed
You undressed first and went to bed.

Walking in Mist

At first the river Noe
Like a snake's belly gleamed below,
And then in mist was lost;
The hill too vanished like a ghost
And all the day was gone
Except the damp grey light that round me shone.

From Lose Hill to Mam Tor,
Darkness behind me and before,
I gave the track its head;
But as I followed where it led,
That light went all the way
As though I made and carried my own day.

Walking on the Cliff

But for a sleepy gull that yawned
   And spread its wings and dropping disappeared
This evening would have dawned
   To the eternity my flesh has feared.

For too intent on a blackcap
   Perched like a miser on the yellow furze
High over Birling Gap,
   That sang 'Gold is a blessing not a curse',

How near I was to stepping over
   The brink where the gull dropped to soar beneath,
While now safe as a lover
   I walk the cliff-edge arm in arm with Death.

The Thunderstorm

When Coniston Old Man was younger
And his deep-quarried sides were stronger,
Goats may have leapt about Goat's Water;
But why the tarn that looks like its young daughter
Though lying high under the fell
Should be called Blind Tarn, who can tell?

For from Dow Crag, passing it by,
I saw it as a dark presageful eye;
And soon I knew that I was not mistaken
Hearing the thunder the loose echoes waken
About Scafell and Scafell Pike
And feeling the slant raindrops strike.

And when I came to Walna Pass
Hailstones hissing and hopping among the grass,
Beneath a rock I found a hole;
But with sharp crack and rumbling roll on roll
So quick the lightning came and went
The solid rock was like a lighted tent.

Long Meg and her Daughters

When from the Druid's Head I came
The low sun doubled tussock-tump
And half in shadow, half in flame
Stood the Stone Circle. Lump by lump
Viewing her daughters Long Meg said,
'Come, stranger, make your choice of one;
All are my children, stone of my stone,
And none of them yet wed;
They wait to play at kiss-in-the-ring
With only now the wind to sing.'
But I, 'No, mother, all are fat
And some too old have fallen down flat.'
Meg frowned, 'You should be dead
To take instead a young tombstone to bed.'

Fields of Asparagus

From their long narrow beds
Asparagus raise reptilian heads
(Even the sand in May awakes)
And men who think that they are snakes
With shining knives
Walk to and fro, taking their scaly lives.

My path goes to the sea
But turning round comes back to me
In clouds of wind-blown sand
Making a desert of the land,
Where men must fight
With purple snakes that grow up in a night.

The Frogs

Each night that I come down the strath
Frogs turn heels-over-head,
And their white bellies on the path
Tell where to tread.

Of fox with brush above the brake
And kestrel pinned to air
And thin dark river of a snake
Let them beware!

Fat acrobats, I watch them turn
Kicking the evening dew,
Till in white waves that ride the burn
I see frogs too.

Ba Cottage

There at the watershed I turned
And looked back at the house I burned –
Burnt, too, by many another tramp
Who sought its shelter, dry or damp.

For coming from the mist-thick moor
I made the window-sill my door
And, wet incendiary, tore up wood
And fed the grate's wide mouth with food.

Then leaning on the mantelshelf
As though a mountain now myself
I smoked with mist and dripped with rain
That slowly made me dry again.

The Falls of Glomach

Rain drifts forever in this place
Tossed from the long white lace
The Falls trail on black rocks below,
And golden-rod and rose-root shake
In wind that they forever make;
So though they wear their own rainbow
It's not in hope, but just for show,
For rain and wind together
Here through the summer make a chill wet weather.

Overtaken by Mist

Like lightning on the mountain-slope
The stalker's path zigzagged,
And climbing it with steps that lagged
I often raised my eyes in hope

To where Scour Ouran's head was bare;
But mist that gathered from nowhere
With a bright darkness filled the air,
Until, both earth and heaven gone,
Never was man or angel so alone.

Idleness

God, you've so much to do,
To think of, watch and listen to,
That I will let all else go by
And lending ear and eye
Help you to watch how in the combe
Winds sweep dead leaves without a broom;
And rooks in the spring-reddened trees
Restore their villages,
Nest by dark nest
Swaying at rest on the trees' frail unrest;
Or on this limestone wall,
Leaning at ease, with you recall
How once these heavy stones
Swam in the sea as shells and bones;
And hear that owl snore in a tree
Till it grows dark enough for him to see;
In fact, will learn to shirk
No idleness that I may share your work.

After the Gale

I pity trees that all their life
Have ivy for a wife
Or with dark mistletoe they bear
Keep Christmas through the year.

So seeing oak-twigs grow on thorn
Where they were never born,
And sprays of ash-keys and pine-cones
Grow on a briar at once,

I blamed the gale that through the night
Had with perverse delight
Quartered rich children on the poor
Like foundlings at their door.

The Flesh-Scraper

If I had sight enough
Might I not find a fingerprint
Left on this flint
By Neolithic man or Kelt?
So knapped to scrape a wild beast's pelt,
The thumb below, fingers above,
See, my hand fits it like a glove.

A Wet Day

Breasting the thick brushwood that hid my track
Diffuse wetness of rain had stained me black;
My clinging coat I hung on a bough-knop
And sodden shapeless hat I laid on top.

With heavy hat and coat left on the bough
I felt a snake that had cast off his slough
And joined the slow black slugs that strolled abroad
Making soft shameless love on the open road.

But, turning on my steps, startled I stood
To see a dead man hanging in the wood;
By two clear feet of air he swung afloat,
One who had hanged himself in hat and coat.

The Stone Eagles

Purple and gold and wet
  To Toller Fratrum, Wynyard Eagle,
Both roads in the sunset
  Shone with a light so rich and regal;
Which choose without regret?

Chance led me by the one
  Where two lean-headed eagles perched
Rain-pitted to the bone
  And the last dregs of daylight searched
With their blind eyes of stone.

What were they watching for?
  Wild eagles that again would fly
Over a waste land or
  Scything wide circles in the sky
Mechanic birds of war?

Hibernating Snails

Here where the castle faces south
The ivy spreading its flat tree
Hides snails in heaps thick and uncouth,
All fast asleep with open mouth,

Although they breathe no air,
Each china throat sealed up with glair;
Yet some will never wake at all,
For two years old or even three
They crawled alive to their own funeral.

The Dunes

These heavy hills of sand,
That marram-grasses bind
Lest they should fly off on the wind,
Hold back the sea from Sea-kings' Land.

Such a waste holds me too
From fields where shadows fly,
Wolds, woods and streams that quote the sky,
All the sweet country that is you.

A Prospect of Death

If it should come to this,
You cannot wake me with a kiss,
Think I but sleep too late
Or once again keep a cold angry state.

So now you have been told; –
I or my breakfast may grow cold,
But you must only say
'Why does he miss the best part of the day?'

Even then you may be wrong;
Through woods torn by a blackbird's song
My thoughts may often roam
While graver business makes me stay at home.

There will be time enough
To go back to the earth I love
Some other day that week,
Perhaps to find what all my life I seek.

So do not dream of danger;
Forgive my lateness or my anger;
You have so much forgiven,
Forgive me this or that, or Hell or Heaven.

Christmas Day

Last night in the open shippen
   The Infant Jesus lay,
While cows stood at the hay-crib
   Twitching the sweet hay.

As I trudged through the snow-fields
   That lay in their own light,
A thorn-bush with its shadow
   Stood doubled on the night.

And I stayed on my journey
   To listen to the cheep
Of a small bird in the thorn-bush
   I woke from its puffed sleep.

The bright stars were my angels
   And with the heavenly host
I sang praise to the Father,
   The Son and Holy Ghost.

The Green Man
(1947)

Hard Frost

Frost called to water 'Halt!'
And crusted the moist snow with sparkling salt;
Brooks, their own bridges, stop,
And icicles in long stalactites drop,
And tench in water-holes
Lurk under gluey glass like fish in bowls.

In the hard-rutted lane
At every footstep breaks a brittle pane,
And tinkling trees ice-bound,
Changed into weeping willows, sweep the ground;
Dead boughs take root in ponds
And ferns on windows shoot their ghostly fronds.

But vainly the fierce frost
Interns poor fish, ranks trees in an armed host,
Hangs daggers from house-eaves
And on the windows ferny ambush weaves;
In the long war grown warmer
The sun will strike him dead and strip his armour.

In Avebury Circle

I see the white clouds blow
From cottages thick-thatched with snow
More clearly than I read
This great stone monster without feet, wings, head:

A huge night-blackening shadow
Set up by kings in this holy meadow,
Where of his fellows most
With those antique Cimmerians are lost.

I wonder if King Sil
Will rise and ride from Silbury Hill,
Where buried with his horse
He sits, a strange invulnerable corse,

And grey wethers that keep
On Clatford Down their lichened sleep
Drive to this ancient fold
And bring again an age of stone and gold.

Field-Glasses

Though buds still speak in hints
And frozen ground has set the flints
As fast as precious stones
And birds perch on the boughs, silent as cones,

Suddenly waked from sloth
Young trees put on a ten years' growth
And stones double their size,
Drawn nearer through field-glasses' greater eyes.

Why I borrow their sight
Is not to give small birds a fright
Creeping up close by inches;
I make the trees come, bringing tits and finches.

I lift a field itself
As lightly as I might a shelf,
And the rooks do not rage
Caught for a moment in my crystal cage.

And while I stand and look,
Their private lives an open book,
I feel so privileged
My shoulders prick, as though they were half-fledged.

Sudden Thaw

When day dawned with unusual light,
Hedges in snow stood half their height
And in the white-paved village street
Children were walking without feet.

But now by their own breath kept warm
Muck-heaps are naked at the farm
And even through the shrinking snow
Dead bents and thistles start to grow.

The Mud

This glistening mud that loves a gate
Was mashed by cows of late,
But now its puddles lie so still
They hold the clouds and trees and hill;

But when the painted cows come out
From milking-shed to grass
And churn the mud up as they pass,
How cloud and tree and hill will dart about!

Spring Flowers

Now we enjoy the rain,
When at each neighbour's door we hear
'How big primroses are this year' –
Tale we may live to hear again –

And dandelions flood
The orchards as though apple-trees
Dropped in the grass ripe oranges,
Boughs still in pink impatient bud,

When too we cannot choose,
But one foot and the other set
In celandine and violet,
Walking in gold and purple shoes,

Rain that through winter weeks
Splashed on our face and window pane,
And rising in these flowers again
Brightens their eyes and fats their cheeks.

In Breckland

Why is it when I cross the warren,
That last year's thistles make more barren,
Rabbits standing upright like men
Dive in their holes again,

And turtle that to turtle purrs
Rises and swerves from the blue belt of firs,
And even the mole that works beneath
Like a small earthquake holds its breath?
Hated by all for others' sins
I bless this rat that only grins,
Stayed by the stiff indifference of death.

A Sussex Ghyll

Primroses thick on its steep floor,
This ghyll deserves a better door
Than an old doubled sack
Flung over the barbed fence's narrow back.

The stream has its own way to come;
And though leaves try to keep it dumb
And even choke it dead,
Like a sick man it lies and sings in bed.

The trees are old: some ivy climbs;
Others like lepers drop their limbs;
But this stream delved the ghyll
Till each bank 'Good-bye' said – a distant hill.

A Shot Magpie

Though on your long-tailed flight
You wore half-mourning of staid black and white,
So little did the thought of death
Enter your thievish head,
You never knew what choked your breath
When in a day turned night
You fell with feathers heavier than lead.

May Frost

It was the night May robbed September
Killing with frost the apple-bloom,
The sunset sunk to its last ember,
I climbed the dew-webbed combe;
There floating from the earth's round rim
I saw the red sun rise.
At first I only thought 'How soon',
And then 'Surely I must be dying;
These are death's cobwebs on my eyes
That make the dawn so dim';
And yet my sight was lying:
The frost had set on fire the full-faced moon.

In Moonlight

Rain pattered in the poplar trees,
   And yet there was no rain;
It was clear moon; the trees' unease
   Made me hear water plain.

It seemed that lover walked by lover
   So sharp my shadow showed;
We never needed to step over
   The tree-trunks on the road.

The moon too on the other side
   From tree to tree flew on,
As though she had forsook the tide
   For her Endymion.

The truest lovers I could have –
So to myself I said –
The shadow marking out my grave
And moon lending a spade.

The Nightingale and Owl

How often had I tried to see
A nightingale, and only seen the tree;
Tonight I went with new belief
That I should see one, looking leaf by leaf.

And I was glad too that I went,
For as I listened, drinking the may's scent,
Another came, drawn by the tale
Of that Greek girl changed to a nightingale.

O Philomela, but for me
Who frightened that dark shadow from the tree,
A further change you had gone through,
Your 'Tereu-tereu' now 'Too-whit too-whoo'!

The Blind Man

Speak of the birds, he lifts a listening finger
And 'chiff-chaff' 'willow-warbler' names each singer,
'Hedge-sparrow' 'robin' 'wren'; he knows their cries,
Though all are nightingales to his blind eyes.

Prospect of a Mountain

Though cuckoos call across the kyle
And larks are dancing everywhere
To their thin bagpipe's air,
My thoughts are of the autumn day
I climbed that Quinaig, monstrous pile,
And striding up its slaggy brow
Stood outside time and space;
It looks so empty of me now,
More years than miles away,
The mountain-cairn might mark my burial-place.

A Mountain Graveyard

Sheep-fold, I thought – till by the dyke
  I saw it lying deep in dock
And knew he never whistled tyke,
  The herd who folded that quiet flock.

The Shepherd's Hut

The smear of blue peat smoke
That staggered on the wind and broke,
The only sign of life,
Where was the shepherd's wife,
Who left those flapping clothes to dry,
Taking no thought for her family?
For, as they bellied out
And limbs took shape and waved about,
I thought, She little knows
That ghosts are trying on her children's clothes.

The Haystack

Too dense to have a door,
Window or fireplace or a floor,
They saw this cottage up,
Huge bricks of grass, clover and buttercup
Carting to byre and stable,
Where cow and horse will eat wall, roof and gable.

In Burnham Beeches

Walking among these smooth beech-boles
With cracks and galls
And beetle-holes
And ivy trickling in green waterfalls,

I noted carvings on their barks,
Faint and diffuse
As china-marks
On Worcester or Old Bow: I wondered whose.

I feared that time had played its part
With those whose token
Was a twin heart,
So many hearts the swelling bark had broken.

Cornish Flower-Farm

Here where the cliff rises so high
The sea below fills half the sky
And ships hang in mid-air,
Set on the cliff-face, square by square,
Walls of veronica enclose
White gladioli in their neat rows
And blue and golden irises;
But though the walls grow tall as trees,
Some flowers from their quiet quillets pass
To mix with wayside weeds and grass,
Like nuns that from their strict retreats
Go visiting the poor in their plain streets.

The Shower

The cherry-pickers left their picking
And ladders through the branches sticking
And cherries hung like gouts of blood
Down the long aisles of white-washed wood.

But now the sun is breaking through
Dark clouds that dry to pools of blue
And the smooth Medway lies uncreased
Except for drops the boughs released.

What is it makes the sun so proud
He will not suck a passing cloud
But needs raindrops to quench his thirst?
Well, let him do his picking first.

At Formby

From that wide empty shore,
No foot had ever trod before
(Or since the sea drew back the tide),
I climbed the dune's soft slide
To where no higher than my hand
Wind-bitten pines grew in the clogging sand.

But farther from the beach
The trees rose up beyond my reach,
And as I walked, they still grew taller
And I myself smaller and smaller,
Till gazing up at a high wood
I felt that I had found my lost childhood.

A Dead Bird

Finding the feathers of a bird
Killed by a sparrow-hawk,
I thought, What need is there to walk?
And bound them on my feet;
And as I flew off through the air,
I saw men stare up from a street
And women clasp their hands in prayer.
'To Hades' was no sooner said
Than a winged Hermes I was there;
And though I peered round for the dead,
Nothing I saw and nothing heard
But a low moaning from a bough,
'Ah, who is wearing my poor feathers now?'

The Revenant

O foolish birds, be dumb,
  And you, jay, stop your mocking laughter;
A revenant I come
  Today as I might come fifty years after.

Why, birds, I am no stranger,
  For as I cross the copse and back,
I feel a double-ganger,
  Who meets himself at each turn of the track.

A better welcome give
  To one who may have bent and blessed
Your fathers four or five
  Laid in the smooth round hollow of a nest.

Come less than fifty years,
  Owls may have cause to mock at one
Who stalks this wood and wears
  A frosty coat that will not stand the sun.

The Beech-Wood

When the long, varnished buds of beech
Point out beyond their reach,
And tanned by summer suns
Leaves of black bryony turn bronze,
And gossamer floats bright and wet
From trees that are their own sunset,
Spring, summer, autumn I come here,
And what is there to fear?
And yet I never lose the feeling
That someone close behind is stealing
Or else in front has disappeared;
Though nothing I have seen or heard,
The fear of what I might have met
Makes me still walk beneath these boughs
With cautious step as in a haunted house.

On the Common

The chaffy seeds by the wind blown
Are here so strangely sown,
That one might almost say
The spider's-webs the bushes wear
Have been put down to hay,
And though no crop they bear
Ploughed and cross-ploughed on empty air,
So thick these hay-fields swarm,
That every gorse-bush is become a farm.

The Blind Children

Where caterpillars ate their fill
On hazels' mealy leaves until
The boughs were stript half-bare
And leaves hung riddled with clear holes of air,

I met with children who upturned
Faces to where the blue sky burned,
Some blinking in the glare,
Some looking up with a white open stare.

I did not need to question which
Should leave the road and take the ditch;
I felt it was small kindness
To children walking arm in arm in blindness.

From their blind eyes I borrowed sight
To see the leaves against the light
Rich and not ruinous,
Set with bright diamonds on the fire-fringed boughs.

On the Hillside

What causes the surprise
That greets me here under the piecemeal skies
Of this thick-wooded scar?
Is it the look that the familiar
Keeps as of something strange
When so much else is constant but to change?
No, it's the thought that this white sun that cleaves
A silvery passage through the leaves
Is the same sun that cleft them
A week ago, as though I never left them
And never went in the sad interval
To my friend's funeral,
Though crossing the churchyard today I shivered
To see how fast on a fresh grave the flowers had withered.

The Rockland Broad

Water too clear to show,
Unless a frown ruffle its brow,
I scarcely feel afloat –
I am suspended in a flying-boat!

Sure, with the land so low
This broad will burst and overflow,
Rush on and never stop,
Till the whole world becomes one water-drop.

Though willow-carrs and reeds
And alders, too, change to seaweeds,
Let Heaven again take note,
Save this new Noah in his flying-boat.

Dundonnell Mountains

Through mist that sets the hills on fire
And rising, never rises higher
Looms a stone figure, gross and squat,
An idol carved out by the weather,
Face, limbs and body lumped together;
And while for none but mountain fox
Eagle or buzzard or wild cat
Its worship may be orthodox,
Death fawning on me from these rocks,
A false step would suffice
To make me both its priest and sacrifice.

The Dead Sheep

There was a blacksmith in my breast,
That worked the bellows of my chest
  And hammer of my heart,
As up the heavy scree I pressed,
  Making the loose stones scream, crag-echoes start.

Rocks, rising, showed that they were sheep,
But one remained as though asleep,
  And how it was I saw,
When loath to leave the huddled heap
  A hoodie crow rose up with angry craw.

Though stiller than a stone it lay,
The face with skin half-flayed away
  And precious jewels gone,
The eye-pits darted a dark ray
  That searched me to my shadowy skeleton.

View from Mountain

When through the parting mist,
That the sun's warm gold mouth had kissed,
The hills beneath me came to view
With lochans gleaming here and there,
It was not like the earth I knew;
Another world was shining through,
As though that earth had worn so thin
I saw the living spirit within,
Its beauty almost pain to bear
Waking in me the thought,
If heaven by act of death were brought
Nearer than now, might I not die
Slain by my immortality?

The Day Ends

The day ends and its heat
Lies in chill dews about our feet;
But though its twelve hours seemed as soon
Gone as the twelve strokes struck at noon,
So much those hours have freed
To blow away for memory's seed,
Will they not still be ours,
Fixed like the church-tower's gilt and holy hours?

At Amberley Wild Brooks

Watching the horses stand
And bend their long heads Roman-nosed,
With thick cheek veins exposed,
So close to where the brook's bank shelves
They almost meet themselves
In the smooth water sliding by,
I think it strange creatures so great
Can be shut in by wooden gate
And brook no deeper than my hand,
And not like Pegasus shoot wings and fly.

By the Erme

No trace of absent years
Water or bank or boulder wears;
All is the same as when I went away.

Even my floating face
Seems looking up from the same place,
More steadfast than the stream that cannot stay.

I might have left it there,
Although I notice that my hair
Now stirs a little foam in the smooth bay.

The Swedes

Three that are one since time began,
Horse, cart and man,
Lurch down the lane patched with loose stones;
Swedes in the cart heaped smooth and round
Like skulls that from the ground
The man has dug without the bones
Leave me in doubt
Whether the swedes with gold shoots sprout
Or with fresh fancies bursts each old bald sconce.

The Salmon-Leap

Leaves, and not birds, now flit,
Brighter than yellow wagtail and coal-tit,
Or on the water lie
Making a sunset of the fishes' sky.

Autumn for salmon-trout
Is spring, and Io Hymen boulders shout,
Spate drawing them to spawn
Where on high hills the river keeps its dawn.

From rock-lipt lynn to lynn,
Shaking the ferns and grasses with their din,
The cascades overflow
And pour in pools to rise as boiling snow;

Tossing their bodies bare
The salmon-trout are seen tasting our air,
For stronger is the flood
That rages in their few small drops of blood.

Lady's Slipper Orchid

Though I know well enough
To hunt the Lady's Slipper now
Is playing blindman's-buff,
For it was June She put it on
And grey with mist the spiders' lace
Swings in the autumn wind,
Yet through this hill-wood, high and low,
I peer in every place;
Seeking for what I cannot find
I do as I have often done
And shall do while I stay beneath the sun.

Twilight

As daylight drains away
And darkness creeps out of the wood
And flowers become too faint to tell,
My eyesight failing me as well
And chill dew watering my blood,
I might imagine night was my last day.

But why need I rehearse
What I must play with my whole heart?
Spectators may be moved to tears
To see me act these now-feigned fears;
While others summing up the part
May with approval say, His lines were terse.

Section 2

Selected Earlier Poems (1910–1931)

From *Songs of Night* *(1910)*

Winter

Time, like an aged gardener,
Still tends the garden of the year,
And, when the summer sweets are lost,
He weaves the scentless flowers of frost.

When, too, the forest boughs have shed
Their generation of the dead,
Against the stars the sacred trees
Spread out their naked traceries.

And in the night an amorous moon
Sings to the sea a tender tune,
And all the star-encrusted sky
Shivers with silent ecstacy.

For Beauty thus not only glows
Within the wine-cup of the rose,
But like a hermit clad may be
In garment of austerity.

The Moon

The Night has risen like the sound
Of solemn music from the ground,
And blackens with her dusky hair
The thin, ambiguous air;

And moonlight lies, a pallid pall,
On sombre woods funereal;
The moon-struck leaves speak mystic words;
And rivers flash like swords.

O white and solitary blossom,
Night wears upon her ancient bosom,
Scentless, a flower of silver light
That only glows by night;

The sword of Winter hath no power
To slay thee, O bright Phoenix-flower!
Thy life is as the changing seas,
Changeless through centuries.

Landscape

Oppressive with its vacant weight,
The moorland stretches desolate,
And like a wound the sunset bleeds
Across a weary waste of weeds.

A tarn is fed by sluggish rills,
Branching like veins across the hills,
And darkened by a wind that flings
The passing shadow of his wings.

Save where one torture-twisted tree
Shrieks out in silent agony,
Oppressive with its vacant weight,
The moorland stretches desolate.

A grey hawk at a dizzy height
Thrills with its sharp suspended flight,
And like a soft, insidious kiss
The snakes within the heather hiss.

To where as in a monstrous birth
The red moon struggles from the earth,
Oppressive with its vacant weight,
The moorland stretches desolate.

Bacchos Chthonios

ὡυτὸς δὲ Ἀΐδης καὶ Διόνυσος,
ὅτεῳ μαίνονται καὶ ληναΐζουσι.
Herakleitos

Lord of the serpent vine,
Thyself the mystic wine
That fills the faint and gives the weary wings:
I also feel the swift
Glad leaping of thy gift,
Wild fire that mayhap was the ancient flame
Of lust and shame
Within fierce lips of courtezans and kings.

Lord of the bright fawn-skin,
Whose kiss is deadly sin,
And gives to Death thy lovers for a spoil:
Yet these red lips are fain
Life's purple cup to drain,
Before I lay my ivy-crownèd head
Where dreamless dead
Are strewn in ashes wet with wine and oil.

Zagreus, twin, sexless, wild,
Bacchos, immortal child
Of mortal mother drawing laboured breath,
No light of star is shed
Above thy lovers dead:
Only lone voices linger like the wails
Of nightingales
In the pale kingdom of the Lord of Death.

Hymn to Zagreus

Zagreus, our Lord,
Who givest a sword,
O Hunter of men who art hunted and slain,
Art thou drunk with the strong
Glad wine-cup's song,
Or with bitter delight of luxurious pain?

Vine-tendrils enmesh
Thy limbs and flesh,
And bite like serpents and bind like thongs;
And we shed dim dust
On the pride and lust
Of thy tigers and women and cymbals and songs.

For our hands and feet
Were fierce with the heat
Of a flame that scorches, a fire that sears;
And we wreaked our will
By hollow and hill
And made thee, O Hunter, the sport of our spears.

Thy wine is a fierce
Sheer sword to pierce,
And our hearts were fulfilled with its purple flood,
And we slew our Lord
With that sharp, clear sword,
And the dark earth was bright with the blossom of blood.

But as garlands of flowers,
In the dance of the Hours,
The shreds of thy red-dripping flesh shall be spun;
And god of the Spring,
Afresh shalt thou bring,
Wild honey and vine-leaves and songs of the sun.

Sleep

The flowers are ghostly white
  Along the dusky lane,
  They sleep and turn again
To tender buds at night.

So, tired with all the pain
  Of songs and sins that burn,
  I, too, shall sleep and turn
Into a child again.

City by Night

Each light is like a flashing gem
Within her guilty diadem;
The night is shed on her like hair
That hides a face's dark despair.

The deadly river, too, glides by
Like some swift tiger, stealthily,
Its sinuous back all painted bright
With quivering bars of golden light.

And far above the city's jars
The ancient army of the stars,
That in a quiet, reproachful mood
Keep watch from God's own solitude.

Night Thought

A little while, and I shall be
At one with earth and air and sea:
A little while, and I shall creep
Where none shall waken me from sleep.

A little while, and life shall pass
And lend a greenness to the grass:
A little while, and these dull bones
Shall be companions to the stones.

And yet the Spirit of God's Love
Is more a falcon than a dove;
And can it be that I shall have
No hiding-place within the grave?

O gracious Lips that I have kissed
And tasted in the Eucharist,
With you alone an answer is,
And yet no answer but a kiss.

The Leaf

Sometimes an autumn leaf
  That falls upon the ground,
  Gives the heart a wound
And wakes an ancient grief.

But I weep not that all
  The leaves of autumn die,
  I only weep that I
Should live to see them fall.

From *Boaz and Ruth and other poems (1920)*

Here and There

Eyes that are black like bramble-berries
That lustre with light the rank hedgerows
Are kindly eyes and within them there is
Love of the land where the bramble grows.

But mine are blue as a far-off distance
And grey as the water beneath the sea;
Therefore they look with a long insistence
For things that are not and cannot be.

On the Cliff

Earth with my little pathway ends
Abruptly, and I stand
Where in a wall of snow extends
The breakage of the land.

White birds, like fragments of the cliff,
Fly on the empty air,
Crying as though from hearts made stiff
With straitening despair.

And far beneath me on the beach
  Sings the incessant sea,
And sighs like love that cannot reach
  To Love's eternity.

Lord, in the weakness of my words
  Let all these pray for me,
The broken cliff, the crying birds
  And the foam-mottled sea.

Chorus from 'Jephthah'

(on Jephthah's home-coming from the land of Tob)

str. I

They say Sidonian sailors dive for purple and sea-pearls
Where the human-headed fish-god lives and the old sea-dragon
    curls;
And go in ships to Ophir by the wide palm-waving capes
For peacocks, gold and ivory, almug-wood and apes,
And, coming by the Red Sea, bring chalcedonies and beryls
And amethysts for feasting kings to quell the fume of grapes.

ant. I

And traders bring from Tarshish in beaked boats on the windy seas
Plates of silver, iron and tin, amber and ambergris;
And camels come from Havilah by the road to Paradise
With mountain gold and cassia, spikenard and sweet spice,
And bring from Sheba silken scarfs and blue-lipped negresses,
Perfumes and dyes and singing dwarfs, incense and golden mice.

ep. I

But though one were a tunny to swim through the ribs of sunken
    ships
And gaze on the wavy glimmer of yellow amber and gold,
Or a stone-eating ostrich to fly to the buried cities of old
With their porphyry cups that dyed king Chedorlaomer's lips,
Yet nothing there is could bless the sight of the eye or yield
Such joy as the hidden treasure that lies in a man's own field.

str. II
O Love, that combest the shaggy locks of the mountain lion's mane
And filest the teeth of the crocodile's jaws in his nest in the water-
cane,
Plucking the sting from the banded wasp and the quills from the
porcupine
And dripping like myrrh from the panther's claws and the horns of
the Jordan kine;
Sweeter than pipes to the horned asp on the lips of a sweet pipe-
player
Or Eshcol grapes to the laughing fox or a honey-comb to the bear:

ant. II
Love, that bringest the plump-fleshed quails to build on the fallow
ground
And blowest the cuckoo's call from the wood like a floating bubble
of sound,
Teaching the crested hoopoe to read where the secret waters run
And rousing the bald-headed eagle's blood to plunge headlong in the
sun,
Making like yellow amber beads the eyes of the cushat-dove
And painting the peacock's outspread tail with a thousand eyes of
love:

ep. II
Love, O king Love, the conqueror of beasts and the tribes of birds
And long-spiked chariots splashed with war, tall crowns and wine-
dark swords,
Though a king should lead an army south and conquer by force or
guile
The untameable heart of the many-mouthed dragon of ancient Nile
And heap on a thousand ox-hide shields the riches of Mizraïm,
He too would lose the last-fought field, for love would conquer him;
Nor could he find in the famous land of the flat-nosed Lubim more
Than the Demon holds in his subtle hands that crouches beneath his
door.

From *The Death of Eli and other poems* (1921)

Daisies

The stars are everywhere tonight,
Above, beneath me and around;
They fill the sky with powdery light
And glimmer from the night-strewn ground;
For where the folded daisies are
In every one I see a star.

And so I know that when I pass
Where no sun's shadow counts the hours
And where the sky was there is grass
And where the stars were there are flowers,
Through the long night in which I lie
Stars will be shining in my sky.

Autumn

When light wakes late and early fails;
And where the catkins swung their tails
Like caterpillars on the trees
Nestle the nuts in twos and threes;
A late owl hooting from the wood
Chills my premonitory blood.

And when the hedges, thick with haws,
Are strewn with the loose harvest straws,
And sullen hips upon the brier
Betray the rose's sepulchre,
The stripped fields in the moonlight glow
White with imaginary snow.

How can I know, how can I know
But something of this winter's snow
Shall fall on me till I become
Dumb as the snow-heaped earth is dumb,
And I myself this year shall be
Part of the year's mortality?

Never again to wake at spring
And see the blackthorn blossoming,
And flowers that later days forget,
Primrose and rumpled violet,
Coltsfoot and gold-rayed celandine,
Outspreading with a silvery shine;

And, where the beds of bluebells lie
Like water that reflects a sky,
That white flower veined with lilac blood,
The three-leaved sorrel of the wood,
The same that to St Patrick was
The Godhead in a house of grass.

Flowers are the dull earth's conscious eyes,
Full of sweet hopes and memories,
Making – O Immortality,
Surely thy image here I see! –
A little outspent sun and rain
Mix with the dust and live again.

Song for Autumn

Come, love, for now the night and day
  Play with their pawns of black and white,
And what day loses in her play
  Is won by the encroaching night.

The clematis grows old and clings
  Grey-bearded to the roadside trees
And in the hedge the nightshade strings
  Her berries in bright necklaces.

The fields are bare; the latest sheaf
  Of barley, wheat and rusty rye
Is stacked long since; and every leaf
  Burns like a sunset on the sky.

Come, love, for night and day, alas,
  Are playing for a heavier stake
Than hours of light or leaves or grass;
  Come, love; come, love, for sweet love's sake.

The Bee-Orchis

I saw a bee, I saw a flower;
I looked again and said, For sure
Never was flower, never was bee
Locked in such immobility.

The loud bees lurched about the hill,
But this flower-buried bee was still;
I said, O Love, has love the power
To change a bee into a flower?

From *Thirty-One Poems* *(1922)*

Epitaph

M.F.H.

A flower herself to flowers she went,
Sharer of Beauty's banishment;
She left us winter, but to her
It was the springtime of the year.

Cuckoo

Cuckoo, cuckoo!
Is it your double note I hear
Now far away, now near,
Now soft, now clear,
Cuckoo?

Cuckoo, cuckoo!
Laughs now through the spring's misty wood
And leaf-winged sap in flood
Your mocking mood,
Cuckoo?

Cuckoo, cuckoo!
So sits among sky-tangling trees
Our Mephistopheles
Singing at ease,
Cuckoo.

Begone, cuckoo!
For soon your bubble-note twin born,
Pricked by the June rose-thorn,
Shall burst in scorn,
Cuckoo.

Waiting

We waited for the spring,
My love and I;
The larks were in the sky,
The lambs were on the hill;
Did we not hear them sing?
Did we not hear them cry?
Yes, yes, O yes, but still
We waited for the spring
My love and I.

We waited for the spring,
My love and I;
Speedwell that robs the sky,
Trumpeting daffodil
And blackthorn's blossoming,
We watched them all go by;
These came and went but still
We waited for the spring
My wife and I.

A Child Sleeping

She is like the sorrel's white bud
That grows in a sun-watered wood
In springtime, opening with brief sun;
But whenever the day is done
Or sky is overcast by cloud
Quickly her slender head is bowed.

But birds are busy in that wood;
They have no time to seek for food;
And sluggish and enormous trees
Pull their green smocks down to their knees;
And even the sun, centuries old,
Renewing youth shakes off the cold.

A Child's Voice

On winter nights shepherd and I
  Down to the lambing-shed would go;
Rain round our swinging lamp did fly
  Like shining flakes of snow.

There on a nail our lamp we hung,
  And O it was beyond belief
To see those ewes lick with hot tongue
  The limp wet lambs to life.

A week gone and sun shining warm
  It was as good as gold to hear
Those new-born voices round the farm
  Cry shivering and clear.

Where was a prouder man than I
  Who knew the night those lambs were born,
Watching them leap two feet on high
  And stamp the ground in scorn?

Gone sheep and shed and lighted rain
  And blue March morning; yet today
A small voice crying brings again
  Those lambs leaping at play.

The Snail

I praise the solemn snail
  For when he walks abroad
He drags a slow and glistening trail
  Behind him on the road.

Clock ticks for him in vain;
  Tick tick tick – will he run?
He hankers not to share men's pain
  Of losing to the sun.

Snail keeps a steady pace,
  Therefore I honour snail;
For if none saw him win a race
  None ever saw him fail.

You say, But in the end
  He fills a thrush's throat.
A life, how could one better spend
  Than for a song's top-note?

Flesh, sinew, blood and bone,
  All that of me is strong,
Blithely would I bury in one
  Short-lived immortal song.

The Dead Sparrow

Today I saw a bird
  Lie upturned on the ground;
It seemed as though I found a word
  That had no sound.

Quickly once that sparrow
  Flew rising through the air;
But quicker flew the flying arrow
  That laid it there.

O strange to see it now
  Lying with sidelong head;
Stranger to think it does not know
  Where it lies dead.

That sparrow asks no man
  To dig for it a grave;
Gentle is death, I thought, that can
  Both slay and save.

At Owley

Dear, I wished you had been there;
It was almost a pain to bear
The beauty of that place alone;
One needed a companion.

You know the hour one trembling star
Anchors off a black belt of fir;
I trembled too, like him unshod
Who saw the flowering of his God.

And I remember came the thought,
Should God by act of death be brought
Nearer than now, might I not die
Slain by my immortality?

Sand Strapwort

When colour lifting from the earth
Catches from trees a dying birth
And in the ivy's yellow bloom
Wasps and blue flies make angry hum,

Here, twenty paces from house-door
Where men so strangely rich live poor,
Where few sea-poppies still unfurl
I set my foot in budding pearl.

Strange joy is mine to know I stand
Here in one spot of our England
Where God and the small strapwort strive
To keep one English flower alive.

Islands

These new songs that I sing
  Were islands in the sea
That never missed a spring,
  No, nor a century.

A starry voyager,
  I to these islands come
Knowing not by what star
  I am at last come home.

From *The Bird-Cage* *(1926)*

Go Now, My Song

Go now, my song,
Let your wing be strong;
Fly and dart and dip
With a chip-chip,
A wren among the thorn
Of the world's scorn.

Never have a fear
Of thorn that would tear
Or the cold stare of men;
O my chitty-wren,
Let not courage fail
Your upturned tail.

January

So thick a mist darkened the wood to-day
My friend, the jay, flashed by two trees away,
  While I stood in a hush
  Seeing each tree and bush
  Hung with buds green and white
  Making unusual light,
Though of the sober green
Less in that wintry wood were to be seen.

That jay I followed, for behind the mist
Two jays, I knew, kept their love's angry tryst;
    And where the track dipt down
    Narrowed and overgrown,
    As I brushed past each bush
    White buds fell in a rush,
One might have said it rained,
While green buds on the barer boughs remained.

Then climbing where with looped and twisted twine
Wild clematis, bryony and woodbine
    And such reptilian growth
    Hung in decaying sloth,
    I stood still thinking how
    Two months or three from now
Those green buds would not tarry
More than the flashing drops of January.

Rooks

In a high wood
Where great trees on their tree-trunks stood,
I seemed as one
Lost with the giants of an age bygone.

A small bird sung
And those old trees were once more young,
Their upper wood
Renewing spring with a faint flush of blood.

I lifted eyes
And saw their tangled tributaries
That to earth sunk
Condensed in the broad river of tree-trunk.

High in those trees
Rooks built their storm-bound villages,
Nest on dark nest
Swaying at rest on the trees' frail unrest.

They cawed and cawed
Till I felt stricken like a man outlawed,
And ill at ease
I sheltered under tempest of those trees.

Then I went out
Where silent grass gave a loud shout;
Looking behind
I saw them like black crosses on the wind.

Green Hellebore

Wind has an edge that cleaves
  Like hook of hedger, for
A blood-stain marks the leaves
  Wind-cut of hellebore.

Green with the loss of blood
  No heavy head looks up,
But in this Easter wood
  Hangs down an empty cup.

Spring

I never noticed, till I saw today
How budding birches stand in their green spray
And bracken like a snake from earth upheaves,
How many in this wood are last year's leaves.

The Wood-Cutter

The white mist made the hanger dim,
  Else I had never heeded
  The spider-webs mist-seeded;
That clinging mist showed me the slim
Shine of each gossamer
That hanging from nowhere hung there,
But hid from sight the sorry wood-cutter.

The preacher stood in his pulpit,
  But not one word was heard
  By any sort of bird,
Wren, sparrow, linnet, finch or tit;
They sang in the wood's fire,
The smoke that thinned out rising higher
To sky as blue as man's farthest desire.

'The spring is come that was to come,'
  So preached the cuckoo-pint,
  But the birds would not stint
Their song that preached the preacher dumb,
Though still that axe rang out
With shout that followed fast on shout;
Whether from axe or tree played with my doubt.

Pasque-Flower

Dear, ask no song tonight,
My heart is heavy with sad delight;
  Beauty's have been these hours
  And yours and the pasque-flower's,
  That having gone are now forever ours.

Forever ours indeed,
Blown away to be memory's seed
And like the pasque-flower still
To haunt on Streatley Hill
Dark with juniper above Streatley mill.

June – To Alison

Rain drizzling in the high blue pines,
A misty tangle of loose lines,
Here in the hollow wood had ceased,
Except when by the wind released
From broad leaves and the bent tree-tops
Rattled a shower of thunder-drops;
Then sudden shafts of light shot through
As the sky dried to pools of blue.

I idled while the hot sun toiled
And thick with steam the moist wood boiled,
Watching on the wet-blackened boughs
Raindrops dark and mysterious
Shining along their silver rows
(Strange as the level eye looked close
Small trees in each to see outlined)
And hazel buds, green, soft and blind.

Four years ago this day of June,
Clear in the sky, a thread-thin moon
I saw you first, you weak, I strong,
As small tit's chip and thrush's song;
Still with increase of strength we grow
Like nut or raindrop in a row,
You fattening in your fringed sheath,
I gathering strength to drop beneath.

July

Darker the track to-day
Than any cloudy March or April day
  When nesting birds sang louder,
For hazels hazels, elders elders meet,
Tangle and trip the sun's pale dancing feet
  That beat it to white powder.

That day in January,
I climbed the hill to this wood's sanctuary,
  The track was plain enough;
But oh, this summer tangle, thistles, nettles,
Goose-grass, fool's parsley, falling privet petals
  And leafy bough on bough.

Then half the sky looked in
Where the track ran, open and wide and thin,
  Though slippery in places;
Now bryony crowds its stars yellow as honey
And close against my face hemp-agrimony
  Pushes its purple faces.

But I may find again
When autumn's fires sink under winter's rain
  A clearer way to pass,
As when that sun with a wan ray of hope
Striking a hollow on the frost-furred slope
  Wet one green patch of grass.

The Young Martins

None but the mouse-brown wren
That runs and hides from men –
Though for a moment now
Clinging with fine claws to a bough
One watches me askance,
Who dimly sit where the loose sunbeams dance –

Trills in these trees today;
All other birds seem flown away,
Though when I scrambled up
Through the thick covert of the combe's wide cup
Shaking down the last dog-rose petals,
My hand kissed by the angry nettles
And clawed by the lean thistles,
Blackbird and thrush flew off with startled whistles.

I see the hillside crossed
By a black flying ghost,
Rook's passing shadow, and beyond
Like skaters cutting figures on a pond
High swifts that curve on tilted wings are drawing
Vanishing circles; but save for the rooks' cawing
And trill of the small wren
Lost in the green again
No birds are singing anywhere,
As though the hot midsummer air
Hanging like blue smoke through the holt
Had driven all birds to sit apart and moult.

Yet when I came up through the farm
Where the stacked hay smelt keen and warm
Heads of young martins, one or two,
Black and white-cheeked, were peeping through
The small holes of their houses;
There where all day the sunlight drowses
They looked out from the cool
Dark shade of eaves and saw the pool
Where white duck feathers raised a storm of foam,
The cock that stood with crimson comb
Among his scraping hens,
The short-legged bull behind the fence,
The line-hung sheets that cracked and curled,
All the sun-laden dusty world;
And nodding each to each
They kept up a small twittering speech,
As though they ready were
To launch out on the air
And from their nests of clay
Like disembodied spirits suddenly fly away.

The Tumulus

Here to the leeward of this Roman mound
  The wind is quiet
As any battle-shout that shook the ground
  Long ago nigh it.

Here the dead sleep in bones through centuries
  With earth for flesh,
Their own long woven in flower-tapestries
  And turf's green mesh.

No bugle shatters sleep for them, so surely
  They keep the peace;
I in their old decease mourn prematurely
  My own at ease.

Findon

This unforgettable place, dear love,
These falling hills, O clear enough;
My memory fits it like a glove.

So stood that one lean row of trees,
So on this slope busy with bees
Frail rock-rose spread its golden fleece.

There in that hollow henbane grew;
Seeing it first I called to you,
Its sluggish beauty to both new.

Calling you now I call in vain;
Your absence works in me like pain
More poisonous than dull henbane.

Now thinking how I stand alone
I ask, Am I the selfsame one
Who made two with you in that sun?

They say these flakes of flesh depart
Till of quick brain and the slow heart
No part remains the selfsame part.

Yet love remains and memory
Of God and you, of earth and sky,
All that is intimately I.

So when it hurts the heart to think
Of that most bitter, abrupt brink
Where the low-shouldered coffins sink,

I ask, should spirit be aghast
That slipt slow bodies in the past
To fling off the whole flesh at last?

You absent from me are most near;
It is such presence with me here
That sanctifies this solemn air.

The Sand Martins

The sand martins were flying,
Flying around and crying;
Till late in the grey light
I watched their twisted flight;
Then with the last light gone
They housed in holes that riddled the sandstone.

I rose and passing by
One thin contented cry,
Chirp of sleep-settling bird,
I heard, and no more heard
Save the late gulls that cried
Down by the wave-lit darkness of ebb-tide.

The Children

Digging a changeful hole
To cast its light on ground or naked bole
This small sun through the crowd of shaking leaves
A doubtful passage cleaves
And looks no larger than the moon;
Though in the early days of June
Green caterpillars ate their fill
Among these hazels' mealy leaves until
Some boughs were stript half-bare
And leaves hung riddled with clear holes of air.

It seems the stranger then
To see this hazel bough budded as when
Hung in bright rows the drops of April rain;
But as I look again
Those small buds young and green
Withered and old are seen
Set on a broken and down-fallen bough;
And seeing them I think of how
The faces of those children were upturned
Withered and old to where the blue sky burned,
Some screwing their shut eyes in the sun's glare,
Some looking up with a white open stare,
For arm in arm those children walked in blindness;
To take the ditch was a small kindness,
For turning with me on the road
With pointing finger those blind children showed

How many lovely things,
White butterflies stumbling with heavy wings,
Ragwort's cheap gold and dusty loose-stringed nettles,
Hedges scattered with rusting privet petals
And freaked with stems of carted hay,
The oats-field rustling its dry spray
And the streaked bindweed bells beneath,
And where my pathway took the open heath
The small round pellets of the rabbits
That are untidy in their habits,
All lovely things that otherwise
I had not seen with my clear-sighted eyes.

Night-Flowering Campion

Close on the bat-crossed hour
I waited for a flower
By light grown visible
Burning the vivid hill.

Pimpernel in night-bud
Showed like small drops of blood;
It was no common flower
I kept late vigil for.

I watched by falling light
Till I saw how with white
And patient petals shone
Night-flowering campion.

So white those petals showed
And such a rich scent flowed,
I said, 'Are we not one,
I and this campion?'

Seeing how for us both
Sweetness followed on sloth
I felt my own song's power
In that night-flowering flower.

But when I came that way
In the clear light of day
I noticed a mean plant
Sticky and small and scant.

Ghosts

When purple on the hill
Struggles the dwarf thistle –
A hand that grips below
Forbids its stem to grow –
From the spear thistle's crown
Shakes loose the thistledown.

Silver against blue sky
These ghosts of day float by,
Fitful, irregular,
Each one a silk-haired star
Blown by the wind at will
O'er the flower-nodding hill.

Vaguely like butterflies
Flowerwards they fall and rise,
Till by a trammelling bush
Caught on their onward rush
And from the wind's aid freed
They settle on their seed.

Not by the famished light
Of a moon-ridden night
But by clear sunny hours
Go these white ghosts of flowers,
Taking from the glad earth
Their burial and their birth.

The Burdocks

No one ever comes here –
Not since last April when the gamekeeper
Choked with lopt boughs this coppice-track
Scarcely distinguished from the black
Tangle of thorn, these autumn gusts
Are stripping cinder-bare,
For only here and there
A last leaf rusts.

So all along this track
Whose length I wander aimlessly and back
With leaf-clogged footsteps that fall dumb
The burdock-leaves hang in foul scum;
But oh those gummy burs are sly,
For brushing by a stem
My coat is thick with them
Withered and dry.

But glad am I to think
Those brown eyes saw in me a badger slink
Back to its earth or the high brush
Of fox dangle from bush to bush
Though none has for an age at least,
Spaniel nor gamekeeper
Nor any walking here,
Seen either beast.

The Seeds

Puffing like smoke over the wood
The old-man's-beard is stained with blood,
And strewn along the pathway lie
Like small open sarcophagi
The hazel-nuts broken in halves
By squirrels, and the old jay laughs.

Now summer's flowers are winter's weeds,
I think of all the sleeping seeds;
Winds were their robins and by night
Frosts glue their leafy cover tight;
Snow may shake down its dizzy feathers,
They will sleep safely through all weathers.

Then with spring's grip, 'Awake, awake!'
The bodies of these seeds shall break
And lo, a wood-spurge or wood-sorrel
Or nettle in hot angry quarrel
Or pale primrose, or it may be
The twin leaves of a young oak-tree.

From *The Cuckoo Clock* *(1928)*

Cuckoo-Bottom

The tunnelling mould-warps
Build their fresh barrows on a kicking corpse;
Where the old barrows linger
This winter sun points no long-shadowed finger.

The thudding race-horse hooves
Print on the sodden soil their lucky grooves,
But wethers chime a bell
Where Briton warriors sleep who sleep too well.

The cuckoo's double note
Loosened like bubbles from a drowning throat
Those Britons do not hear –
Cuckoos in Egypt call this time of year.

Rother in Flood

Between twin banks the Rother
    With slow contentment goes;
Bush-sprinkled lakes spread this side and the other
    Flowing as the wind flows.

High on the upper lands
White-cowled oasthouses stare
And piled poles in hop gardens seem like hands
Whose fingers point in prayer.

Gathered by stormy weather
The rooks and sea-gulls meet
Like black angels and white mingling together
At God's last judgment-seat.

The Long Man of Wilmington

What figure, drawn in chalk, strides with his pole
Across the Downs, as naked as a soul?
Odin or Balder? Time will solve the doubt
And mail-clad robots look on a Boy Scout.

The Moon

'What gars Garskadden luk sae gash?'
Kilmardinny said to one,
While late into the early morn
They sat drinking on.

'Garskadden's been wi' his Maker
These twa hours,' said he;
'I saw him step awa, but, faith,
Why spoil gude company?'

Kilnaughton Bay

From the black rocks
  Whose shadow with the waving water swings
A heron squawks
  And floats away on widely-flapping wings.

Lighthouses wink,
  One winking slowly with a blood-shot eye;
Stars rise and sink
  As, seeking light, earth whirls from sky to sky.

Dead Leaves in Spring

These beech leaves in their courses
Are like withered sea-horses;
They do not change at once
To fibrous skeletons;
Brown and brittle and thin
They keep a sun-tanned skin.

Stuck at a rabbit's bury
They peer a moment and scurry,
As though they frightened were
And loved the sunny air
And glistening grass that waves
More than dark gaping graves.

So they rattle and run
Before the wind and the sun
And when, as dancers do,
They pause a minute or two
It is the wind falls slack,
Not any breath they lack.

The Old Tombs

What are those tables for,
Stone table set by stone table
Under the east gable
Of this old church, Saxon and Norman,
With Death always the foreman?

Do the dead at Bishopstone
Rise from the ground like moths
And sit at white table-cloths
The moon at Easter spreads for them
Or the Star of Bethlehem?

In Balcombe Forest

Earth wakes again stretching thin arms of bracken,
From sleepy fists the silken fingers slacken;
These and that purring rattle of nightjar
Hint age, as children do, so young they are.

Osea Island

I came in sight of Osea Island
  Walking the turfed sea-wall;
To right mud-banks chirped like a cricket,
  To left I heard sedge-warblers call.

I never went to Osea Island,
Perhaps I never shall
More than those crabs with sun-bleached bodies
That through the grey sea-purslane crawl.

I took the road to Osea Island
Soft to my feet and green
As any road that through a wood-ride
Vivid with summer grass is seen.

Before I came to Osea Island
The seaweed on the road
Rose in the tide that from the mud-flats
Flowed through culverts and overflowed.

Why do I think of Osea Island?
Perhaps I am afraid
Some foaming tide may overtake me
Walking a blossom-dropping glade.

The Ant-Hill

I stand here like the sun
And look down on this vast metropolis
Where the small emmets run;
I almost think it is
The same sun that looks down
On London now or any other English town.

Yet I know well enough
That clapping dove is no dove but a culver
And under the sheen bough
Of – no, not holly, hulver,
These heavy cows that lurch
Call with a hollow bell to some lost pagan church.

But matters it so much
  If like those kissing brimstone butterflies
We too a moment touch,
  And whither each one flies
We do not know nor whence;
Just so to touch our first and final prescience?

Kingley Bottom

Beneath these bine-looped yew-boughs
  Gorse blossom is outspread
Like gold that lies unguarded
  By dragons that hang dead.

All but one pterodactyl
  That hid in mist and rain
High over Kingley Bottom
  Hums like an aeroplane.

The Old Man

I listened to the grasshoppers
  Like small machines mowing the hay,
Hot and content to think myself
  As busy and idle as they.

A woman sat under a tree
  Cursing the flies that tormented her;
I did not stop with 'Which is the way
  By Herbert's Hole to Ballinger?'

I thought of that old man I asked
  Who saw each meadow, stile and lane
Clear as pebbles washed by the Chess
  And never shall see them again.

Wicken Fen

Nothing is here but sedge-cut skies,
Azure of darting dragon-flies
And horse-flies settling on my flesh
Soft as the touch of spider's mesh.

A plunging pike rocks with a wave
The white-spoked nenuphars that pave
With smooth round leaves the loose-mired lode
That through the fen drives its straight road.

And as the wind blows back the stream
Shaking the buckthorns from their dream,
Time flows back here at Wicken Fen
To swine-steads and blue-woaded men,

Small shaggy men that plunge again
Through sedge and the black rotting rain;
And I too shudder as I feel
The whole earth shake under my heel.

Ben More

Two ravens from the summit rise and croak
Sailing in circles over the hill-smoke;
Why do their raucous cries strike on my ear
Less than those motor-horns I cannot hear?

Denholm Dene

Chaffinches dropping on the oats
Toss up and down like little boats
And blue geraniums with their bill
Peck at the winds from cleuch and hill.

The winds blow down from Rubers Law
And sweeping over holm and shaw
The Teviot and its white townships
Break on that crag-perched tower, Fatlips.

Downland Shepherd

While stable-boys go thundering by
Slinging dark divots at the sky,
Like a wind-hover he stands still
Beside the sun, late on the hill,
And chin on hands, hands on his crook,
Tegs, shearlings, yoes cons like a book
Or sees them pass slow as a cloud,
Four hundred heads with one prayer bowed.

The Hanger

Stubble the ploughshare narrowed
Lies as bare earth, seeded and harrowed,
Loose clods and upturned stones
And flints scattered like pigmies' bones.

Crisp leaves across it roll;
A sun-greened jacket on a pole
Guarding the seeds from harm
Salutes the wind with broken arm.

Black eyes in elder bushes
Are half picked out by thieving thrushes;
No green save ivy lingers
That crawls and climbs with small webbed fingers.

Why do I grieve at fears
And make these falling leaves my tears?
These trees do but undress
To wrestlers clad in nakedness.

Half of the wood is blue
Where in wide rents the sky falls through;
A second Adam, I
Walk in the compass of its eye.

The Oak-Wood

Tree behind tree they stand;
  Their slavish roots roll through the ground
And veined like the flat ivy's hand
  Their heavy boughs lean out around.

Is it not thus and thus
  The branched veins issuing from the heart
Like tentacles of an octopus
  Go up and down through every part?

How many saps have sunk?
  How many more shall yet run fresh
Till these trees too like this dead trunk
  Shall turn to touchwood, soft as flesh?

On the Beaulieu Road

Oaks stand bearded with lichen
  Like witches that knot the birch;
But hark! the cow-bells chiming
  That call no one to church.

Oak-leaves to crown an empire
  Lie sodden as brown dulse,
While chiming bells in the distance
  Die like a fitful pulse.

At Oxford

Though cold December rains draw vanishing rings
  On the choked Isis that goes swirling by,
These academic gowns flap like the wings
  Of half-fledged blackbirds that attempt to fly.

From *The New Shepherd* *(1931)*

On the Ridgeway

Thinking of those who walked here long ago
On this greenway in summer and in snow
She said, 'This is the oldest road we tread,
The oldest in the world?' 'Yes, love,' I said.

The River Dove

Now it is I
Who on the frost-furred grass go by
Through these sheep-coloured walls
Where ice in long stalactites falls
And limestone scaurs and rocks
Are the old unchanging flocks.

It is not mine
To stroke you with a fly and line,
But where I see a soft gloom lie
You see me with a soft black eye;
I hear too as it were a voice
That breaks through your stone-trammelled noise.

You run, I walk
And no word catch of your scattered talk.
O Dove, do you remember some
Who by this way forget to come?
Mourning for them you make me glad,
If you mourn not I am not sad.

Castle Rocks

Look! on Fin Cop a castle stands
Guarding the dale, not made with hands;
The wind that built himself a house
Could only build it ruinous.

Now when young ashpoles rise and twist
Thin flames in the amethystine mist,
What is the silence listening for –
The falling of that wind-built tower?

The Stour

I followed each detour
Of the slow Stour,
Stopping at times to throw a stick
Lest I should go too quick,
But lost the race,
I could not keep so slow a pace.

Though last snow in the copse
Was first snowdrops,
I could not rest even there
Where the weir combed the river's hair
At Flatford Mill;
I wonder if I ever will.

O Spring!

I did not think nest-hiding spring
Could have so sharp a sting;
Where blossom from the wild pear shakes
Too rare a china breaks;
O spring, turn back,
Where hope still droops by the rain-driven track.

That thrush that notes the passer-by
With beadlike eye,
Is she not warming with her breast
A brood to rob her nest,
While cuckoos shout
The name they will forget ere June is out?

I watched on olive-coloured ash
Buds like an inky splash;
Those black eyes turn to jealous green;
I would not so be seen.
Spring, turn or stay,
For once too often will you come this way.

Kinderscout

O heart, why did you knock
So loudly on that sky-bound wall of rock?
Was it to see again
Behind the weeping rain
No, not the Edge of Kinderscout,
But visionary hills long since burnt out?

Here is nothing but black peat-hags
Where a slow Lethe drags;
Peat-hags pitted and pitted by frost
As though a flock were lost
Or in the mist
With shepherd kept a hidden tryst.

Round Barrows

The prophet's cloudy hand
Was not so small
As those grave-howes that stand
Along the skyline of the rig,
No, nor so big
Now as the shades of evening fall.

But what of those dead bones?
Not stiff and stark they lie,
But as a family,
Fathers, mothers and sons,
With indrawn knees
They lie or lean or sit at ease.

The Hill-Wood

Who was it laughed just now?
Or was it but a creaking bough
Or wind-blown rook
That tosses like a black Satanic book?

Why should they laugh at me,
An old, old man who with bent knee
And doubled back
Creeps under boughs that overlean his track?

I stand upright again
Where caterpillars drop like rain
From hazel boughs
Whose mealy leaves hang bare and ruinous.

Let a light gust go by,
A rabbit dive – I turn my eye
At every sound
Alert as a bright light-spot on the ground.

Who is it that I fear
Shall one day crash down on me here
Loud as some beast
Or blackbird stepping through dead leaves at least?

The French Coast

Across the sea what lovers walk,
  And what sweet things are planned and vowed;
But what to them is solid chalk
  To me appears a low white cloud.

On Dartmoor

I said, 'Now that I am
Walking by her sweet sister, Yealm,
Shall I not see the Erme?
A seven years' term
Is it not long enough
To stay from that brown stream I love?'

But as I stoop to drink
The Erme slips by me while I think,
Although no trace it wears
Of those seven years
And so far from the sea,
This stream might now taste salt to me.

In the Wood

Where trees were sloping on the hill
I stood and wondered where
All this that I now saw and heard
I saw and heard before;
Beyond the path as through a door
The busy light of open day
That seemed so far away,
The silence broken by a bird,
A restless bird among the boughs,
The idle sunlight in the gloom;
And then I knew;
We stood and sat around the room
With sunlight falling on the floor,
Black silent figures listening to
Those stealthy noises here and there,
Those slow steps on the stair,
The day the dead man left his house;
Yes, there I waited still
Musing that all was now the same,
Silence and gloom and sun's sick flame,
As when the dead man went his way.

The Flint-Breaker

After the rain was gone
The wind among the trees rained on;
I listening to that scattered tread
Heard what the old flint-breaker said
(Two years or three before):
'Some flints have water at the core.'

Did I walk that sea-bank
Where flints with fluid mouths once drank
The drop they hold apart
In rusty hollow of their heart,
And lingers too in me
One drop of that old Nummulitic Sea?

A Windy Day

What is your haste
To heap the wood with leafy waste
Confusing to the eye
Starlings and leaves that fly?

Whoever you are,
You made one wind-poised leaf a star
That still lingers behind
The leaf that went on the wind.

The Teasels

How could I feel a stranger here
Who know all changing seasons of the year
  From buds that speak in hints
  To frost that sets the flints
  As fast as precious stones?
  I know them all at once,
For when on thinning boughs the birds are dumber
My memory can make a full-leaved summer.

But now today out of the trees
Flies and falls down a flock of greenfinches
    And on some teasels lighting
    Cling with crying and biting,
    Till tugged and torn by them
    Each fringed brown-headed stem
Shakes like the wand tossed by a thyrsus-bearer
And I stand looking on, a strayed wayfarer.

The Long-Tailed Tits

I stopped to hear it clear,
The sound of water tinkling near,
Although I knew no dowser could
Turn hazel-fork in that beech-wood.

Then on the high tree-tops
With rising runs and jerks and stops
Like water stones break into bits
Flowed the cascade of long-tailed tits.

Grime's Graves

Here where the dark earth heaves
    Like a tossing sea
And frost shakes down the leaves
    From the Judas tree
And on the warren lie
    The broken flints,
On which like a snake's eye
    The green moon glints;

At first I thought, Perhaps
As it only seems
That a flint-knapper knaps,
So all is dreams
And we two are not here;
And then you spoke
And we were standing there
In the moon's white smoke.

In the Spinney

When I had stopped to mark
How scrub in winter sheds its bark
And how the privet's eyes of jet
With laughter in the sun were wet,
A hand touched me behind;
I turned and lo! a bough swung on the wind.

Why is it that I stand
Half hoping that it was a hand
That struck the gentle blow?
One thing at least I know,
Beauty on earth I do not seek
More than I sought it on my mother's cheek.

Restalrig

Now maist o' us maun sleep in earth
Until the Judgment Day,
But wi' that traitor Restalrig
God wot it wasna sae.

Whiles he was sleepin' in the earth,
   Weel-happit wi' the grass,
Word cam unto the Lords o' Council
   He a foul traitor was.

He didna bide the angel's trump
   Nor twinklin' o' an e'e;
They howkit him oot o' his grave,
   A three-year corp was he.

They brocht him into Edinboro court,
   'Fause traitor,' cried they a';
Now God preser's lest sic a thing
   Should ever us befa'.

Section 3

Unpublished and Other Miscellaneous Short Poems

Late Summer

Old? No, I am not old nor young,
I am like honey-suckle swung
Midway the wild flowers' year
From March to October.

With violets I felt the smart
Of murmuring rain on my near heart,
Felt too the ravishment
Of rain-delivered scent.

Now loose on the least breeze is blown
The seeded silk of thistle-down
And bird's-foot trefoil shows
The black print of her toes;

And the round-headed rampion
Unsheathes her blue claws in the sun
Clutching at every wind
That leaves her still behind.

I know that I am no self-heal,
But oh, dear God, give me to feel
One small chill drop again
Of primrose-lightened rain.

Sea-Birds

With a thin earth for crown
The rising cliff falls down
Bathing its rocky knees
In the foam-netted seas.

Sea with slow waves a-crawl,
Marbled round this rock-wall,
Roars with the thoughtless voice
Of dull incessant noise.

When to this cliff I come
Sound of the sea dies dumb
Drowned by the shriller cries
From bird-disordered skies.

Foam of the foam are they
Tossed up like a white spray
Bright on the cliff below,
Dim in the air as snow.

Though with these birds I share
Sea, cliff, nor hollow air
At my appearing form
Awakes this white sea-storm.

Friston Church

From Friston Church down to the Tiger
  Path through the field runs to and fro,
Scored with the feet of happy children
  Dead men and women long ago.

Church Field, the field; the scented orchis
  Shoots from the grass in rosy spire;
Such odour of sanctity was wafted
  Never from stone church with white choir.

Rain summoned me to church's shelter;
  Baring my head I entered in
And from last pew kneeling on hassock
  Waited for service to begin.

No priest was there, nor any people
   Nor rows of washed white-surpliced boys;
The Book left open on the lectern
   Read with no aid of human voice.

I sat and listened to the lesson
   Till through the roof beamed with black oak
Old and worm-eaten, spaced with plaster,
   The rain of Heaven began to soak.

It fell through roof and sturdy rafter
   On hands and on hand-hidden face;
Never knew I such shower of blessing
   As dropped on me in that same place.

I left the church; a swinging gateway
   Led my steps to the road beyond.
Surprised I noticed how the raindrops
   Winked in circles on Friston pond.

The Cobweb

Where idle cobwebs mist the furze
And shake with the least wind that stirs
Their outspread pattern on twig-fork,
Belying the keen spider's work,
Against one trembling web has blown
And struck a starry thistle-down.

Hid in the shadow of a leaf
I see that spider nurse his grief,
A close-hunched ball; content enough
I spring the crafty cobwebs of
My labour and my idleness
To catch a star by its silken tress.

This Cuckoo Still Will Talk

This cuckoo still will talk,
Mechanic as a cuckoo-clock,
Confusing all the hours
The half-hours and the quarter-hours
Of day and night
And driving them in hurried flight,
A flock of swallow-tails
Across a dark sea, white with sails
Of swiftly-foaming waves
That fail and fall in hollow graves;
O cuckoo, cuckoo stop
And leave that old man with his bill
And back as crooked time to kill
The yellow turnip-flowers,
The aftermath of the greencrop
Caught when I watched the apples drop,
And me a moment more
To see the white anemones
And the dun shadows of the trees
Make of this wood a dancing-floor,
And violets before they fall
Keep their own purple funeral.

In the New Forest

With branch on sighing branch reclined
And wild rose beckoning wild rose,
I lose my way, only to find
That no-one here his way can lose.

At Newlands Corner

The poets knowing what the public wants
Writing of fairies drove them from their haunts;
Now windscreens flash their light from down to down,
And God takes up his residence in town.

Drosera Anglica

Through bogs as black as iodine
I hunted that fly-catching flower,
Hateful to some, being in fine
Too like themselves – a carnivore.

While Doubters Ask

While doubters ask 'Is God asleep?'
And 'Why does He not help us now?'
His presence is in men who keep
Strong hearts, clear eyes, and a calm brow.

By a British Barrow in Wartime

Let me lie down beside you, prince,
And share – no, do not wince –
Your grave for a short hour at noon
Shaped, with molehills for stars, like the full moon.

Man in this moon of turf and chalk,
If you can hear me talk
And understand a Saxon stranger,
Listen! today our country is in danger.

Does that not stir you, man of bones?
Your country it was once,
Yours when you strode across these downs
Where walls still wave about your hilltop towns.

Or is the news stale in your world
Where hosts are hourly hurled?
Perhaps you learnt from one of these
Who by his death gained a victorious peace.

You do not hear, man in this moon;
The skylarks might as soon
Hear me as you who are not there;
I waste breath that were precious now in prayer.

The Bleeding Nun
(a Ghost Story)

The lovers plotted
How she, her parents' prisoner, could escape.
She told of the castle's ghost, how each May-night,
Soon as the clock struck one, appeared a Figure,
Veil on her face, blood trickling from her bosom,
Lamp in one hand and dagger in the other,
The Bleeding Nun. The castle-gate that night
Was left wide open to entice her out,
But always she returned to haunt the room.
The lovers spied a hope in the superstition;
May-night was near; veiled and with blood-stained habit,
With lamp and dagger, she would be the Nun!

No one would peer too closely as she passed
To join her waiting lover. The night came;
The clock struck one; a light in the haunted room
Flashed and was gone; then at a staircase window
It flashed again, descending from the tower;
A nunlike figure slowly crossed the courtyard,
Passed through the gate. The lover sprang from the shadow;
The lamp and dagger clattered to the ground;
The lovely ghost was in his arms. She breathed,
'With all I trust you', and 'Forever thine,
Body and soul', he cried. Safe in the carriage,
Huddled together on the rocking seat,
The lovers sped into the night. But when,
All danger past, he called to slacken pace,
The horses flew the faster, flinging the driver.
A storm burst on them; slanting raindrops slapped
The carriage windows. Lightning blushed and thunder
Cracked and spread trampling round the sky. The horses,
Maddened by the night's terror, speeded on
Through hedges, over ditches, precipices,
Till in a rending crash the lover's head
Thudded against a rock.
He woke to find himself in a rush-lit room;
Of what had happened in his stony sleep,
Who brought him to the inn, how long he slept,
He never questioned; she was his only thought.
He had not long to wonder; as a clock
Struck one, he heard a slow step on the stair.
He started up to see a nunlike figure
Stand at the door. She ran to his outstretched arms
And sank in them with a contented sigh;
'Forever mine, body and soul', she whispered
And raised her veil. It was the Bleeding Nun!

The Crow

With heat that hung blue in the holt
Driving the birds to sit and moult,
I felt the whole earth was forsaken,
And when suddenly overtaken
By a black shadow in the meadow
With no one there to cast the shadow,
What could I think but that I saw
The Devil too withdraw,
Until I heard the crow's mocking 'Craw-craw'?

Suilven

Throw, Suilven, your dark shadow,
And never let a day go down
Without that monstrous mountain thrown;
For, waking in a darker meadow,
Still your inveterate lover,
I may shake off earth's cover
And flying in ghostly escapade
Mingle your shadow with my colder shade.

Hymn

Lord, by whose breath all souls and seeds are living
With life that is and life that is to be,
First-fruits of earth we offer with thanksgiving
For fields in flood with summer's golden sea.

Lord of the earth, accept these gifts in token
Thou in thy works art to be all-adored,
For whom the light as daily bread is broken,
Sunset and dawn as wine and milk are poured.

Poor is our praise, but these shall be our psalter;
Lo, like thyself they rose up from the dead;
Lord, give them back when at thy holy altar
We feed on thee, who art the living bread.

In the Dingle

As the spring darkened into summer
This dingle rill grew dumber,
Till only sand and gravel
Showed sullen pools the way to travel;
And now no water flows
But what by root and tree-trunk goes,
Sinking and rising up
To bathe a leaf or fill an acorn's cup.

At Grime's Graves

These flints that on the warren lie
And glint in moonlight like a snake's eye,
Though chipped by knappers for flint arrows
That flew away like sparrows,
Are still so fresh that one might say
Those dead men were on holiday;
'Few poems keep as fresh as flints,'
The green-eyed moonlight hints;
'Yours will not last as long;
They will not even go for an old song.'

The Blind Man

How often it comes back to me,
The small white cottage looking out to the blue sea
Over the bents blurred with an oily heat,
And seated on the rustic seat
The old, old man with thick
Fingers bunched on his varnished walking-stick;
But he looked out on nothing – he was blind,
Blind to all but the sunny wind
Whirling the two jack-tars on their tall pole,
That round and round would roll
In their blue jackets and white trousers;
Whichever way the wind went,
Those wooden sailors were no drowsers,
Though he would sometimes sleep in the hot scent
Of stocks, moss-roses, southern-wood and sweet-william;
But when he raised a listening finger,
Each bird-note in the silence seemed to linger,
Till to the bird he gave a name;
Wren, chaffinch, robin, tit, he knew their cries,
Though all were nightingales to his blind eyes.

Pevensey

With waves that up the shingle shoot
In haste to lick my foot
How false and fawning is the sea,
Like him who crouches on bent knee,
Waiting till bass or ling too late
Discovers the sly bait.

Now as I walk away
Across the flats of Pevensey Bay,
My footsteps on the desert beach
Keeping up a stony speech,
I fear the sea, leaving the shore,
Follows my heel to dog me to my door.

At Arley

The Severn sweeping smooth and broad
A motion to the hillside gives
Till it too liquifies and lives,
For glancing from that rushing road
I see the solid hill
Flow backward for a moment and stand still.

In Wingfield Manor

As clocklike in the crypt
The water from the stone boughs dripped
And I stood thinking how,
Though it was summer now,
This still was winter rain
Taking so long to drain
That splashed on the earth floor,
Time in a moment slipped
Backward through half a year or more.

Two Prose Poems (from *The New Poly-Olbion, 1967*)

The Hesperides

Poets have made Hebrides a magic word; sailing for the Outer Isles you hope to light on the Hesperides. The Barra Islands look strange, but they are hills half-sunk in the sea. And once gigantic waves heaving against the six-hundred-foot cliff of Barra Head left small fish on its summit; there are no such storms in the Isles of the Blest. South Uist is mainly rocks, bogs and lochans. The lochans are lively in the wind, tossing white water-lilies and mute swans, but the island has a half-created look, land and water not fully separated and vegetation scarcely begun. Benbecula, its low flat neighbour, appears to be rising from the sea; and it is subject to mirages, a beach tilted like a cliff and off-shore an islet hanging in the air; it is a small piece of creation still unstable. North Uist is even nearer chaos; it has a road, and there are peat-tracks, but you would need wings to explore the watery wilderness. Harris and Lewis are not islands, unless they are Siamese twins. Mountains and long sea-lochs give Harris a grandeur unsuited to human beings, at least more suited to red deer and seals, while in Lewis the Callernish Stones, that in their lonely setting make Stonehenge seem suburban, have a heathenish look; neither could be an Isle of the Blest.

But you need not lose hope of the Hesperides, least of all in North Uist with its Machair Leathann. A machair is merely flat land and a sandy shore, but the one is so verdant and the other so snowy, that spring and winter rub shoulders. The sea only shows itself when it breaks into white ripples; on the beach you step into invisible pools. But some evenings the sea becomes jovial, opal near the shore, turquoise farther out, and where it meets the sky, mocking it with cobalt blue. But that adds nothing to the machair; it takes from it, spoiling the appearance of something fresh from creation, simple and very beautiful. A machair by itself would be a Hesperis.

Cold Cotswolds

Crocuses in gardens were awake, stretching themselves and yawning; if daffodils are the spring's trumpets, as poets tell us, every garden had its brass band; the flowers even trespassed on public roads. But it was still winter on the wolds; the long lines of beeches were shamelessly naked, shivering in a wind you could see; even violets shivered in their purple hoods. There were no primroses, for those sweet Infantas of the year keep off the cold wolds. I felt coldly towards them myself. But I warmed myself with old memories, of chambered barrows, from the Whispering Knights, a denuded skeleton, to Hetty Pegler's Tump, so far from a skeleton that Hetty looks plump, even pregnant. And with memories of buildings in the Tudor tradition, from manor-houses with an ambiguity as to what they are, domestic or ecclesiastical, to small houses that have a dignity that makes you feel inferior to their owners; the Royal Family could live in Chipping Campden's almshouses.

But the cold Cotswolds added a new memory. Driving over the Edge in twilight, I saw what was apocalyptic. Dark cloud shadowed the sky and the Severn Valley lay in deep shade, but between cloud and shadow burned a sunset, a long sea of fire. There, if anywhere, were 'the flaming ramparts of the world'. Or was I seeing farther, not a sunset, but a sunrise on another world? No, it was too lurid; it was a reflection from some infernal region. And I was hastening down to it, leaving not only the Cotswolds, but the earth itself. Drawing closer to my companion, the sharer of old memories, I said silently,

> You have so much forgiven,
> Forgive me this or that, or Hell or Heaven.

Section 4

Longer Poems and Verse Plays

Memorial Verses
(1918)

I

Leaving the open wind-swept fields, I sank
  By a steep path to where the alders grew
  Black in the darkness. Here the stars were few
For half of them were hid by either flank
Of the deep chasm, and to my upward view
  The Plough was tilted on the higher land.
  I came to where a bridge, half-broken, spann'd
A stream – a birchen railing and a double plank.

II

The moonlight in the trees, straggling and sparse,
  Created for the eye a double wood
  Of trees and tree-like shadows. Where I stood
The gales, that blustered overhead, now scarce
Were heard; they seemed as mothering birds to brood
  Above an eyrie of young winds, that played
  Like nimble squirrels in the boughs, and made
A soft commotion in the leafless twigs and stars.

III

The moon that shone from the black water was
  Like a white flower. The clouds in silent race
  Swept over it, and suddenly earth's face
Grew dark; it struggled from their thinning mass,
And earth was bright. So long in that one place
  I stood, that the moon slowly moved and cross'd
  Towards the bank, and, reaching it, was lost,
Spilt like a vain milk-offering in the dim grass.

IV

It passed: and in its place arose and shone
  A light upon my introverted eyes,
  A light of richer glooms and ecstacies,
A light that, broken also and withdrawn
Like this white moonbeam, but to other skies
  Lit by no kindliness of stars or boon
  Of pilot light, sails like a phantom moon
And slowly steers toward the uncompromising dawn.

V

It was thy life I saw; for once with thee
  On this old bridge I stood. And now I stand
  Alone, and turn my eyes on every hand
To look for what I know they cannot see.
Love shall not find thee in a living land:
  Thy presence is become an empty space,
  Thy voice is choked with silence, and thy face
Lives only in the falling dusk of memory.

VI

On many a sweet path our feet have gone
  Together; the white edges of the sea
  And the brown hills have heard such things as we
Drew from our heart to speak. But there was one,
Where dimmer eyes than thine could better see
  The way: thou hast blown down it like a wind,
  And left the daylight and our love behind
And taken thy dark uncompanioned way alone.

VII

Love knits our hearts so close, but Oh how far
  We still are separate! That moment when
  Thy face among the faces of all men
Darkened, how was it that we felt no jar
In our life's even courses? Were we then
  Asleep or waking? Or perhaps we dreamed
  Or smiled, so thoughtless of the shell that screamed
Between the two thunders of the hoarse throats of war.

VIII

And though our absent hands laid not the wreath
   Of sacred custom upon thy dear brow,
   Yet thou, in dying for thy soldier's vow,
Foundst something more than death. So we bequeath
Thy spirit unto sleep in hope that thou
   Shalt hear the birds at dawn: for so we deem
   That sacrifice sufficient to redeem
Thy spirit from the dread autocracy of death.

IX

And still I say, But surely I shall find
   Thee there (in such and such a place I know),
   Or happen on thee as we come and go.
I know the year has gone and left behind
Nothing of all its flowers or leaves or snow:
   And yet I cannot understand that thou
   Art gone with them, and that the sweetest bough
Was broken from my tree by the rough Autumn wind.

X

Of all dear things that with the fall of year were fled;
   Flowers and leaves and lights and the austere
   Dews of the dawn, that not the sun's bright spear
Or moon's round shield could save, and now are dead
With thee: nothing so holy or so dear
   Shone in the sky or blossomed on the land,
   As that deep love thou heldst within thy hand
And dim divinity that lay upon thy head.

XI

Why wast thou held of such unequal worth,
   That these lived the full shadow of their sun
   And had their noon-day ere their day was done;
And thou who wast of finer sky and earth
Sawst not the fullness of thy sand-glass run,
   But darkness fell upon thy rising noon,
   And dawn upon the waxing of thy moon,
And sudden death came on thee as untimely birth?

XII

And they shall waken when Spring comes and bids:
The fields shall dry beneath the April showers
And soft winds whistle to the sleeping flowers.
But heavier than the weight of pyramids
Sleep lies upon thy head; no voice of ours
Can stir the silence of those eyes that sleep
And yet are sleepless, and no tears we weep
Can wash away the dust from off their blinded lids.

XIII

We know that when thy spirit went it shed
Something that lives within the hearts of friends,
And quietly pursues the steadfast ends
That here before it had elicited.
Such is the hope we have that partly mends
Life's broken purpose, but is not enough
To satisfy the deep desire of Love,
Or pay the heavy mortgage held upon the dead.

XIV

And so, at nightfall, when the day is done,
From out of nowhere steals the Star of Love,
And heeds not that the thickening dews reprove,
And darkness melts the sky and earth in one
And all familiar shapes of things remove:
And for a hope to shine upon our night
Up to the drifting moon there leaps a light
Out of the sepulchre of the deep-buried sun.

XV

Still we remember thou hadst much too brief
A day, to see thy deeply laboured land
Come to its reaping-time and bring to hand
The hoped-for harvest of the Autumn sheaf.
Or shall we think it was more wisely plann'd
For thy life's beauty that swift Death should steal
Thy May-time bloom than that thy age should feel
The Winter's bloody stab on its deciduous leaf?

XVI

We think it so; for we were much to blame
  If we mistook in what life's fullness lies;
  For as the lightning's bright unlidded eyes
Exceed in glory the slow-lapping flame,
So thy brief life, consumed in sacrifice,
  Exceeds in fullness of fair glory those
  That linger on toward a dying close,
And leaves for legacy a more remembered name.

XVII

And for that sacrifice we love and bless
  Thee, as we never blessed or loved before.
  What matter though we see thy face no more?
Our little sacrifice – to acquiesce.
Thou gavest all thyself; and all thy store
  Was poured for thy dear land, as the rich rain
  Is poured on the green ranks of springing grain,
To fill the undawned days with fruit and thankfulness.

XVIII

It was this land, this land thou lovedst, although
  Sundered by the steep fathoms of the sea
  From her warm side, thou fellst: and now for thee
She mourns, and bids the wandering moon to throw
On thy French grave her whitest fleur-de-lys;
  And bids her bend her waxen countenance
  To mark thy cross in the sad land of France,
Sad land of France, where only wooden crosses grow.

XIX

France! saddest of words, that was the sweetest once;
  Saddest of words that fall on English ears.
  Now, as I think, after these dreadful years
There are no birds or flowers beneath the suns
Of France to-day: they have been choked by tears;
  Choked by *our* tears, that drift in dismal rain
  Across the sea, and fall upon the slain,
Now more removed than we from the world-shaking guns.

XX

Are these not charged with other shells that come,
   Shot off in a transverse trajectory,
   Singeing the darkness of the mediate sky,
To fall on England? then women's hearts become
Fuller of death than the dead men's who lie
   In France. And for each shot that brings a date
   To some life that is dear, a duplicate
Lodges its lead deep in a softer breast at home.

XXI

Did thy heart not remember, when it threw
   Its utmost on the hazard of the dice,
   That not itself would live to pay the price,
But her's, thy mother's? Ah, too well it knew!
This was to thee the hardest sacrifice
   Of all. Yet now unto the common day
   She shows clear eyes; clearer for tears that may
Keep secret fellowship with the night-shaken dew.

XXII

But thou wast loved beyond the common lot
   Of men. And for thy sweet companionship
   And all dear things that passed from lip to lip
We thank thee now with tears; tears that may not
Show on our eyes, but shall in silence slip
   Down to the blood-washed bases of our heart
   Forever; till its waves shall fall apart,
And with the earth and sun thou too shalt be forgot.

XXIII

O Thou to Whom we say, Thy will be done,
   When lo, it is already done and past!
   O Thou to Whom our weak wills yield at last,
As to the sea all vagrant waters run!
Giving Thee back what Thou already hast,
   Restoring what is gone beyond our reach,
   We bow to Thee, as waves break on a beach
Or heavy brown-eyed sunflowers bend before the sun.

XXIV

Now with this prayer turning from where I stood,
There on the water, as I stepped aside,
Again I saw the moon. And then I cried
With a loud heart, Oh that my spirit could
Take such a step as this! Might it not slide
Into some interstice of time or space
And be confronted also with the face
That it had known and loved in former flesh and blood?

XXV

So when I passed to climb the windy slope,
I found my heart, climbing a steeper hill,
Was shouting louder than the wind that still
His spirit lived, and in some place of hope
Waited and watched with quiet heart, until
The universe should break apart in pain,
And earth and sun and moon and stars again
Be mixed and shaken out in their kaleidoscope.

XXVI

Here all was wild: leaves swirled about my knees
And, running, pattered on the road like rain:
And wood and gale were wrestling in the strain
Of violent war; the great winds surged in seas
Against the elms; the branches creaked in pain
And waved wild signals; all the ground was strewn
With broken twigs: the wind's ally, the moon,
Splintered a thousand lances in the thundering trees.

The Adversary (1923)

Part One: Morning

The scene is outside Job's House.

SATAN enters.

SATAN

Someone was up betimes building this altar;
These bright-cut faggots are undarked by dew;
Hot kiss of torch will set them leaping in flame.
Clearly Job intends an early sacrifice.
I have hit the moment:
I see the long gash of dawn in the sky;
The stars are melting like a hasty rime.
The whole earth awakes, trees, birds and insects;
And Job awakes – to what?
My sudden ear hears stirring in the house;
A thread of light burns from under the door.
The matter now will come to a brief proof.
Does Job serve God for naught?
His meekness, loud in men's ears, what is it?
Sly beggar's cloak seeking an alms of God.
His charity – that lash of poor men's backs?
Arrow aimed at a far-sighted target,
Casting of careful bread upon the waters.
But hush! footsteps and drawing of a bolt;
Here till they end their sacrifice
This tree will shade me from encroaching eyes.

JOB AND SERVANTS enter from the house.

JOB

O sight for angels! the sun's golden shears
Clipping the fleecy vapour from the slow hills.
Birds are loud awake already,
Whistling like rapid milk that sings in pails.
Bring leaves and straw; set to the torch.

The fire is kindled.

JOB

Thou Who didst slay the Dragon,
The deep sea-coiling Dragon,
And bind that foolish Huntsman,
The starry-sworded Orion,
In yoke of fruitful stars,
Glory to Thee, glory, glory.

SERVANTS

Glory to God, glory, glory.

JOB

O nightingales of Egypt,
That falling out of Egypt
Unload on our hills' springtime,
On flaming wharves of flowers,
Your cargo of sweet song,
Give to God glory, glory.

SERVANTS

Glory to God, glory, glory.

JOB

Leopards that leap from mountains,
Like cataracts from the mountains,
Dim wolves, night-faced hyenas
And long small-headed serpents
That suck the she-goat's milk,
Give to God glory, glory.

SERVANTS

Glory to God, glory, glory.

JOB

And all ye wavy fishes,
Both great and little fishes,
That curtained by green water
Do breathe strange pearl and amber
Under the deep sea,
Give to God glory, glory.

SERVANTS

Glory to God, glory, glory.

The sacrifice is offered.

HYMN

O Name unknown, O Word eternally unspoken,
  Revered and feared and loved and more than all adored,
From Whom the light of day as daily bread is broken,
  Dawn and set of sun as milk and wine are poured:

Thou art the Lord of life, the Life and the Life-giver,
  Breath of all living things that living live in Thee,
Bright air and flowery earth, field and flashing river,
  Round sun and crumbling moon and time-observing sea.

Giver of all gifts, we offer Thee thanksgiving,
  Across their glorious dust marking Thy finger-trace;
But most of all for man, great miracle of living,
  Whose frailer dust upholds a mirror to Thy face.

Servants go into the house.

JOB

That man under the apple-tree?
A beggar if his cloak speaks truth.
Beggar? More like a wandering king,

One who still carries on his brow
The shadow of a fallen crown.
Closely he watched me; watches me closely still,
Silence the doubting threshold before he speaks.

JOB approaches Satan.

Stranger, your eyes are asking me a question;
Would telling of my name give you an answer?

SATAN

You, Job, I know, though unknown to you.

JOB

Will you tell me whence you come?

SATAN

I come from going to and fro in the earth
And from walking up and down in it.

JOB

Will you enter my house and rest?
Will you sit down with me and eat bread?

SATAN

Neither I need:
I rest like the incessant waterfall
That sleeps in the steady thunder of its motion;
Your food too, is it likely to serve my taste?
My soul feeds on strong marrow from the bone.

JOB

I find your prelude strange.

SATAN

Think well if the event prove no stranger.

JOB

Tell me at least what it is you seek,
And why seeking it you have come to my door.

SATAN

Perhaps I come as much to give as to take;
Getting and giving in some things are alike
So that one gets in the measure one gives.

JOB

Can I think then that you are a merchant
From Saba, Arabia, Elam, or Egypt
Come here to trade in gums, stones or blue pearls?

SATAN

I trade in things not bought or sold in markets;
Thoughts are more to me than sea-mined pearls
Or any Arabian stones of kings
That can charm the trooping spirits of air;
Men's tears are more to me than weeping balsam
And crushed hearts more than opobalsamum.
But to narrow the matter now to a point:
I observe here your altar;
I saw you offering a salted cake
And heard the song of your servants and maid-servants.

JOB

And what question would you make?

SATAN

I have travelled much;
The world has been to me as a single path.
I have seen among men many strange customs:
Some think of God as a very old man,
Others think of Him as a warrior youth;
Some worship Him even as a cow-horned goddess,
Others again as the strange head of a cat.

Now this diversity of men's opinion
Has grown a burr that catches on my mind,
Is there any steadfast truth as can be known
Or is men's worship mere imagining?

JOB

Are you a man that ask this of me a man?
Have you no heart to give your heart an answer?
But none can speak for any but himself;
One man may be to another as a foreign land
Different of speech and thought and custom,
As perhaps you are to me.

SATAN

Did I not say so?
Truth for men is variable as a star
Continually changing colour to the eye,
A rosy fire, a sapphire or a tear;
And therein lies my doubt and question:
Men look on truth as their desire dictates,
Most filling their eyes with enchantment of moonlight,
Fearing to look at the snake-hatched cockatrice
That strikes with death.

JOB

What man are you?

SATAN

Like truth I am a star,
Not changing instantaneous robes of light
Like any common star of the multitude;
I am the solitary morning star,
The silver whisper of day's awakening;
The first bird that shakes off her faltering dreams
And wakens others with her song.

JOB

Stranger, if I take your meaning,
I am such an one as needs awaking,
A head-hung bird that feeds her heart on dreams.

SATAN

Dreams hang in your mind like bats in a cave.

JOB

I do not doubt but all things are a dream
Woven on the sleeping loom of creation;
But intruding in men's dreams and causing them
Come broken fragments of truth like outside sounds
That agitate the dreams of sleeping men.

SATAN

Would you be willing to wake now from sleep?

JOB

I wait the gentle shake of death. How else?

SATAN

By what I come to bring you and seek from you.

JOB

The truth? your truth?

SATAN

The truth that drives my blood as water a wheel;
That sends me out to pluck to flying pieces
The rich fabric of dreams that from themselves
Men continually spin like the Chinese worm.

JOB

Do you not seek falsehood rather than truth?

SATAN

By seeking the falsehood I find the truth.
I prick all sky-reflecting bubbles
And let loose the empty nothing of air;
I overturn the old mossy stones of custom
Uncrushing for men's eyes their crawling life.

JOB

Your words have heat of unknown argument;
They are like smoking springs
That rise out of dark sources in the earth.

SATAN

True, my friend; you have hit a surprising truth.
I do not judge by the slender veils of sense,
By thin appearance flashing on the eye;
I sink deep wells of thought;
The truth I drink is filtered through the mind;
I cannot drink like placid oxen
That muddy with their mouths the azure pool.

JOB

A man can think too much,
More deeply than is good for life;
To such thought becomes a disease.
Thought springs out of its value as a use;
It cannot of itself judge what it serves.
Man lives by other things;
By the strong labour of his articulate hands,
By the glad earth and forgiving dawn
And the blossoming air that cages a thousand birds;
By love that knits the heart of man and man,
Man's faith in faith and hope for hope
And that believing that is God Himself.

SATAN

You speak in broken sleep.
These things you speak of – faith, hope, believing –
Dream of a dream!
The echo of a man's unanswered prayers;
An unpromising rainbow painted on his tears;
A thin mirage cast on life's emptiness.

JOB

You look on life with dark obliquity,
The shadow of some hate, I know not what,
Eclipsing for your eyes the light of truth.

You cannot find the life by slaying it;
Probing at the dead carcase of the truth
You miss the life, the breathing form, the beauty.

SATAN

Beauty!
It is not beauty that I seek but truth,
And these two are adverse as water and fire.
Beauty is never truth; it is the mask
With which men cover up the face of life,
Hiding the twisted shadow of its sin
And the slow burning of its frozen tears.
What lovely tale was ever yet told
Of all those timeless ages whose dead leaves
Are overgreen on poets' brows
Since the wild sunset of the morning world:
What tale of kings or white-browed queens;
Of queens who changed their lovers with the moon,
Or kings who dangled empires on their knees
But slipping once upon a little blood
Sleep a long night among the slippered dead;
Or what sad tale of lovers who had drunk
Too deeply of each other's eyes to see
As others saw who slew them both in hate;
What tale in all the world,
Tale that was true or was too true for truth,
Was not the tale of sorrow or of sin?
And all such tales under their beauty's mask
Hide from the face of men the face of truth
That is too terrible and full of death
For living men to look upon and live.

JOB

Stranger, your eyes are brighter than a bird's;
And yet your face is sad as though you kept
The kisses of dead things on your lips.

SATAN

These words I have spoken, are they fire or wind?

JOB

Not knowing you I know not what you say.

SATAN

What do you mean?

JOB

God's eyes reflect the truth, perfect and whole,
Man's darkly and in part; what a man sees
Is partly truth and partly too the man;
Therefore I say that by not knowing you
I do not know the truth of what you say.

SATAN

When God made man He made a fool.

JOB

But there are three men on their way here now,
Eliphaz, Bildad, Zophar: they are my friends
And wiser men than I –

SATAN

Did you not bid me in your house?

JOB

If talking of other things –

SATAN

Then lead the way.
For I can tell of wonders: snowy mountains
Mistaken for clouds among the clouds,
Where no bird's foot ever sets delicate arrow;
Deserts so full of a great emptiness
That silence lies in them like sleeping thunder;
Seas where men look on the black bones of ships
Waving like wind-blown branches; cities too,
Where honey-coloured men walking in gardens
Blow kisses to the sun –

Satan walking behind Job flings off his cloak and renders himself invisible.

JOB

What was that light? You saw it, stranger,
The sudden light that flashed before us?
Why, what is this?
I see the house, the door, the steps, the trees;
The stranger, has he gone? gone like a dream?
If this should be a dream?
But no, I see his dark cloak lying there.
A mystery? – Well let him go;
I am not sorry he went by my door.

Job goes into the house.

SATAN

And so with the off-flinging of my cloak
I leap into a density of light
Too shrill for mortal eyes. Pure flame again,
No weight of heavy blood withholds me now
To pass from here to earth's extremity
Moved by the simple impulse of my will.
But I have work to do with Job. So first,
As swiftly as a shooting star that lives
For a bright dying moment on the night
I rise to the angelic consistory,
Where God seated upon the heaped-up ages
That lie like drifts of everlasting snow
Still chides His angels charging them with folly
And ponders with the frown of mountainous brows
This ball of trembling dust men call the earth;
And if I find my will at one with His,
Then Job, ah Job!
For I going about to do my Master's will
Shall come again close on the fall of night.

Part Two: Evening

The scene is as before.

SATAN enters.

SATAN

He said that at my fall
A tear fell from the great Father's face
On heaven's burning pavement; such a tear
Might compass the salvation of a world,
And yet it scalds my heart. I am content;
I could not be another than myself
To abdicate the kingdom of my mind,
No, though I were to die
Breaking my heart on my unbroken will.
Ah, I see a thing!
A mystery, a shadow on the ground.
It moves; I cannot shake it from my feet.
Is it my SHADOW?
But how can I, a spirit compact of light,
Suffer eclipse and trail a mortal shade?
Michael spoke truth:
'Satan, thy throne is quenched,' he said,
'God's sons go sighing past it.'
So it was not for nothing the noon sun,
Obstructed by the interloping moon,
Grew visibly dark in mutilated light,
And men who saw the shadowing hand of God
Stared at their own fear in their neighbours' faces.
But I, knowing the cause of things, cannot know fear;
And if I am forbid to pass this sun
That bathes with blossoming light earth's upturned face,
Here I remain,
Constant always to men as their own shadow,
Spreading the swift contagion of my thought,
Proclaiming in ways as various as the wind
That adorable goodness sits not on heaven's throne.

That truth like a wild beast leaping from my lips
Shall work such havoc in the slow flocks of men,
That God at last shall confess failure,
And tearing this written legend of creation
Drop it piece by piece into forgetful silence.

First messenger enters.

SATAN

Ah, a thief?

FIRST MESSENGER

No, sir, a hind, one of Job's servants.

SATAN

What news do you bring that brings you here?

FIRST MESSENGER

The oxen were ploughing and the asses feeding
And we were with them in the field;
We looked for nothing,
Till looking up we saw a cloud of dust.
It blew towards us from the desert
With the shaking thud of camels' feet;
We saw bright spears in the sun
And faces of black men with snowy teeth
And ear-rings tinkling in the wind –

SATAN

In brief,
Your fellow-hinds were slain and you escaped
And those Sabean warriors are richer
By certain scores of oxen and she-asses
And Job is so much poorer.
Go now and tell this to your master.

First messenger goes into the house.

SATAN

A man has nothing, neither goods nor children,
But what he borrows from the lender, Fate;
He pays dear interest of daily care,
He robs his sleep, his peace of mind to pay it,
Yet knows that any hour the hour may strike
When he shall give all back, his best and dearest,
And in the end be left life's bankrupt.

Second messenger enters.

SECOND MESSENGER

What man are you?

SATAN

I am an astrologer.

SECOND MESSENGER

What man is that?

SATAN

One who can cast the stars.

SECOND MESSENGER

Could you say something to my profit?

SATAN

Two silver shekels chinking in my hand
Sing like the nightingale.
Find me here when it is dark.
Come now, what news do you bring to Job?

SECOND MESSENGER

It chanced I went across the hill for water
Leaving the herdsmen with the sheep and camels
Locked in a narrow glen;

As I came back on the other side of the hill,
I felt my face pricked by a sudden heat;
I heard a nimble crackling of thorns and thistles;
Then at my feet a serpent –

SATAN

Ah, caught in the trap
Your fellow-herdsmen and their cattle
Were no more to that blind-eyed fury of fire
Than other snakes, mice, lizards, scorpions,
That perished too.
Go; enjoy the pleasure of telling evil tidings.

Second messenger goes into the house.

SATAN

I have a fear for Job; the man is old
And stands supported like the Indian tree
By his own branches that have taken root;
I fear the next axe hewing at the props
May bring the old trunk with them.

Third messenger enters.

THIRD MESSENGER

O God, the sight that I have seen!
I see it still:
The whirlwind from the desert,
The dancing pillars of dust,
The swaying house, the rent of bulging walls,
The twisted limbs, the flowers, the wine, the blood –
They are all dead, they are all dead.

Third messenger goes into the house.

SATAN

Is it too much?
What if so great a gust should blow clean out
The weak flame sheltered in that earthen lamp?

There is a pause.
Then Job with a cry comes running from the house and falls at the altar.

SATAN

He does not move.
Can I have feared too well?
O God, is it Thy spite to let this man
Make easy passage into death by prayer?

Satan approaches Job.

Is there a heart that measures its slow time
Within the flooded prison of those ribs
And like a captive tramping in his cell
Limps on across vast continents of pain?
Is it the breathing body of a man
That kneels there at that deaf indifferent altar,
Giving and taking air to keep alive
The working lungs and the incessant heart,
Each speaking pulse and that self-seeing light
That dwells between the eyeballs and the brain?
Or has death set his cobwebs on those eyes
And with a shut-in gloom and gathering dust
Darkened the inward pictures of the mind,
So that what once was man is such no longer
But something less than the night-loving moth
That shall survive him till the setting moon?

JOB

Oh, oh!

SATAN

He lives; that was a sigh that slipped his lips
Like a thin bubble from a drowning man.

JOB

O let me die and let this be the end;
Let not the torture of a new day's light
That wakens others waken me.

SATAN

He rises, stretching hands in a blind prayer
As though to embrace the empty form of God.

JOB

Ask not that I should take this burden up;
I cannot lift it; its bewildering weight
Crushes me like a world.

SATAN

He staggers like a tree that feels the axe
Deep at its roots. Now with this man, this child,
This aged child that looks as old as God,
Have I to wrestle.

JOB

Friend, lend me your hand.

SATAN

You know me?

JOB

Ah, the stranger.

SATAN

And your friend.

JOB

I thank you if you are; my grief is great,
My grief is more than I can bear.

SATAN

Tell me, is this thing true I hear?

JOB

I cannot speak it; what you hear is true.

SATAN

Servants and cattle in one day destroyed?

JOB

That too is true; I had forgot it.

SATAN

Then learn, my friend, to find in what is left
The greater blessing. You have your children still,
And therein lies your world.
For love though tender as a tear or dewdrop
Can be as hard as diamond to resist
The world's worst hurt or envy.

JOB

Oh!

SATAN

Why do you cry?

JOB

My sons and daughters!

SATAN

What of them?

JOB

I slay them all a second time to tell it.

SATAN

Speak; am I not your friend?

JOB

They feasted in their elder brother's house;
A whirlwind, a great whirlwind from the desert,
Smiting the corners of the house –
And they are dead, dead, all dead.

SATAN

Your children dead? your sons and daughters dead?
Slain by the hand of God?
And not one left to keep your name alive
And save your blood from running to an end?
O that is the last evil of all evil,
When the flame dies down on the household hearth
And the oil is spent in the cruse.

JOB

Have pity on me, O my friend, have pity.

SATAN

A man's footsteps are blind from birth to death:
As man is blindly born and blindly goes
To death's strong-posted door, so all between
Is blindness; for O how blindly you have walked
To set your foot in this flower-smothered trap.

JOB

A trap?

SATAN

The fox, O Job, what of the trap-caught fox?
The iron teeth are fixed; they bite like fire;
It drags a blood-stained track across the hills,
As you must drag –

JOB

O God, have pity on me.

SATAN

The sheep, the goat, the rat, the toad, the snake,
Tortured by imminent death, move man to pity,
But man move God – ?

JOB

God's ways are dark.

SATAN

The darkness is in man, in man himself;
The bowed head and self-blinded eyes of prayer
Make all the darkness.

JOB

You are God's enemy.

SATAN

And if I am, I am the more man's friend.

JOB

God's enemy is not my friend.

SATAN

Will you still pray to this child-slaying God?
Did He not slay your children?
Break them like playthings, fling them in the fire,
Beat them like singing locusts from the vines?

JOB

And you, what would you have me do?

SATAN

A man can act by his indwelling light,
That whisper of the truth that makes him man,
Not like the blind-eyed beast that sees a spot;
Man has a more discerning gift
To take life or refuse it as he will.

JOB

What do you hint at?

SATAN

A wise man who has drunk of life's top sweetness.
Will fling away the dregs.

JOB

You hint at death?

SATAN

Death is the sacrifice man pays for life,
Requital of sin and seal of lasting peace.

JOB

O if it might be, how sweetly would my body
Mingle with death in his promiscuous bed
And crumble back into slow earth.

SATAN

Is it not one act? one swift sudden act?

JOB

With self-destroying hand?

SATAN

That way at least is open;
A man can make one safe escape from life
Cleaving a desperate passage through his heart
And winning death's invulnerable tower.

JOB

To slay the body, is it to slay death?
No, death is God's gift;
Now should we snatch it, setting in one balance
His will and ours, a breath against a wind,
A stream choked by a rising sea?

SATAN

What is it that you fear?

JOB

I fear to kill the God that dwells within.
I fear too with some reason;

For if man's soul can be so fugitive
That in his sleep which is death's breathing image
Strange forms of terror can intrude to lift him
To fiery wrestlings in the heat of dreams,
To what strange lands beyond this hiding sun
His spirit loosened from the blood-locked body
May by death's winds be blown
To face unknown and spectral forms of sin?

SATAN

Is it then with such wild words as these – ?

JOB

Not wilder at least than your spray-spattering words.

SATAN

O were you less of man and more of woman!

JOB

What do you mean?

SATAN

A woman has too piercing sight to blind;
Give her her children, she has God enough,
But take her children and you take her God.
In woman's heart the lioness and lamb
Lie down together; lay hand on the lamb,
The blood-hoarse lioness will start.

JOB

You are a man one might have cause to fear.

SATAN

O Job, were I as you,
In whom God's bloody knife has cut so deep,
What prayers would I make that this same God,
Who sits now like a mountain on His throne,

Might tumble down, a dead world on the world,
And I
Like a wild prophetess under her tree
Might sing to Him my sweet love-hymn of hate.

JOB

Silence!
I will not hear you further; these words you speak
Have a more dreadful sound than the black wind
That brought the house down on my children's ruin.
Enough is said; more than enough is said.
If you have come, if you have sought me out,
As it appears, to tempt me from my God,
You come too late.

SATAN

Too late?

JOB

Death is the price we pay at last for life.
Is it too great a price?
If I have purchased at the price of death
The gift of those dear children that I loved,
Richer before, I am no poorer now.

SATAN

What gift is there to take where one has given?

JOB

In what remains, the very pain of love,
That teaches us the greatness of the gift,
Not to be changed for any lesser joy.
But, stranger,
This is no house to ask a guest to enter;
There is one here that bids us be alone –

SATAN

Are you a man?

JOB

I am a man,
Not less nor more; dust of the earth indeed,
But a strange dust blown by the breath of God.

SATAN

God!
What do you know, what can you know of God?
Is it from earth, green-gushing spring or autumn,
The stars or the cold cruelty of the sun,
Or that white moon baring her milkless bosom,
You draw this ineradicable dream?

JOB

No, but from where close by the heart of God
Man's heart can lie apart and listen and know.
Friend, you have come too late; you should have come
Not now, but in my better happier days.
My love for God, my love for them, my children,
Was one; with one half gone, by so much more
I need the other.
Forgive me if I close the door.
Farewell.

Job goes into the house.

SATAN

When God made man He made a fool.
O God, bend down Thy star-reflecting eyes
And single out this world among all worlds
And see this Job, a man after Thy heart.
For me it is enough.
O must it ever be that God and man
Shall strive together and that Chance with both
Shall strive, and there shall be no end? For one
Shall lose, and that is neither God nor Chance,
But man. Therefore I pity this man, Job;
Pity all men indeed; though there is good,
Mingled with greater evil in man's life,

This may at least be said: man wakes too late,
Sleeping through happiness, waking at evil,
To see the happiness he missed; as now
From that black rose-tree the night-sheltered bird
Awakes too late and mourns to see the day
Embalmed like a dead queen in barks and spice
Breathe odours on the air, while silent night
Nails down her coffin with a thousand stars.

Rizpah (1923)

Argument

For three years there has been a drought in the land of Israel. Inquiring of the Lord, David learns it is on account of Saul's massacre of the Gibeonites. He asks the Gibeonites what atonement can be made, and they demand the death of seven of Saul's sons. Accordingly these seven men are sacrificed at Gibeon, and their bodies hung from a tree till the rain shall give the sign that atonement has been made. Rizpah, the mother of two of them, watches by the dead bodies throughout the summer, driving off the wild beasts and birds. The poem begins after the first rain has fallen.

The scene is the hill behind Gibeon. There is an altar-stone and a tree from which hang the bodies of Saul's seven sons. Rizpah sits under the tree. The Chorus, women of her house, have come from Gibeah of Benjamin to take her home. It is night when they arrive, having climbed the hill.

Chorus enters.

SEMI-CHORUS I

Which way, sisters, which way?

SEMI-CHORUS II

No way is here.

SEMI-CHORUS I

The track?

SEMI-CHORUS II

Slipped like a snake from eye and foot.

SEMI-CHORUS I

Stumble we all night on the hill?

SEMI-CHORUS II

What hope,
Unless the moon appearing shoot a shaft?

SEMI-CHORUS I

A sign, a sign! See where she gores the clouds,
The cow-horned one.

SEMI-CHORUS II

O happy blossom of light!

SEMI-CHORUS I

Sidonian women offer raisin cakes
To twin-horned Ashtaroth.

SEMI-CHORUS II

Good words, good words;
The Stone of God is here, the great Stone of God.

SEMI-CHORUS I

The Stone anointed by the filial blood.

SEMI-CHORUS II

What blood?

SEMI-CHORUS I

Of Rizpah's two and Merab's five.

SEMI-CHORUS II

The Stone has ears; silence is best for all.

SEMI-CHORUS I

O God!

SEMI-CHORUS II

Why do ye cry? what have ye seen?

SEMI-CHORUS I

Lift up your eyes.

SEMI-CHORUS II

To what, to what?

SEMI-CHORUS I

The tree!
O heavy sight that breaks the moon.

SEMI-CHORUS II

What tree?

SEMI-CHORUS I

The tree whose roots are as earth-cleaving serpents
Striking to hell to bear upon its branches
This sevenfold fruit of death.

SEMI-CHORUS II

O that my hands
Could pluck the fruit of this forbidden tree,
A fruit too ripe, too ripe; but it is death
By stoning or by sword –

SEMI-CHORUS I

Look what is here;
This is no stone, it is a crouching woman.
Rizpah!

SEMI-CHORUS II

Asleep?

SEMI-CHORUS I

Too deep for voice to waken.

SEMI-CHORUS II

O is she dead, the mother of dead children?

SEMI-CHORUS I

What shall we do, what shall we women do?

SEMI-CHORUS II

Sit we by her and mourn and mourn and mourn.

SEMI-CHORUS I

Uncover not the sackcloth from her face;
I fear to look on the dead woman's face,
Sitting alone in the moon's bright danger.

CHORUS

Was it for this we wove a crown
Of saffron and sweet-smelling dill
And led her through the clamorous town
With sound of flute and smoking torch,
The self-vowed victim, willing thrall,
A snow-white heifer of the hill,
And brought her to the rose-clad porch,
The shouts of men and the lighted house of Saul?

The smoke was blindness to our eyes,
Our ears were deaf with the sounding flute,
The cries of men and the women's cries,
Or we had slain her where she stood,
Plucking from the deep-browed door
The heavy lintel ere her foot
Stept on the flowers that bright as blood
Lay in a dazzling pool upon the floor.

RIZPAH

O woe, woe!

CHORUS

Someone speaks, who is it speaks?
A living voice? a death-tied tongue? I fear,
Greatly I fear, knowing not what to fear.

RIZPAH

Go from me, ye that wake the dead.

CHORUS

Rizpah!
Is it not Rizpah's voice? She lives, she lives;
Her sleep was but the overwork of grief.
And see, her face unclouding like the moon,
As lost and dead and patient as the moon.

RIZPAH

O is it ye, the women of my house?

CHORUS

Thou seest us, thou knowest us.

RIZPAH

Alas,
Why have ye come? what do ye seek?

CHORUS

O Rizpah,
Girding our robes in haste, we came this day
From Gibeah.

RIZPAH

And why? what have ye heard?

CHORUS

The rain crying with shrill voice from the ground.

RIZPAH

The rain, the rain, what to me is the rain?

CHORUS

Heaven shed sweet tears of pity in the rain.

RIZPAH

My eyes were sooner kinder to my sorrow.

CHORUS

Men shouted, hearing the reluctant rain.

RIZPAH

They shouted, but I raise no joyful shout;
For they have vines and olives, but for me
The fruit hangs black and withered on the bough.
What hope is in the rain?

CHORUS

Trusting the rain
Had washed from these dead bodies of thy sons
The shadow of the blood that cursed the earth,
We came.

RIZPAH

And have I not shed tears enough
To loose from earth the fastest-clinging curse?
And whence is this blood-shadow? Blood met blood;
If so be that Saul wrought a deed of blood
His house has given a piteous bloody answer.

CHORUS

No question make we one way or another;
It is the hate of Gibeon is strong.

RIZPAH

The hate of Gibeon is beyond all hate;
Savage destroyers of the dead, they shoot
Across death's boundary a poisonous arrow
At the unburied dead, pursuing hate
To endless end.

CHORUS

O was it for Gibeon,
Who tricked him with the tale of mouldy bread,
That Joshua bade the sun and moon stand still
Over the Amorites in Ajalon
And shut the five kings in a living tomb,
Hanging their bodies after in the sun?

RIZPAH

And I through a long summer, sun and moon,
Keep watch by these dead bodies of my sons,
Driving the obscene beasts and bitter birds.

CHORUS

Evil, thrice-evil race of Gibeon!
And what of those two with pretence of wheat,
Who passed the sleeping portress at her mill
And slew at noon the young king on his bed,
Whose spear-borne head was laid in Abner's tomb?

RIZPAH

But one I hate more than all Gibeon.

CHORUS

Whom more than all Gibeon dost thou hate?

RIZPAH

David.

CHORUS

O lay thy hand upon thy mouth
If thou wouldst speak of him, the Lord's anointed.

RIZPAH

Anointed by what oil?

CHORUS

From Samuel's horn.

RIZPAH

No fragrant oil of myrrh and calamus
Anointed Jesse's son.

CHORUS

How so, how so?

RIZPAH

Too bitter was the smell.

CHORUS

Then say what oil.

RIZPAH

The blood of Saul's seven sons.

CHORUS

What dost thou hint?

RIZPAH

He slew them at the mere excuse of rain,
Not by his own hand but by Gibeon,
That safer he might ride their father's throne.

CHORUS

One son he spared at least, young Mephibosheth.

RIZPAH

Lame on both legs! a lame man for a king!

CHORUS

O Rizpah, not for strife of words we came.

RIZPAH

Why have ye come?

CHORUS

We came to take thee hence
To eat thy bread once more among the living.

RIZPAH

My tears are sweeter while I watch the dead.

CHORUS

Thou wilt not come then?

RIZPAH

Here beneath this tree
My grief has taken root, and like the nightshade
Brings forth its poisoned berries; day and night
I eat that fruit, living by my own pain.

CHORUS

This rain has opened graves for thy dead sons.

RIZPAH

When they go back to Gibeah, I go.

CHORUS

Thou wilt not come?

RIZPAH

Shall I forsake the dead?
Their spirits haunt these leafy trees, by day
Hanging like light-dazed bats, but at nightfall
Flittering to and fro in the brown air,
Crying for easeful burial.

CHORUS

Is this the end?

RIZPAH

It is the end? no further word I speak.

CHORUS

They say that under this sacred Stone,
Raised by the Zuzim and Zamzummim,
Giant pest-peoples that lived of old,
Crouches a maiden unnamed, unknown,
Bending forward, chin upon knees,
Locked together limb to limb,
A victim buried alive to appease
The Baal that gives increase to corn-field and sheep-fold.

Woe for the luckless lot of her,
The girdled girl, unwooed, unwon,
Lying alone in her straitened bed,
With apples unplucked and no sweet myrrh
Scenting her skirts with borrowed breath;
But woe for the heavier lot of one,
A woman wed to incestuous death,
That labours in second pangs to bear the unborn dead.

SEMI-CHORUS I

What are those dancing lights?

SEMI-CHORUS II

They climb the hill.

SEMI-CHORUS I

Wild beasts with eyes like wandering stars,
Hyenas, wolves or jackals?

SEMI-CHORUS II

Dawn is near;
I hear the rapid noise of birds.

SEMI-CHORUS I

Nay, lamps,
That dart sharp questions at a doubtful way.

SEMI-CHORUS II

Hither?

SEMI-CHORUS I

So seems it, and I hear men's voices.

SEMI-CHORUS II

What cause have we to fear?

SEMI-CHORUS I

The event will show,
And soon.

SEMI-CHORUS II

One man I see who leads the rest;
He beckons back his following and comes.
O do I dream?

SEMI-CHORUS I

Nay, it is he, the king.

King David enters with Attendants.

DAVID

Who are ye women gathered at this tree?
I scan your faces, but the face I seek,
I see not. Are ye silent?

CHORUS

O great king –

DAVID

Say on.

CHORUS

I am a reed, shaken by wind.

DAVID

What dost thou fear?

CHORUS

The swift gust of thy presence.

DAVID

Fear no such fear. Come I with ill intent?

CHORUS

How can I know?

DAVID

Should I then come myself?
A king has in his servants a long arm
To do a needful evil. Fear not, but say,
Ye are her women surely, where is Rizpah.

CHORUS

She looks at thee, O king.

DAVID

That crouching stare
That seems about to spring? O never think
Thou hast a cockatrice's eye to kill;
I bear upon my breast a righteous gem
Against enchanting eye. And art thou Rizpah,

The watcher by this empty tomb of air,
The mother who has nursed these seven dead men
Through the dark summer heat? Thou wilt not speak?
Why then on my side is no cause to speak.
But I have charm for the deaf adder's ear;
Speak thou for me, my sword; both deaf and dead
Shall hear the seven sharp words that thou shalt speak.

CHORUS

O wilt thou slay her?

DAVID

Nay, I slay her hate.

CHORUS

How, how?

DAVID

Cutting these bodies from the tree.

RIZPAH

Jackals, wolves, foxes, kites and bearded vultures
Have I with crying hands through summer vigil
Kept from these bodies; but now springs a beast,
A fouler and more carrion-loving monster,
Waving death in his sword. O women, women,
Share with me the shrill pleasure of my death,
Fighting to save these dead.

DAVID

Be silent, sword;
Thou hast too sharp an edge of speech; sleep thou,
Imbedded in thy sheath. With softer words
This box, opening its dumb mouth, will speak.
Ye watching women I address; come hither;
Look ye; see what is here, say what ye see.

CHORUS

What, what? how can I tell?

DAVID

Touch not these bones.

CHORUS

O do I look on fire-burned bones?

DAVID

The ashes
Dug from the trec at Ramoth-Gilead.

CHORUS

Of Saul and Jonathan?

DAVID

All but the head
Hung with the armour in Astarte's temple.

RIZPAH

What do I hear?

DAVID

What thou canst see.

RIZPAH

O God!

DAVID

These are the dead bones of thy husband, Saul,
And Jonathan, his son, who was my friend,
Reduced by fire.

RIZPAH

O woe is me, O woe!

CHORUS

See, she bends over them with weeping hair.

DAVID

One tear at least thou sparest from thy sons
To fall on these poor bones; I too shed tears
Over that silver dust. Tear has met tear;
Our tears have touched, thy tear and mine; O Rizpah,
Have we not in this mingling of our tears
Together made a covenant of salt?

CHORUS

O mistress, O dear mother, give good heed.

RIZPAH

Am I now in a dream, a slippery dream,
Twixt sleep and waking?

DAVID

Put thou forth thy hand.

CHORUS

Ask thou of him; for me, I fear to ask.

RIZPAH

What should I ask? I know not what to ask.

CHORUS

Why he unyoked the power of these dead bones?

RIZPAH

The hand was rash.

CHORUS

Or the intent was good.

DAVID

Father and sons shall sleep within one tomb.

CHORUS

I see a ray of hope.

RIZPAH

In Gibeon?

DAVID

Better that tree, their growing sepulchre
At Ramoth-Gilead.

RIZPAH

Where then?

DAVID

In Zelah.

RIZPAH

The tomb of Kish?

DAVID

Saul's father.

RIZPAH

This thou swearest?

DAVID

My oath shall be the stone that seals their tomb.

CHORUS

Rejoice, Rizpah, rejoice; we too rejoice.

RIZPAH

Was it for this thou camest?

DAVID

Swift as rain.

RIZPAH

Yet thou didst let them die?

DAVID

At word of God.

RIZPAH

Who sent the drought.

DAVID

And the releasing rain.

RIZPAH

If what thou sayest is in truth the truth,
My steps shall go along with these dead men.

DAVID

Then out, my sword, and speak; nay, sing a song
For Rizpah's ear, neither too harsh nor sweet.

King David cuts down the bodies from the tree.

SEMI–CHORUS I

Is it an airy dream
Or some enchantment I behold:
A vapour from the cold
Ox-horned, malignant moon,
Or phantasy that soon
Will shrivel like a sunbow on a stream?

SEMI–CHORUS II

I feel as though a wand
Thrice had waved before my eyes,
And this wizardry that dyes
The alien light of day
Would swiftly shrink away
And vanish at the waking of my hand.

CHORUS

From Jesse's rod there sprang a stem,
(Rejoice, rejoice, O Bethlehem,)
A stem, a sapling and an oak,
(Rejoice with harp and dulcimer,)
Tossing in tempestuous smoke,
Scattering stars and thunder from his hair.
(Let us rejoice, rejoice with them
Who sing aloud for Bethlehem.)

Crowned with a star-set diadem,
(Be glad, be glad, O Bethlehem,)
O see that stem of Jesse stand,
(Raise a glad shout and bend the knee,)
Lifting his rod across the land,
Shaking a flowery sceptre on the sea.
(Let us be glad, be glad with them
Who sing aloud for Bethlehem.)

Nicodemus: A Mystery (1937)

PERSONS

JOHN as an old man
JOHN as a young man
NICODEMUS
A BLIND MAN
SIMON PETER
JUDAS
CAIAPHAS, the High Priest
ANNAS, formerly the High Priest
Clerk and Members of the Sanhedrin
Constables
SAUL
An angel

Prelude I

In a house. Darkness; then a spot of light discloses JOHN, *as an old man, writing his Gospel: he sits at the side.*

JOHN: Now when he was in Jerusalem at the passover, in the feast day, many believed in his name, when they saw the miracles which he did. But Jesus did not commit himself unto them, because he knew all men, and needed not that any should testify of man: for he knew what was in man. There was a man of the Pharisees, named Nicodemus, a ruler of the Jews: the same came to Jesus by night and said unto him –

What did he say? –
Where are the notes that Peter sent from Rome?
– He too was crucified – . I see
He writes a sprawling hand like Paul. – 'Rabbi,

We know thou art a teacher come from God.'
And what did Jesus say? 'Except a man
Be born again – '; that puzzled Nicodemus.
'How can a man be born when he is old?'
I was not born till I was nearly thirty;
Poor Nicodemus had a lot to learn.
Then Jesus spoke about the wind. 'The wind – '
He said, 'it bloweth where it listeth – '
That was a night of wind; I thought the wind
Would blow the Paschal moon out of the sky;
Trees kept their backs to it, bending like divers.
But we were snug indoors; we felt it strange,
We fishermen, to be there in the city,
Not in the wave-lit darkness of the lake.
It was the night that Simon cooked the supper;
He raised the cover from a dish of eels;
'See, they have lost their heads like John the Baptist,'
Said Andrew; and we all looked grave at first,
Till Jesus smiled, and then we burst out laughing.
Fishers of men!
We little thought of the rich lustrous fish
That even then was nosing at the net.
Supper was ended and we sang our hymn;
The hymn we often sang;
We were a happy band of brothers then;
'Behold how good a thing it is,
and how becoming well' –
No sooner had we sung it than a knock
Came at the door. 'Go, John,' the Master said,
'We have a visitor; see who he is.'

Scene I

Outside the door of a house. It is a windy night with a full moon. A hymn is being sung in the house.

(NICODEMUS *enters during the singing*)

Behold how good a thing it is,
and how becoming well,
Together such as brethren are
in unity to dwell!

Like precious ointment on the head,
  that down the beard did flow,
Ev'n Aaron's beard, and to the skirts
  did of his garments go.

As Hermon's dew, the dew that doth
  on Sion's hills descend;
For there the blessing God commands,
  life that shall never end.

(NICODEMUS *enters hesitatingly, knocks at the door, and* JOHN, *as a young man, opens it*)

NICODEMUS: Is this where Jesus lodges?
JOHN: Nicodemus!
NICODEMUS: Hush, do not shout my name. I see you know me.
JOHN: Know you? Surely I know you; only –
NICODEMUS: You are surprised to see me. Have I not
Seen you with Jesus? You are His disciple?
What is your name?
JOHN: John.
NICODEMUS: A relative of John the Baptist?
JOHN: A distant cousin.
NICODEMUS: Indeed? John was a most outspoken man,
And he is dead. It does not always do
To say too much. Is Jesus in the house?
JOHN: You think He says too much?
NICODEMUS: He might say less; and yet I do not know.
JOHN: Is He in danger? Is that why you come?
NICODEMUS: No, not immediately; but who can tell?
JOHN: You come to warn Him?
NICODEMUS: Listen! what is that sound?
JOHN: Only the wind.
NICODEMUS: No, no; that other sound; that tap-tap-tapping.
JOHN: I hear it; somewhere down the street.
NICODEMUS: Now it has stopped; no, it begins again.
JOHN: It sounds like someone knocking.
NICODEMUS: There, someone has passed that lighted window.
JOHN: It is his stick that taps.
NICODEMUS: He stops; he peers about him like a bird.
Stand in the shadow till he passes.
JOHN: No need; the man is blind.

(*The* BLIND MAN *enters*)

BLIND MAN: Who says that I am blind? If I am blind,
I see you well enough, you standing there.
I raise my stick; ah, does that frighten you?
You will not speak lest I should beg for money;
I do not beg at night when I am rich.
Listen; these coins chink sweeter than house sparrows,
They sing like nightingales.
Will you not speak?
God curse this world; I say God curse this world
Where blind men make the others deaf and dumb.
I see you there; you think that I am blind;
I am not blind except I cannot see.
God gave me eyes; I feel them with my finger;
They died the day that I was born. Alas,
That you should stand and feel me with your eyes
And my eyes should be dumb and cannot answer.
I know the dogs better than I know men;
We share the street and have our meals together;
They do not even know that I am blind.
I know you stand there, for you stand so still.
A curse upon you, you that I heard speak
And you that have been silent like a spirit.
But I know someone who will speak to me,
And one day I shall meet him – Jesus the Prophet.
Have you not heard He gives sight to the blind?
He is not such as you who grudge us sight.
You mock at me because you think me blind;
My eyes are only blind until I see Him.

(*The* BLIND MAN *goes out*)

JOHN: What shall I do? Shall I go after him?
NICODEMUS: No, let him go; I know the fellow well;
He sits all day at the Gate Beautiful;
His blindness is a profitable business.
Your Master has more sense than heal him – yet,
Why not, why not? Quick, call him back.
JOHN: You want him back?
NICODEMUS: I want to see a miracle.

JOHN: Blind man, blind man! – I cannot hear his stick.
Blind man, blind man! – can he have gone so far?
NICODEMUS: The man is sly; he listens like a mouse.
JOHN: Blind man, blind man, if you would have your sight –
It is the wind that blows my voice away.
Blind man! Hello! Jesus is here.
NICODEMUS: Hush, you will wake the street. The man is gone;
Perhaps he will come back. In any case –

(SIMON PETER *comes out from the house*)

SIMON PETER: Who calls on Jesus?
JOHN: Simon!
SIMON PETER: John, was it you? I thought it was your voice.
JOHN: I called to a blind man who passed just now.
SIMON PETER: What did he want?
JOHN: Simon, go in; I will explain.
SIMON PETER: Who have you there? Someone stands in the shadow.
JOHN: Go in just now; we have a wonderful guest.
SIMON PETER: What guest? Who is he?
JOHN: Someone whose name you know: it is —
NICODEMUS: Tell him to close the door.
SIMON PETER: The wonderful guest tells me to close the door.
But hurry, John; your supper will get cold.

(SIMON PETER *goes into the house, closing the door*)

NICODEMUS: Who is that man?
JOHN: His name is Simon; Jesus calls him Peter.
NICODEMUS: Peter; that means a rock.
JOHN: I know; He says that on this rock –
NICODEMUS: What rock? You mean that man?
JOHN: I know that it sounds strange; He said –
But no; you would not understand. Come in.
Jesus would like to speak to you.
NICODEMUS: He is at supper; I will come again.
JOHN: Will you not join us?
NICODEMUS: I have already supped.
JOHN: Not even in a cheerful cup? I know
That Jesus will be disappointed.
NICODEMUS: Tell me one thing; why do you follow Jesus?

JOHN: It was because of John the Baptist first.
NICODEMUS: But why because of him?
JOHN: One day, when we were standing by the Jordan,
John and my cousin Andrew and myself,
We saw a man pass by, tall as a spirit;
He did not see us though he passed quite near;
Indeed we thought it strange;
His eyes were open but he looked on nothing;
And as he passed, John, pointing with his finger,
Cried – I can hear him cry it now –
'Behold, The Lamb of God!'
NICODEMUS: And He, what did He say? What did He do?
JOHN: Nothing; we watched Him slowly climb the hill;
His shadow fell before Him; it was evening.
Sometimes He stopped
To raise His head to the home-flying rooks
Or greet a countryman with plough on shoulder.
NICODEMUS: John said, 'Behold, the Lamb of God'?
JOHN: He said so.
NICODEMUS: And from that day you followed Him?
JOHN: No, that was afterwards in Galilee.
NICODEMUS: But tell me why; why did you follow Him?
JOHN: I think it was our feet that followed Him;
It was our feet; our hearts were too afraid.
Perhaps indeed it was not in our choice;
He tells us that we have not chosen Him,
But He has chosen us. I only know
That as we followed Him that day He called us
We were not walking on the earth at all;
It was another world,
Where everything was new and strange and shining;
We pitied men and women at their business,
For they knew nothing of what we knew –
NICODEMUS: Perhaps it was some miracle He did.
JOHN: It was indeed; more miracles than one;
I was not blind and yet He gave me sight;
I was not deaf and yet He gave me hearing;
Nor was I dead, yet me He raised to life.

(JUDAS *enters from the house and looks about suspiciously, opening and closing the door carefully. He looks about him and goes out*)

NICODEMUS: Who is that man?
JOHN: Judas Iscariot.
NICODEMUS: Is he one of your company?
JOHN: He is.
NICODEMUS: Why did he look like that? Where is he going?
JOHN: I do not know. He often walks at night.
NICODEMUS: If he has left the house, supper is ended.
JOHN: Listen; they sing the hymn.

(*A hymn is sung from the house*)

The Lord's my Shepherd, I'll not want,
He makes me down to lie
In pastures green; he leadeth me
the quiet waters by.

My soul he doth restore again;
and me to walk doth make
Within the paths of righteousness,
ev'n for his own name's sake.

Yea, though I walk in death's dark vale,
yet will I fear none ill:
For thou art with me; and thy rod
and staff me comfort still.

My table thou hast furnishèd
in presence of my foes;
My head thou dost with oil anoint,
and my cup overflows.

Goodness and mercy all my life
shall surely follow me:
And in God's house for evermore
my dwelling-place shall be.

JOHN: Nicodemus!
NICODEMUS: Nothing, nothing; the music wrought on me.
I shiver too in the night wind;
And that man who went out, he bodes some evil.
The night is growing late; it is too late;
Tomorrow I will come –

JOHN: Tomorrow He returns to Galilee.
NICODEMUS: But He will come again.
JOHN: But not this hour. O Nicodemus, look!
A miracle; you asked a miracle;
Look, look, the wind has blown the door wide open.
NICODEMUS: A miracle?
JOHN: He used the wind to work a miracle;
Even the wind obeys Him.
NICODEMUS: I scarcely think it is a miracle.
JOHN: It is, it is.

(SIMON PETER *appears at the open door*)

SIMON PETER: John, John, will you stop railing in the street?
There is no miracle about the door.
I opened it myself. The wind's hand too
Plucked at it; we both opened it at once.
I told the Master of our visitor;
Why do you keep him standing at the door?
What is that sound?
JOHN: The blind man coming back; you hear his stick
Tap-tapping; he is coming down the street;
Now it has stopped.
I will stay here and speak to him. You, Peter,
Take Nicodemus in, if he will go.
SIMON PETER: Nicodemus!
NICODEMUS: I – I will go in.

(PETER *and* NICODEMUS *go into the house;* JOHN *waits till the* BLIND MAN *enters*)

JOHN: Blind man.
BLIND MAN: Ah, voice, we meet again. Still standing there?
Have you no feet to walk about?
Good voice, take care of your invisible throat;
Voices can catch a cold and cough and spit.
Voice, be a voice and speak. Where are you?
I cannot see to hit you with my stick.
JOHN: Keep your stick quiet.
BLIND MAN: A stick? a serpent; this is Moses' serpent;
Jump quick or he will bite your heels.
JOHN: Listen. I heard you ask –

BLIND MAN: And why did you not answer? Tell me that.
And where is your voice's friend, the other voice,
The dumb voice that cannot speak? Is he about?
Hiss at him, serpent.
JOHN: Keep your stick quiet and listen.
BLIND MAN: Listen? What does a blind man do but listen?
I listen like an echo in a cave;
I am a drum that listens to be struck.
And when did you, you paste-faced hypocrite,
Listen to me? Have you not seen me sit
Outside the Temple, mewing like a cat,
'An alms, an alms, for God's sake give an alms;
Pity a poor blind beggar.' And did you listen?
JOHN: I might say something for your good.
BLIND MAN: All day I sit there with my sleeping eyes
And look up at the sun. God thinks I pray.
But when night comes
And I can rattle money in my purse,
Ah, then I am a king; night is my kingdom.
O I can see to spy a tavern door,
And there I meet my friends; I know their voices;
Some blind like me, some deaf or dumb or halt;
One has a palsy, he trembles like an earthquake;
And there is one that often drops down dead;
And there we sing our – well, not our psalms.
JOHN: I do not doubt it, friend.
BLIND MAN: You cannot see by night, but I can see;
O that my eyes could see that Man called Jesus.
JOHN: Perhaps they will; I think they will;
But not tonight.
BLIND MAN: No, not tonight; I will be healed by day;
I should be only half-healed in the dark.
My eyes must look up at the blessed sun.
They say it is no bigger than an apple
And made of fire. How can a fire be round?
I do not understand about the moon;
How can men see the moon when it is night?
No, it must be by day my eyes are born.
How they will sit on either side my head,
Those new-born twins, and look up at the sun!
But with two eyes will I not see two suns?

JOHN: Both the same sun.
BLIND MAN: But, God forbid, what if one brat should die,
Should I see half the sun?
JOHN: You will see all the sun.
BLIND MAN: For I have heard men say that they saw only
Half of the moon.
JOHN: No, with one eye you would see all the sun.
BLIND MAN: Well, God is wise, giving the blind two eyes.
I must see Jesus.
JOHN: If you see Jesus, you will see indeed.
Goodnight, my friend.

(*The* BLIND MAN *goes out;* NICODEMUS *comes from the house*)

JOHN: Nicodemus!
NICODEMUS: My name! Who speaks the name I had forgotten?
My eyes are stupid coming from the light.
John, is it you? Have you been waiting here:
Still waiting? O how long ago it is
Since you and I stood talking at this door.
It was another life. I did not know
Your Master then; O John, I know Him now.
I had a mother once and she is dead;
I think she did not bear me till this hour.
Or 'born again' was what the Master said;
Have I been born again? O God, I pray
I be not cast out like a stillborn child.
He is to blame to let me go – But no;
I cannot now go back; never again.
It was a stillborn child my mother bore,
But I am come alive tonight. O John,
Not only I am born again tonight,
The world is born again. Look at the stars;
Though small they jostle in the sky for room,
Shining so bright, they drop down through the air;
Are they not born again? Look at the street;
The stones are nestling down to their hard sleep,
Stone nudging neighbour stone, whispering 'Friend,
Are we not born tonight?' Look at the door,
An open sepulchre; I went in dead,
Now I come out again and walk in heaven.

Who could have thought that our poor earth was heaven?
I kiss you, John, my brother.

(JUDAS *enters, looks at* NICODEMUS *and slowly passes into the house*)

NICODEMUS: Who was that man?
JOHN: Judas;
I told you that he often walks by night.
NICODEMUS: Can corpses walk in heaven?
JOHN: What do you mean?
It was the moonlight on his face.
NICODEMUS: I fear that man.
JOHN: Why do you fear him? He is one of us.
NICODEMUS: Of us? he too? Has he been born again?
JOHN: Why do you ask of him?
NICODEMUS: I do not know;
I cannot tell you more than that I ask;
Or is it that I ask about myself?
No, no; go, brother John, back to the Master
And tell Him that I walk tonight in heaven.

(NICODEMUS *goes out;* JOHN, *looking after him, enters the house, and closes the door*)

Prelude II

As in Prelude I

JOHN (*writing*): Then they sought to take him: but no man laid hands on him, because his hour was not yet come. And many of the people believed on him, and said, When Christ cometh, will he do more miracles than these which this man hath done? The Pharisees heard that the people murmured such things concerning him: and the Pharisees and chief priests sent officers to take him.

How clearly I remember; I was there
Outside the door, where Nicodemus told me;
He said that he might call me as a witness;
He did not call me.
I saw the constables go out to take Him;

'Make way, make way,' they cried, pushing a path,
Until the people closing in like water
Hid them from sight; I saw them come again;
They shuffled in with slow uncertain steps,
But Jesus was not with them. –
How costly is this parchment that I write on;
I must write nothing but the words He spoke,
Lest men living in far-off lands and ages
Should read this Gospel I am writing now
And blame my wasted words. –
I think it was the third day of the Feast;
I never saw so great a throng before.
I heard the Levites blow the silver trumpets,
And all the people waving myrtle branches,
That stirred the sleepy dust about their feet,
Flowed on toward the golden Candelabra
Singing the harvest hymn. When that was ended,
Nicodemus came and gripped me by the arm;
We looked more than we spoke.
And then the Council entered; Caiaphas,
As High Priest for that year; then Annas followed,
His white beard streaming like a waterfall,
Then Summas, Alexander, Datan
And others that I could not name.
They took their seats. Then Caiaphas arose,
Lifting his hand, and all stood up to pray.

Scene II

The Hall of Hewn Stones

(JOHN *stands at the door, which opens to the Temple court. Outside people pass, waving branches and singing a hymn*)

Thou crownest the year with thy goodness: and thy clouds drop fatness.

They shall drop upon the dwellings of the wilderness: and the little hills shall rejoice on every side.

The folds shall be full of sheep: the valleys also shall stand so thick with corn, that they shall laugh and sing.

(NICODEMUS *enters*)

NICODEMUS: John.
JOHN: Nicodemus.
NICODEMUS: What does the Master say?
JOHN: His hour is not yet come.
NICODEMUS: You are prepared to be a witness?
JOHN: I am. But, Nicodemus –
NICODEMUS: But what?
JOHN: Remember when you came to Him that night.
NICODEMUS: Remember! How can I forget that night?
I live there yet;
No sun for me has risen on that night;
It is still night; that night.
JOHN: Then be yourself the witness; why not now
Come out into the light as His disciple?
NICODEMUS: I will, but – is the time now ripe?
He says His hour is not yet come.
Here in the Council I am a listening ear;
I can report. And meantime I can work
In other ways. Joseph of Arimathea,
Last night I sounded him – But see, they come,
Caiaphas, Annas and the rest.

(CAIAPHAS, ANNAS, *the* CLERK *and other members of the Sanhedrin enter*)

CAIAPHAS: Why, here is Nicodemus.
NICODEMUS: The High Priest's servant; and, Annas, yours.
ANNAS: Mine too? As Master of the Waterworks
Take care there is no poison in the water.

(*All take their seats.* CONSTABLES *stand near the door*)

CAIAPHAS: Rise, let us pray.
True is it that Thou art the Lord our God and the God of our fathers: our King and the King of our fathers: our Redeemer and the Redeemer of our fathers: our Maker and the Rock of our salvation. A new song did they that were redeemed sing to Thy name by the sea shore. For the sake of our fathers who trusted in Thee, and Thou taughtest them the statutes of life, have mercy upon us and enlighten our darkness. Blessed be the Lord, who in love chose His people Israel. Amen.
ALL: Amen.

CAIAPHAS: Apologies for absence.
CLERK: Gamaliel writes to say he has a cold,
And Joseph of Arimathea writes to say
He has a chill; both beg to be excused.
NICODEMUS: Why are these brethren absent from our Council?
CAIAPHAS: One has a cold, the other has a chill.
NICODEMUS: I fear they do not favour these proceedings.
ANNAS: No more do you; yet you are here.
CAIAPHAS: The Clerk will read the minutes of last meeting.
CLERK: On the eleventh day of Tishri, in the Hall of Hewn Stones; at which time and place the Sanhedrin met and was duly constituted by prayer; the High Priest presided, and there were also present Annas, Nicodemus, Summas, Alexander, Datan, Gamaliel, Joseph of Arimathea, Nepthalim, Cyris and other members. The High Priest reported that on the Day of Atonement he had entered the Holy of Holies. Estimates for repairing the pipes that drain the High Altar were submitted; these were referred to the Finance Committee. Following a report sent from the Sanhedrin of Capernaum and the hearing of witnesses a discussion arose about a man called Jesus, said to be an agitator of the people. Nicodemus moved that the report be left on the table; this was not seconded. Annas then moved that as Jesus might be present at the forthcoming Feast of Tabernacles the matter be brought up at the next meeting. This was seconded and carried. There being no other business the Sanhedrin adjourned to meet on the eighteenth of Tishri in the Hall of Hewn Stones at the hour of Evening Sacrifice. The meeting closed with prayer.
CAIAPHAS: Is it your pleasure that I sign these minutes?
ALL: Agreed, agreed.
CAIAPHAS: The only business rising from these minutes
Is the report concerning this man, Jesus.
Since the last meeting of the Sanhedrin
I took it on myself,
Seeing the charges made in the report
Were of so serious a character,
To have it copied out and circulated
Among the members; it is in your hands.
NICODEMUS: Has this Man come up to the Feast?
CAIAPHAS: I hear He came two days ago.
NICODEMUS: And yet I see the charge against Him here,
That He observes no Sabbath-days or Feasts;
How can that be if He comes to the Feast?

ANNAS: He is a most notorious Sabbath-breaker.
CAIAPHAS: That matter was discussed at the last meeting.
Fathers and brethren,
I take it you have studied the report;
Are you prepared to come to a decision?
ALL: Agreed, agreed.
ANNAS: Then, Caiaphas, I rise to make a motion.
I need not now take up the Council's time
Traversing what I said at our last meeting;
My views were clearly voiced on that occasion;
So at this juncture I will merely move
This Jesus be sent for and brought before us.
NICODEMUS: I, Caiaphas, would second that. But first,
Before you put the motion to the meeting,
I have a witness.
CAIAPHAS: Another witness? We have heard enough.
NICODEMUS: Those witnesses were on one side.
ANNAS: The right side.
NICODEMUS: That does not yet appear.
ANNAS: It shall.
CAIAPHAS: Order! I call you both to order. Fathers,
Is it your will to hear a further witness?
NICODEMUS: I claim the right; can you deny my right?
ANNAS: Or mine?
CAIAPHAS: You too? You too would call a witness?
ANNAS: Why not, if Nicodemus claims the right?
CAIAPHAS: We will hear both. You, Annas, call your witness.
ANNAS: Fathers, at the last meeting of our Council
We heard such evidence of this blasphemer
It burnt our ears; it might have singed our beards;
Who would have thought we needed to hear more?
But Nicodemus says 'All on one side,'
As though white were not white and black not black.
That he would call – mark the effrontery! –
One of this Man's disciples as a witness,
A lying tongue in our holy convocation,
An angel whispered in my ear.
NICODEMUS: An angel? A spy, a snake;
Behold a High Priest changed to a snake-charmer!
He keeps a garden full of snakes.
ANNAS: You, Nicodemus, hide behind your wealth,

But God will call you one day to account.
CAIAPHAS: Order! Proceed.
ANNAS: And so I am prepared.
I have a witness; fathers, take note of him,
A young man with a future, Saul of Tarsus.

(SAUL *enters*)

CAIAPHAS: Your name is Saul? you come from Tarsus?
SAUL: Saul is my name; I come from Tarsus.
NICODEMUS: Why is he blinking like an owl?
ANNAS: He is half-blind with studying our Law.
CAIAPHAS: What is your occupation?
SAUL: A student.
CAIAPHAS: Who is your professor?
SAUL: Gamaliel.
CAIAPHAS: Gamaliel is not here to vouch for you.
ANNAS: He has a cold, a most convenient cold;
But I can vouch for him.
CAIAPHAS: You know the Man called Jesus.
SAUL: I know Him; I am His disciple.
CAIAPHAS: What!
SAUL: None follows Him more faithfully than I.
CAIAPHAS: What are you saying? Are you mad?
Here, Annas, is a change of wind.
SAUL: No, Caiaphas, I am not mad.
I follow Him about like His own shadow;
I drink His words as a dog drinks water;
They change to gall and wormwood in my belly.
CAIAPHAS: Another change of wind. – What do you mean?
Are you this Man's disciple, Yes or No?
SAUL: Is it not written in our Holy Law
That the Lord said to Moses, Send out men,
One man of every tribe, to spy the land?
CAIAPHAS: Well, what of that?
SAUL: And God, who leads men by a way they know not,
Sent me from Tarsus to spy out this Man.
NICODEMUS: A spy and self-confessed!
SAUL: Those spies came bringing from the brook of Eshcol
Clusters of mighty grapes, pomegranates, figs;
I bring you Dead Sea fruit, apples of Sodom.

CAIAPHAS: I cannot make out what you say.
NICODEMUS: The man is fortified in lunacy.
CAIAPHAS: I ask again, are you this Man's disciple?
SAUL: The hunter on the mountain stalks the hind,
The hawk pursues –
ANNAS: Come down from your high mountain and talk sense.
Fathers, this man is no disciple.
He means – the thing is plainer than a post –
That he has watched the heretic; set himself
To watch Him closely and catch up His words;
This man can tell you the whole lying truth.
CAIAPHAS: Then let him tell us; let the man speak plainly.
Come, witness, speak.
SAUL: Caiaphas, Annas, Fathers of the Council,
I have your leave to speak and I will speak.
Though born in Tarsus, which is no mean city,
I am a man that am a Jew; for, know,
After the strictest sect of our religion
I was brought up a Pharisee –
CAIAPHAS: You must not make a speech.
ANNAS: Say what you said to me last night.
What does this Jesus say of us?
That is the point. Fathers, listen.
SAUL: His word is in mine heart,
As a burning fire shut up within my bones,
And I am weary with forbearing.
ANNAS: Stop quoting scripture and speak sense.
NICODEMUS: Why must we listen to this ranting fellow?
ANNAS: Come, tell us what He says of us.
SAUL: Hypocrites!
ANNAS: Ha, now we get the truth.
SAUL: Blind leaders of the blind!
ANNAS: We are blind leaders of the blind!
SAUL: Whited sepulchres!
ANNAS: You hear it? We are whited sepulchres.
You hear this truthful witness, what he says.
I knew that we would get the truth.
CAIAPHAS: So we are whited sepulchres, hypocrites,
Blind leaders of the blind; is this the truth?
SAUL: It is the truth.
CAIAPHAS: He says these things of us?

SAUL: These words with which I have defiled my mouth
Tickle the people's ears and make them laugh.
CAIAPHAS: This is hot blasphemy.
ANNAS: It is indeed;
Blaspheming us he blasphemes God.
CAIAPHAS: What does the Council say?
ALL: Blasphemy, blasphemy!
Let Him be sent for; we have heard enough.
NICODEMUS: Caiaphas.
CAIAPHAS: Silence! Let Nicodemus speak.
NICODEMUS: Fathers, I wonder an old man like Annas
Should mock us in our holy Convocation
With this play-acting fellow. You heard him say
'I have defiled my mouth to speak these words';
But with what relish did he speak them! A witness?
Behind the false face of his evidence
The fellow leered at us; in shrewd pretence
Of holy zeal he plucked us by the beard.
Annas, if old in years, is young in wisdom
To be deceived by such a mocker. Why,
He owns himself a spy; you heard him own it;
And being so great a student of our Scripture
He quotes it to approve his vile profession.
You saw the serpent flick his double tongue,
'I am and I am not this Man's disciple';
You saw too how the serpent turned and twisted,
No one could catch his meaning. Look at him,
This man called Saul, whom God has sent from Tarsus,
This young man with a future –
No, do not blink at me and work your hands;
I know that they would clutch my throat. Listen!
Have you no fear of God to play this part,
To spy on this most righteous Man?
ANNAS: Most righteous man! Listen to Nicodemus.
If Jesus is most righteous, what are we
But hypocrites, blind leaders of the blind?
CAIAPHAS: Order, order!
I rule that we are finished with this witness.
You, Saul of Tarsus, leave the Council.
ANNAS: But wait outside the door.

(SAUL OF TARSUS *goes out*)

CAIAPHAS: You have a witness, Nicodemus.
ANNAS: Why need he call another witness in?
Let Nicodemus call himself as witness.
CAIAPHAS: Himself?
ANNAS: Why not?
Am I in order if I ask a question?
CAIAPHAS: What is your question?
ANNAS: I ask of Nicodemus –
CAIAPHAS: What?
ANNAS: Is he too a disciple of the Man?
CAIAPHAS: Let Nicodemus answer if he will.
NICODEMUS: The question – does not seem – in order.
ANNAS: No, it is not; it is far out of order
That I should need to ask it. Caiaphas,
I, who am old in years and young in wisdom,
Think I can gauge the feeling of the Council.
If Nicodemus will not speak himself,
We will not hear his mouthpiece.
CAIAPHAS: Are you agreed?
ALL: Agreed, agreed.
ANNAS: I made a motion – it was seconded –
That Jesus be sent for and brought before us.
Is it not time you put it to the meeting?
CAIAPHAS: I put that motion to the meeting –
NICODEMUS: Wait!
CAIAPHAS: Well, we are waiting.
NICODEMUS: No; put the motion.
CAIAPHAS: All those in favour?
ALL: Agreed, agreed.
CAIAPHAS: Go, constables, and bring the Man before us,
The Man called Jesus; if He will not come,
Bring Him by force.
A CONSTABLE: Here is a crowd and with them a mad fellow
Who dances as he walks; they all are crying,
'A miracle, a miracle.'
ANNAS: Why, this may be the mystagogue Himself.
CAIAPHAS: Hold back the people.
CONSTABLES: Back, back; stand back, stand back.
CAIAPHAS: What do they want? Let one man speak.
CONSTABLES: What do you want? Let one man speak.
CAIAPHAS: What do they say?

A CONSTABLE: They say they bring a miracle to show you.
CAIAPHAS: A miracle? What kind of miracle?
A CONSTABLE: A man; the dancing fellow.
CAIAPHAS: Then bring this dancing fellow in before us;
But keep the others back.

(*The* BLIND MAN *enters*)

CAIAPHAS: Who are you?
BLIND MAN: Truly the light is sweet and a pleasant thing
It is for a blind man to see the sun.
Where is the sun? I cannot see the sun.
O friends, I hope I have not lost the sun.
ANNAS: This man is drunk.
NICODEMUS: No, no, he is not drunk. Look, Caiaphas,
I call you all to look; this man was blind
And now you see his eyes are open.
ANNAS: A trick, a trick! The man was never blind.
NICODEMUS: But I have seen him begging.
ANNAS: Why, any man can shut his eyes and cry,
'An alms, an alms, pity the blind.' A kick
Is all the miracle such fellows need
To give them sight enough to skip.
CAIAPHAS: Go, constables, and bring the Man called Jesus;
As for this fellow, leave him here with us.
BLIND MAN: Good constables, go bring the Man called Jesus;
That Jesus is the Man that I would see.
CAIAPHAS: That you would see, you, fellow?
BLIND MAN: And why should I not see? Have I not sight?
My eyes were dead, but they are living now.
O I can see so much I scarcely know
If I am here or there or where I am.
I see so many things that I would need
A hundred hands to tell me what they are.
I see you there; I see you seeing me;
You are the Sanhedrin, High Priest and all;
The holy men. God tells me you are men,
Or else I should not know it.
CAIAPHAS: Constables, stop staring at this man and go.

(*The* CONSTABLES *go out*)

BLIND MAN: Go, constables; no, stay and take me with you.
Where are you, constables? God curse these eyes;
Why do I stumble when I try to walk?
I must be blind again to see my way.
ANNAS: I say the man is drunk.
BLIND MAN: Ho, ho; a voice says I am drunk. Who spoke?
I have been often drunk; God pity me,
But what else would He have a blind man be?
But not today; no, I am worse than drunk;
Today I have my sight and see.
ANNAS: You have been drinking at the Feast.
BLIND MAN: O you are speaking; you with the long beard;
A holy man. Where are the prayers that drip
Like gravy from your beard? You look like God. –
But where is God? I had not thought of that.
Now I have eyes, I must see God as well.
Where is the Temple where they say He lives?
I used to know but now I have my sight
I lose my way.
CAIAPHAS: Stay where you are.
BLIND MAN: What, would you have a blind man not see God?
Why have I eyes then? Why should I not see Him?
Ha, ha, perhaps you have not seen God either.
Perhaps you frighten Him; I should not wonder;
Perhaps when you, the priests, go in the Temple
God scampers like a little careful mouse
And runs and hides Himself behind the curtains.
I must go to the Temple and see God.
Besides, now I remember, Jesus said
I must go to the priest and show myself.
He said it; I must go.
ANNAS: Here is the priest, the High Priest.
BLIND MAN: And here am I. Look well at me, High Priest;
The people praise me as a miracle,
And so I am. Lift up your voice in prayer;
Offer a prayer of gladness and thanksgiving.
I know that you can pray;
I know by your long beard and scowling face.
How could a poor blind beggar pray himself?
CAIAPHAS: Be quiet, fellow.
BLIND MAN: I will be quiet; I do not want to speak;

When I have sight, why should I want to speak?
CAIAPHAS: Now listen to the question of the Council;
Do you say this Man, Jesus, gave you sight?
BLIND MAN: I say He made the clay, as God made Adam,
And laid it on my eyes and gave me sight.
CAIAPHAS: You say that to the Council?
BLIND MAN: No, no; I do not say it; I am dumb;
A poor dumb beggar who can only see.
Where is the door? The light must be the door.
My eyes are tired; my eyes are tired with seeing;
O I must close them and be blind again.
Where are you, friends? Here is your miracle.
Jesus and God, I have a lot to see.

(*The* BLIND MAN *goes out, and the people cry,* 'A miracle, a miracle!')

CAIAPHAS: Bring back that man. Where are the constables?

(*The* CONSTABLES *enter*)

A CONSTABLE: Here, here; shall we bring back the miracle?
ANNAS: Be careful, Caiaphas;
The people count him as a miracle.
CAIAPHAS: No, let him go. Bring in the Man called Jesus.
Where is He? Why, fools, are you dumb?
Have you not brought Him?
Why do you stand there shuffling on your feet?
Is this another miracle?
A CONSTABLE: We went to take Him –
CAIAPHAS: Well, did you not take Him?
A CONSTABLE: But no man ever spoke as that Man speaks.
His words were living things, part of Himself;
They were an arm stretched out to hold us back.
NICODEMUS: O Caiaphas, let me fill up the silence.
I see you staring at these men; they say
That no man ever spoke as that Man speaks.
You think that they are foolish ignorant men;
But what if I, a member of the Council,
As having spoken with the Man myself,
Should say the same, that no man ever spoke
As that Man speaks, what would you say?

ANNAS: Nothing; there is no need to say. From now
We know you, Nicodemus; this Man too;
The thing is plain as a whitewashed sepulchre;
I say this Jesus must be put to death.
NICODEMUS: Our Law can judge no man before it hear him.
ANNAS: He has resisted our authority;
I at the proper time will vote for death.
He is as good as dead. You, Nicodemus,
Are you too His disciple? Why then, go
And buy some unguent to anoint His body;
The Man is dead already.
NICODEMUS: Caiaphas, I protest.
ANNAS: I know my words have the cold sound of death
In Nicodemus' ears; and why is that?
Have I not said, he too is a disciple?
If he is not, he needs only to say it.
We know this Man's disciples who they are,
A pack of fishermen from Galilee;
Can any good come out of Galilee?
Tax-gatherers and other publicans,
And wicked women too. Come, Nicodemus,
You are this Man's disciple, are you not? –
Fathers, you hear his silence?
NICODEMUS: I say again
Our Law can judge no man before it hear him.
ANNAS: He shouts so loud that you can hear his silence;
Jesus is dead and buried in that silence.
Fathers, let us be joyful. Hark, the music!
Here is a happy ending to our Council.
The flutes are playing in the Temple court.
The night grows brighter as the day grows darker,
Young priests have climbed and lit the Candelabra.
The people sing and join the holy dance;
You hear their voices lifted in the psalm,
And God can hear the shuffling of their feet.
See how the gold light treads across the chamber;
Come, let us join the dance. But wait;
Let Caiaphas first close the meeting.
CAIAPHAS: Is it your will I close the meeting?
ALL: Agreed, agreed.
CAIAPHAS: Then let us pray.

Praised be Thou, Lord, who bestowest abundant grace and rememberest the promises to the fathers, and bringest a redeemer to their children's children, for Thy name's sake, out of love. O God, who bringest help and salvation, and art a shield, praised be Thou, O shield of Abraham. Amen.

ALL: Amen.

ANNAS: Fathers, step out; I too will shake my beard,
Joining the people in the holy dance;
Come, Nicodemus,
And dance as David danced before the Ark,
No Michal looks out through her lattice window.
The Spirit of the Lord lifts up our steps.
You, foolish constables, can dance as well;
But close the door behind.

(*The Members of the Council dance out with slow swinging movement, singing the hymn.* NICODEMUS *remains behind*)

He will not suffer thy foot to be moved: and he that keepeth thee will not sleep.

Behold, he that keepeth Israel: shall neither slumber nor sleep.

The Lord himself is thy keeper: the Lord is thy defence upon thy right hand;

So that the sun shall not burn thee by day: neither the moon by night.

The Lord shall preserve thee from all evil: yea, it is even he that shall keep thy soul.

The Lord shall preserve thy going out, and thy coming in: from this time forth for evermore.

(*The* CONSTABLES *close the door behind them*)

Prelude III

JOHN *sitting as before writing his Gospel.*

JOHN (*writing*): For these things were done, that the scripture should be fulfilled. A bone of him shall not be broken. And again another scripture saith, They shall look on him whom they pierced. And after this Joseph of Arimathea, being a disciple of Jesus, but secretly for fear of the Jews, besought Pilate that he might take away the body of Jesus: and Pilate gave him leave. He came therefore, and took the body of Jesus. And there came also Nicodemus, which at the first came to Jesus by night, and brought a mixture of myrrh and aloes, about an hundred pound weight.

About an hundred pound! Why, Mary's gift
Was but a pound, and Judas thought it costly,
And that was to anoint His living feet;
And this, an hundred pound of myrrh and aloes
Was to embalm His body for a night,
One night, for Jesus was no sleeping Pharaoh.
My lamp burns down;
The flame lies on the oil and soon will die;
And this old body that grows cold with time
Has no more life left than that floating flame.
How different was it on that Easter morning,
That first of Easters;
We raced together to the sepulchre,
Peter and I, and I outran my friend.
But Peter has outrun me in the end;
His course is finished, he has gained the crown.
James too and brother Paul and all of them
Have left me far behind. I am the last.
Yet not so far behind; no, not far now;
I run a race where old age outruns youth;
My weakness is my strength, my slowness speed,
And I am hastening on towards the mark.
How strange I am the last,
The only one now living on the earth
Who saw and talked with Jesus as a friend.
If I should die, would He not die again?
No, He will live still in His living Church. –
I must be writing. But I cannot see
By this small dying flame.
Caius may be awake still; I will ring. –
So Nicodemus, the same who came by night,
Came with his hundred pound of myrrh and aloes;
Alas, he came too late.

(*An* ANGEL *enters*)

ANGEL: You struck the bell.
JOHN: But who are you?
ANGEL: I am the one who rolled away the stone.
JOHN: The stone?
ANGEL: I rolled it from the sepulchre; God said,
'Go, take an earthquake, roll away the stone.'
JOHN: Are you a servant of the house?
ANGEL: I am the angel of the sepulchre.
JOHN: An angel!
ANGEL: Body and clothes are one material;
I put them on just now outside the door.
Give me your hand, for you must come with me.
JOHN: You come to take me? I must die tonight?
ANGEL: Tonight: some other night; it is the same.
JOHN: I think you are God's angel; it would not matter
Though you were not; you could not take me far.
I see that I must die.
Well, I will go with you; here is my hand.
But this is not like dying; though I am old.
How can I die when I am still alive?
ANGEL: No, you mistake me; this is not your hour.
It was another died tonight.
JOHN: Another of us martyred?
ANGEL: Nicodemus.
JOHN: Nicodemus!
ANGEL: Killed by the Jews; his spirit fled to heaven;
I met him on the way.
JOHN: O God be praised! You came to tell me that?
ANGEL: I came to tell you that; I also came
To lead you back through fifty years and more
To that dark morning at the sepulchre
And show you something Nicodemus saw;
Though Mary and the women went there early
He was the first.
JOHN: He told us nothing.
ANGEL: It was forbidden him to speak;
For once when he might have spoken he was silent.
Hold fast my hand and we are there.

Scene III

Outside the Sepulchre.

(*Two* CONSTABLES *stand at the door. Two other* CONSTABLES *enter*)

1ST CONSTABLE: Halt! Who goes there?
3RD CONSTABLE: The Temple guard.
1ST CONSTABLE: Then pass the word.
3RD CONSTABLE: May angels guard the constables.
1ST CONSTABLE: Why are you so late in relieving us?
3RD CONSTABLE: We came the moment that the captain sent us.
Is this the sepulchre?
1ST CONSTABLE: Did you hear music on the way?
3RD CONSTABLE: We heard the soldiers singing in the castle.
1ST CONSTABLE: But afterwards; here in the garden?
3RD CONSTABLE: We heard the nightingales.
1ST CONSTABLE: That is not music. No, music in the air,
High in the air; sounds without instruments,
Voices without people, as though the air
Were playing of itself and singing too.
3RD CONSTABLE: No, we heard no such music.
1ST CONSTABLE: We are well quit of it;
It sounded too like heaven for my taste.
Good night and a safe watch.
3RD CONSTABLE: Good night and a sound sleep.

(*The first two* CONSTABLES *go out*)

4TH CONSTABLE: What is this music in the air?
3RD CONSTABLE: They must have dreamt it.
4TH CONSTABLE: They would not sleep on guard.
3RD CONSTABLE: They would not sleep – do you think that, young friend?
Why does the captain set us two and two,
Except that one should sleep and one should wake?
We will take turns; and I will sleep first.
But pass the cider.
4TH CONSTABLE: The bottle is three-quarters empty.
3RD CONSTABLE: That is their music in the air.
I will hear music too, music for nothing.
Good health, a long life and fat purse.

4TH CONSTABLE: I am too cold to sleep; it is the dew.
They say dew falls; I never felt it fall;
I think it rises from the ground.
3RD CONSTABLE: It is the heat that makes the dew.
4TH CONSTABLE: How can heat make the dew? The dew is cold.
3RD CONSTABLE: I do not know. I wish I were a dog,
That wakes and listens while he's still asleep.
4TH CONSTABLE: It will be morning in an hour.
Do you remember –
3RD CONSTABLE: Remember what?
4TH CONSTABLE: The day they sent us to arrest Him?
3RD CONSTABLE: The Council? I remember.
4TH CONSTABLE: And we came back without Him;
And we could only stand and tell the Council
That no one ever spoke as that Man spoke.
3RD CONSTABLE: Death was a better constable.
4TH CONSTABLE: I did not think He would be crucified.
3RD CONSTABLE: He went about it the right way.
4TH CONSTABLE: Perhaps He lies there on the shelf and listens.
3RD CONSTABLE: But He is dead.
4TH CONSTABLE: A dead man lies so still he seems to listen.
The dead are far more cunning than the living;
I think too that they have the sharper hearing,
Although they never will let on they hear.
3RD CONSTABLE: He could not hear us from behind the stone.
4TH CONSTABLE: Perhaps a spirit can pass through a stone.
3RD CONSTABLE: A stone would be an open door to spirits,
If there were spirits.
4TH CONSTABLE: You think there are no spirits?
3RD CONSTABLE: No, there are none.
4TH CONSTABLE: But if there are no spirits, why do you say
A stone would be an open door to spirits?
3RD CONSTABLE: Because I speak of nothing.
4TH CONSTABLE: But if there were no spirits, how could you say
There are no spirits?
3RD CONSTABLE: In the same way that I can speak of nothing.
4TH CONSTABLE: To speak of nothing would be not to speak;
If you can speak of spirits, there are spirits.
Listen, Listen!
3RD CONSTABLE: I hear it.
4TH CONSTABLE: The music in the air.

(*A hymn is heard in the distance*)

I bless the Lord, because he doth
   by counsel me conduct:
And in the seasons of the night
   my reins do me instruct.

Because of this my heart is glad,
   and joy shall be exprest,
Ev'n by my glory; and my flesh
   in confidence shall rest.

Because my soul in grave to dwell
   shall not be left by thee;
Nor wilt thou give thine Holy One
   corruption to see.

Thou wilt show me the path of life;
   of joys there is full store
Before thy face; at thy right hand
   are pleasures evermore.

4TH CONSTABLE: Angels, angels!
Were these not angels singing?
3RD CONSTABLE: They were not jackals or hyenas.
4TH CONSTABLE: Perhaps they sing because of Jesus.
3RD CONSTABLE: They do not sing because of us.
4TH CONSTABLE: What shall we do?
3RD CONSTABLE: We cannot cheer them as we cheer a circus
And ask for it again, no, certainly.
4TH CONSTABLE: We must do something; they were angels.
3RD CONSTABLE: Go and arrest them then.
4TH CONSTABLE: Shall we report it to the captain?
3RD CONSTABLE: Why not report it to the priest?
Come, take a drink of cider; you will feel better;
Let me drink first. Health to the angels,
Though no need to wish immortals a long life.

(*The* BLIND MAN *enters with a sack*)

BLIND MAN: I come in time; leave some for me, good friend.
3RD CONSTABLE: Halt, who goes there?

BLIND MAN: I halt; and why should I not halt?
I have come fast enough. You, sack, lie there;
O how the earth smells sweet, struck by the sack;
It smells of flowers and roses.
3RD CONSTABLE: The dancing fellow!
BLIND MAN: The singing constables! I heard you sing.
Who would have thought you had such pleasant voices?
Or did you bring the Temple choir? Where are they?
3RD CONSTABLE: What have you in the sack?
BLIND MAN: It might afflict your noses. Myrrh and aloes;
Surely it stinks enough. It makes the place
Smell like the holy Temple. Bees will wake
And come and sting us. A hundred pound;
Lift it; a hundred pound of precious smell.
Samson could not have carried it. O, I
Shall stink of it for ever. I am a garden;
A sweet herb-border like the Shulamite.
I shall not need to die; I am embalmed
Like an Egyptian mummy. But tell me, friends,
Is this the sepulchre of Jesus?
3RD CONSTABLE: What is His sepulchre to you?
BLIND MAN: Why, surely, you are the wise constables
To ask what is His sepulchre to me.
Did you not know this Jesus gave me sight?
For how could I have known that I was blind
Unless He gave me sight?
Perhaps it was His own sight that He gave me;
He lies so blind there in the sepulchre.
3RD CONSTABLE: Why have you come here?
BLIND MAN: To see you, constables; was that not right?
Now I have eyes I must see all I can.
My eyes are blest to see such men as you.
3RD CONSTABLE: We know you; you are one of His disciples;
We saw you at the Council: the dancing fellow.
BLIND MAN: And I saw you; they sent you to arrest Him;
Why was it that you did not bring Him back?
3RD CONSTABLE: Are you not His disciple?
BLIND MAN: Why should you think it?
3RD CONSTABLE: He gave you sight.
BLIND MAN: Why did He give me sight? Come, tell me that.
Why did He take away my livelihood?

When I was blind, could I not eat and drink?
I did not need to close my eyes to sleep.
I had no sins; a blind man cannot sin.
Earth was a heaven that I could not see
And men who had their sight were walking angels
Or devils when they cursed me.
3RD CONSTABLE: Why have you brought this sack?
BLIND MAN: That sack, too, is a problem; I must work;
I must do this and that for Nicodemus;
You see I have to work both day and night;
I am a servant.
3RD CONSTABLE: Servant to Nicodemus?
BLIND MAN: Why not? He is a good man, Nicodemus,
Although he makes a blind man work for money.
And he is kind; I think he pities me,
Now I have lost my blindness.
3RD CONSTABLE: Why have you come?
BLIND MAN: It is this dead Man in the sepulchre
That I would speak to, if He is alive.
Jesus, Jesus, wake up and answer me,
Why did you take away a poor man's blindness?
Was I not a great blessing to the city,
Stirring the spirit of alms-giving?
Misers have wept to see me. Now, alas,
For want of a blind beggar to give alms to
The rich must die and go to hell.
4TH CONSTABLE: He mocks the dead.
3RD CONSTABLE: Or he is mocking us.
4TH CONSTABLE: I think he plays for time.
3RD CONSTABLE: It is some trick, we must arrest him.
BLIND MAN: Wake up, and save me from the constables;
Make them as blind as the vile men of Sodom
Who wandered round the door.
3RD CONSTABLE: Come, we arrest you, fellow.
BLIND MAN: Leave go, leave go!
3RD CONSTABLE: Come, come.
BLIND MAN: Well, have you got me fast; what will you do?
3RD CONSTABLE: How can we tie him up?
4TH CONSTABLE: We passed a vineyard; I could smell the blossoms;
The young vine-shoots would tie him safe enough;
It is close by.

3RD CONSTABLE: Then go and pull them.
4TH CONSTABLE: This eel will wriggle from your hands.
3RD CONSTABLE: Then let us take him with us.
4TH CONSTABLE: We cannot leave the sepulchre.
3RD CONSTABLE: We shall not be long gone.
BLIND MAN: Hold, I must wait for Nicodemus here.
3RD CONSTABLE: When you are tied up you will wait the better.

(*The two* CONSTABLES *go out with the* BLIND MAN. NICODEMUS *enters*)

NICODEMUS: O Jesus, if your spirit haunts this place –
I feel that you are here, here in this garden,
Where they have brought and planted your poor body,
But not to rise again – forgive, forgive me!
You see me kneeling here, my sin as dark
As the black shadows of this moon-washed garden.
I tried and yet I did not try to save you;
Something I said and yet I did not speak.
O had I spoken boldly, or even said,
'I am this man's disciple,' I do not think
They would have dared to do what they have done.
My silence was the witness that condemned you.
I was afraid; afraid of nothing, for me
They could not crucify as they did you.
I was afraid of nothing but to speak,
Afraid to tell them what they knew. That silence
Became a weight upon my lips, a chain
That bound me, a dumb devil that afflicted me;
And now it is become a wilderness
Where I must ever wander and be lost.
I thought that you would save yourself at last;
I thought – O God, I even thought – that day –
Only two days ago – when I went out
And looked towards the crowd at Calvary
And saw you stand above the people's heads
That you had saved yourself – and then I knew
It was the cross that held you in its arms.
I come again by night; but now too late,
For I can only come to your dead body.
This is a vain work that I come about,
Bringing this useless load of myrrh and aloes;

For to embalm your body with these unguents
Is to perpetuate the wounds and blood.
It is your death that I would keep alive;
And it was I who crucified you, I
Who might have spoken and did not speak.
Forgive me, Lord. Why do I call you Lord?
Is it that in some majesty of death
Your spirit has grown greater than a man's?
Or was it always so, and now in death
I know you, what you are?
Lord, Lord, forgive me, Lord!

(*The two* CONSTABLES *enter with the* BLIND MAN *bound*)

3RD CONSTABLE: Here is another at the sepulchre.
BLIND MAN: Nicodemus!
NICODEMUS: What, is that you?
BLIND MAN: The constables have taken me.
NICODEMUS: Leave go my servant. Who are you?
3RD CONSTABLE: The Temple guard.
NICODEMUS: Why are you here?
3RD CONSTABLE: We watch the sepulchre.
NICODEMUS: Well, I commend your watching; but this man,
He came here at my bidding. Set him free.
BLIND MAN: I told you, fools.

(*The* CONSTABLES *unbind the* BLIND MAN)

NICODEMUS: You constables, come here and lend a hand;
I want the stone rolled from the sepulchre.
3RD CONSTABLE: We have no orders from the captain.
NICODEMUS: Take them from me, then.
3RD CONSTABLE: We were sent here to guard the body.
NICODEMUS: I do not come to steal but to embalm.
Come, help my servant to roll back the stone.
4TH CONSTABLE: The music in the air!
NICODEMUS: What is that music?
4TH CONSTABLE: It is created music, made from nothing.

(*A hymn is heard from the air*)

Ye gates, lift up your heads on high;
ye doors that last for aye,
Be lifted up, that so the King
of glory enter may.

But who of glory is the King?
the mighty Lord is this;
Ev'n that same Lord, that great in might
and strong in battle is.

Ye gates, lift up your heads; ye doors,
doors that do last for aye,
Be lifted up, that so the King
of glory enter may.

But who is he that is the King
of glory? who is this?
The Lord of hosts, and none but he
the King of glory is.

(*An earthquake, with thunder and lightning*)

BLIND MAN: O master, master, look! the earth is drunk;
It is not I this time.
The earth is turned to sea; we rock like boats;
It gives me a cold rising stomach.
NICODEMUS: This is an earthquake.
BLIND MAN: The constables are shipwrecked; they have fallen.
NICODEMUS: Kneel down, kneel down.
BLIND MAN: O master, I am frightened.
The ground is rising up to swallow me.
NICODEMUS: Look at the stone, the stone!
BLIND MAN: What stone?
NICODEMUS: There at the sepulchre; it moves.
BLIND MAN: O God, the stone is frightened too.
NICODEMUS: It trembles like a curtain.
BLIND MAN: It will fall back and crush us.
NICODEMUS: Look! it is rolling like a wheel.
The light, the light!

(*A lighted Altar is disclosed*)

BLIND MAN: O master, is this heaven? am I dead?
NICODEMUS: The tomb is full of light.
BLIND MAN: Or am I blind again to see this sight?
Only the blind could see it.
NICODEMUS: Light, light; nothing but light;
The tomb is empty; He is gone.
BLIND MAN: Where is He gone? Go in the tomb and look;
He may be there.
NICODEMUS: The Lord is risen.
BLIND MAN: But He was dead; could the earthquake wake Him?
NICODEMUS: Waken these sleeping men; they too must see it.
BLIND MAN: Waken, waken! They will not waken;
They seem alive and dead at the same time.
NICODEMUS: Then let them lie; this sight is not for them.
BLIND MAN: But where is Jesus? Call on Him;
If He is gone, He cannot have gone far.
NICODEMUS: Go, leave me here.
BLIND MAN: Go where?
NICODEMUS: Back to Jerusalem.
BLIND MAN: He may be going there.
NICODEMUS: Go quickly; I will follow soon.
BLIND MAN: I am afraid to meet Him, a dead man;
He may come walking to me through the trees;
I wish I never had received my sight.

(*The* BLIND MAN *goes out*)

NICODEMUS: O risen Lord,
I do not ask you to forgive me now;
There is no need.
I came tonight to speak to your dead body,
To touch it with my hands and say 'Forgive',
For though I knew it could not speak to me
Or even hear, yet it was once yourself;
It is dissolved and risen like a dew,
And now I know,
As dawn forgives the night, as spring the winter,
You have forgiven me. It is enough.
Why do I kneel before your empty tomb?
You are not here, for you are everywhere;
The grass, the trees, the air, the wind, the sky,

Nothing can now refuse to be your home;
Nor I. Lord, live in me and I shall live.
This is the word you spoke,
The whole earth hears it, for the whole earth cries,
I AM THE RESURRECTION, AND THE LIFE: HE THAT BELIEVETH IN ME THOUGH HE WERE DEAD, YET SHALL HE LIVE: AND WHOSOEVER LIVETH AND BELIEVETH IN ME SHALL NEVER DIE.

Excerpts from *The Sirens* (1939–40 unpublished)

ODYSSEUS: That silver bay
Stretching beneath the tall white waterfall,
That waves against the cliff, is where they live;
And there mingled with sand and purple pebbles
Are bones, broken-nosed skulls and empty ribs,
The sun-bleached bones of sailors they have eaten.

EURYLOCHUS: I see the silver bay,
But not the Sirens; where are they?

PARAMEDES: If they are goddesses,
They may have changed themselves to rocks or trees.

ODYSSEUS: Attend to me and hold the rudder steady.
Their green hair waving in the wind like water,
There all the day they lie like lazy seals
Basking in the hot sun; but when their ears
Catch far-off the slow rise and fall of oars
They sit up with a green light in their eyes
And feet and fingers sharpen with long claws;
Then from their throats bubbles a song so sweet,
So killing-sweet that all things stop to listen,
Waves with bent heads, the stiffened waterfall
And birds on boughs that winds forget to swing;
The ship stops too; then with high hurried strokes
Oars smite the sea, the ship runs up the beach,
The frenzied sailors tumble over the gunwale,
And drawn down to the Sirens' foul embraces –

EURYLOCHUS: Look, yonder, in the bay,
Those two white shapes . . .

⋆ ⋆ ⋆

ODYSSEUS: Sing, Sirens, sing; I am the wise Odysseus,
Who by good-will and ill-will of the gods
Have travelled land and sea to the one end,
To hear you sing. Sing, hawk-faced nightingales;
You see my ship with oars digging your bay.
They say that at your singing ships stand still,
The mast remembers that it was a tree
And puts forth leaves, and on the hanging oars
Vines clamber with sweet blossoms. These are dreams.
Perhaps what maddens men is not your voices
But foolish things you sing about.

SIRENS: Rest, sailors, on your dripping oar
And watch the moving shore,
The rocks and trees that glide along,
And listen to our honey-hearted song.

Calm is the water of our bay,
Its depth as clear as day,
Where red star-fish stretch in the sun
And green crabs scuttle off with sidelong run.

Here let the waves' soft sudden beat
Be music to your feet,
And gaze on calmer clearer skies
Bending above you in the Sirens' eyes.

⋆ ⋆ ⋆

But something more we have to tell;
We cannot sound it like a bell;
You must come near, you must be here,
If we would whisper in your ear.

What is the thing that all men seek,
Soldier, sailor, Trojan, Greek?
When fingers fold a lump of gold
All happiness they clasp and hold.

O sailors, when we sift this sand
What bright thing glitters in our hand?
You must come near if you would hear,
Our soft lips whispering in your ear.

* * *

If our lips are not red enough to please,
Though red and soft as sea-anemones,
Yet like a murmuring shell set to the ear
They whisper what the heart dances to hear.

If our hands are not white enough to charm,
Though white and soft as the sea's floating barm,
Yet like a silver rosebud they unfold
To show in their pure cups a secret gold.

* * *

ODYSSEUS: Back, you evil birds,
Nest on your withered bones. – The keel is crunching;
The ship is free; it dances on the water.
High Zeus be praised. Look at those savage creatures,
Biting their mouths and clawing at their breasts
Because they cannot follow. Paramedes,
Eurylochus, stand on your feet and see
What I have saved you from and praise the gods.

EURYLOCHUS: So all, Odysseus, was a trick to save us,
The lies you spoke, the blow you gave us.

PARAMEDES: And I believed you when you said
That you were not afraid.

ODYSSEUS: You were not wholly wrong. I was afraid,
For who would not fear evil? Yet to say
That I was not afraid lessened my fear
As though the falsehood changed into a truth.
So from our story let us draw the moral:
To be afraid of evil and to say
'I fear no evil' is a golden lie;
Such a falsehood the truthful gods will bless.

Out of the World and Back (1958)

Into Hades

1 The Funeral

One midnight in the Paris Underground
Walking along the tunnel to a train,
I saw a man leaning against the wall,
Eyes shut, head sunk on chest; selling newspapers
He had fallen asleep, but still stood on his feet.
Just so I must have stood,
When drowsily I heard, as from a distance,
Forasmuch – Almighty God – unto himself
The soul of our dear brother here departed,
We therefore commit his body to the ground;
Earth to earth, ashes to ashes – Half-asleep,
My mind took time to gather in the meaning;
Than I began to wonder, and awoke.

By an open grave
Lined with the undertaker's verdant grass,
Their backs toward me, priest and people stood.
The verger, who dropped the clods, dusting his hands,
Why, it was Fred! And this was Stonegate Church!
These were my friends, the priest the Rural Dean;
Did they think I lay ill in the vicarage,
Too ill to bury a parishioner?
Could they not see me standing in the road?
But when I saw the Three,
Who after the priest's '*I heard a voice from heaven*'
Drew closer to the grave's brink and gazed down,
I gasped and cried, 'Stop! there is some mistake;

You cannot bury me; I am not dead'.
But no one turned, for no one heard my cry.
Terrified by the silence of my own voice,
I sank down with a shudder by the lych-gate.

2 The Prison

It was like waking
In a strange room; I almost hoped to hear
The opening of a door, a slippered step.
The funeral came slowly back as though
A scene from last night's play. I lay and listened
For night's stealthy noises, swaying curtain,
Sigh of spent cinders in a fire-place; but all
Was silent as myself. No wind outside
Drew its loose fingers through a bush; farm-cock
Still slept like weather-cock.
But I could wait. Soon a window would grow pale;
Already I could see my hand, my body.
I had no fear, thinking of nothing more
Than the strange novelty of being dead.

Often I had waked
Thankful to be alive after an air-raid;
I was as thankful now to wake and to be dead.
I even grew light-headed; I had made
The long night journey in a sleeping carriage;
I had not changed at Crewe. Where was my watch?
What was the time now in Eternity?
The funeral was a hoax; how false that coffin
They slowly lowered with its puppet. Why,
It was my conjurer's box, with which I showed
The Vanishing Parson; played the trick so well
I had deceived myself. Scared by the audience,
Affected by the flowers, unconscious bouquets,
I had been seized by stage-fright and cried out,
'You cannot bury me; I am not dead'.

Would someone come?
The place must have its routine, a new arrival
Causing no sensation. I should hear voices soon,

Friends at the door. Which should we be in heaven,
Our parents' children or our children's parents?
We might be both. Time could be a clock,
No foolish face, only a pendulum,
Swinging us to and fro, backward and forward,
From age to youth, from youth again to age,
The psychological clock, our minds had lived by
In the interchange of memory and hope.

This dusk was ambiguous;
Would it thin to dawn or thicken to darkness? I waited,
Longing to hear a bird's first doubtful chirp
And then another and the whole kindled chorus.
But no birds sang that morning – if it was morning.
Birds had no time to sing, for while my eyes
Were fumbling with informal cloudy shapes,
Light entered with a step, and it was day,
Wide-open, unabashed. I stared in wonder
At what had the appearance of a prison
With thick-ribbed vault and iron-studded door.
Yet it seemed hardly real;
More like a dungeon in an opera,
Fidelio or *Faust*. What made it stranger,
I saw no window for the light to enter.

Frightened, yet half mocking,
I sat and viewed it. Was this one of those fits
That often seized me? Objects of themselves
Melted away to their own images,
An insubstantial world; or it only needed
That I should say, 'I see what I am seeing',
To feel that what I looked on was unreal,
Nothing was changed, but all was visionary,
And I was in a waking dream. But this time
My sight was in reverse and what looked real
Was visionary. Reaching out my hand
To put it to the proof, I touched a stone;
It was as soft as mist; my hand went through it,
Boring a hole. This was mere make-believe,
Stuff of myself; like a silkworm I had spun
My own cocoon. I understood this prison;

A symbol of the womb, it was the presage
Of my new birth. No midwife would be needed
For this confinement; precocious embryo,
I should prick the pregnant bubble. These stones would vanish,
The prisoner escaping with the prison.

From this side death
Ghost tales seemed credible; could I not go back
To the vicarage? show myself to the Three,
Who thought they left me in the lowered box?
Would they be psychic? A determined ghost,
I should be palpable, besiege the house,
Lay ambushes in the garden, look through a window –
But at the thought I stiffened!
A picture came to my mind – was it from something
I had seen or read? or was it not imagined? –
Of a dead man, live ghost, who came and stood
Outside a lighted window of his house,
Face crushed against the glass, white as a mushroom,
Eyes burning like a moth's, and gazed within
On wife and children, who were so unconscious
A daughter rose and looked out on the darkness
And, seeing nothing, drew the blind. I was frightened
By that picture so intolerant of hope;
It even woke new fear.

3 The Body

I had seen a tree-trunk,
That hurt the ground with its dead weight, sprout leaves
Not knowing it was dead; I had caught fish,
Flounders that flapped, eels tying and untying
Slippery knots, slow to drown in our air;
Was I too living out my life's last remnant,
Not living, only lasting? Was Death a monster,
A cat that toyed with a mouse, caught but not killed?
The thought seized my brain, a fear so tumultuous
That, afraid of itself, it died in fascination,
A crouching, a yielding to the softened paw,
The sense I was safe – not to escape.

Or was I not yet myself,
Not recovered from my illness, cured by death,
Still convalescent? How had I died?
Had death come as a storm, tornado, razing
A tract of memory? There was a gap,
Days, weeks and months torn from the almanac.
I remembered my father's death;
How I had watched the hard, humiliating struggle,
That made me half ashamed that I, his son,
Spied on his weakness. I remembered her,
Who held her son's last letter in her hand
Like a passport to heaven. I remembered too
Thinking that some time I should go their way;
But had I then believed it?

Why, even now
The sight and touch of my accustomed body
Compromised the truth. Here it was out of place,
An obvious mistake. Raising my hand
I recognized a white scar on my wrist;
I felt my heart; shut in its cage of bones,
That songless lark kept time. But the funeral!
The coffin with its cargo! I was confused;
Were there two bodies, two scars, two bird-cages?
Paudricia in *Palmerin of England*
In place of her lover, still alive in prison,
Buried his effigy. Trust the undertaker
Not to bury a guy.

As I looked at my body,
It stared back with a strange impertinence,
Familiar, hostile, superfluous proof I was dead.
It, too, was make-believe, stuff of myself,
Old use and wont expected, therefore seen.
I was my own Pygmalion!
A fungoid outgrowth, it was not like that other
I left in the churchyard, that stiff, straight soldier
Who kept good guard in his fallen sentry-box.

I must not sleep again;
Nothing to hold it, my body would be gone,
And, body gone, should I not also go?

The thought alarmed me; it was high time to answer
The long-unanswered knocking at my mind's
Back-door. I had heard it since I first awoke,
Steady as a clocklike dripping in a crypt.
Now I bustled about and with shamefaced 'Welcome, stranger,
You should have come up by the garden path',
I greeted my terrific visitor,
The thought of God.

4 *The Prisoner*

The thought was surgical,
But could I not disarm it of the knife?
Had I no grievance I had been kept waiting
So long in an ante-room? *O bona Patria,*
Num tua gaudia teque videbo?
How often had I sung. Not patriotic
Like Bernard de Morlaix, I yet had tasted
The honey of the land in his sweet *Rhythm*.
Where was that land? where was the mystic city?
What had I seen? A ghost with a white scar,
An opera prison.

But nothing happened,
Time lazy, stale, dammed up by a long moment.
Was I here forever, or till the Judgment Day?
Which was this cell, convict's or anchorite's?
The prison irked me; though it looked determined,
It was stage property. What I had conjured up
Could I not conjure down? Calling to myself,
'These are the prophet's stones of emptiness',
I tried to wave it away. It answered back,
Stones shooting out on elongated necks
Fantastic gargoyles. It was like a church
Turned outside in. Waving their serpent heads,
They reached towards me, tugging at the walls;
I was seized by my oldest fear, to be buried alive,
And gave a nightmare cry.

I outstared them in the end;
Grinning acknowledgment, they relapsed to stone.

I was their Gorgon's head!
Yet I was afraid; it was dangerous to be dead.

5 *The Lover*

Why had I waked?
There was no future in this future life,
Nothing to do, no prayer, no repentance.
Dante set out to walk from hell to heaven
For his soul's health, but mine had caught a cold.
And Dante came back! Why was I singled out?
What was peculiar? What the truth, the value?
Was it in that young lover,
Who pitched his tent in heaven and read Plato?

I had the strange feeling
Someone that moment, in looking through my relics,
Had found a ring, a ring of twisted silver
Carved with a letter, and had paused to wonder
Whose name it stood for, what the cheap treasure meant.
How little did he guess
She had been nothing I could see or touch
And had no other name than that I gave her
Unless among the angels. Unlike Psyche
Lighting her penny dip, I asked no sight
Of the flying Eros. Hermits and virgins,
Who in the love and proof of chastity
Slept side by side in the Egyptian desert,
Had not so pure a passion. Joseph and Mary
Might have been the witnesses, when at our wedding
I placed the ring, for our marriage was by proxy,
On the third finger – of my own left hand.

Her speech a responsive silence,
(Though in undertones of streams I caught her voice),
She was the charm of woods, my Adam's rib,
My Muse, my shadow on the sunny side.
She mocked me on mountains; where hands and knees clasped rocks,
She glided as a ghost; yet in a mist's
Rich loneliness she was singularly present.

I found her most in Paris;
In the twilight, in the evening, when, behold,
A woman at the corner, she cooled my blood
More than the corpses set up in the Morgue
Like fashion dummies in a milliner's window.
I starved my body that the loosened spirit
Might break out to the prospect, the fulfilment;
Indulged in the thought of death, feeding on Plato;
For though he argued of the life to come
With only half his head, he was himself
The better argument.

With no gross brain
Steadying it, my mind clutched at a hope;
Though I had broken my noviciate's vows,
Fallen from that envied self, now my despair,
Might she not trespass on a timid star
And, euphrasy on her eyes, see how her lover
Struggled in this strait-jacket? That Platonic love
Was withered seaweed, crawled over by bleached dead crabs,
Busy with sand-hoppers; yet it had floated once,
Waved with the water, lustrous, stranger than earthplant.
Believe what you see not and you shall see
What you will not believe: If in the words
There was heavenly logic, might she not come?
I outbid hope; she would come laughing, mocking
My artificial body, 'not one true limb,
Poor Dresden china shepherd'. But what came instead
Was sleep, an irresistible sleep —

6 *The Ghost*

Morning was late that day,
Delayed by thick fog. Trees, their tops out of sight,
Scattered irregular rain: dew-hoary cobwebs
Drooped with false geometry. Over the hedge
The mist drew round the coats of coughing sheep
A halo of silver light: they might have been
Hyperion's. How I came in the garden
Was denser fog. A moorhen on the pond,

Jetting its head with red phylactery,
Pushed forward in widening angles. Seeing a man,
It would have croaked and run with dripping legs
To shelter in the reeds: but it swam closer.
I was a ghost; I could go up to birds
And pick them like a barn-owl from a bough.
That it was my own garden I was haunting
Filled it with stinging nettles. The old boat,
Upturned with gaping wounds, was not so dead;
It came to life in summer, growing warm
And raising tarry blisters.

The sun itself was a ghost,
A pallid ball that came and went in the haze
It helped to thin. I saw the vicarage
Across the pond; but where was my ambition
To haunt it? Achilles' horses could shed tears,
But mine were raindrops on a winter bough,
That freeze and forget to fall. For something told me
I was warned away, a trespasser in my own garden.
I had come home to learn
With how true an instinct I had dedicated
The ring of twisted silver in the end.

The bell rang for the Celebration.
It had an absent sound, but I would be present;
All mornings for a ghost were All Saints' Night.
Why, when they brought St Germain's body to church,
Choir tapers lit themselves. And I wore my cassock!
Had they buried me like a Carthusian monk
In his usual habit? And the feast was ghostly;
I should feel at home, see with St Chrysostom
The Word born on the altar; I should kneel
And worship like the Magi at the manger.

The bell stopped ringing,
As I took the road. The boy with Sunday papers
Came cycling down; I would have said 'Good morning',
But he rode past, eyes fixed ahead. I turned
And saw him jump off at the garden gate
And, feeling for a paper, disappear.

He had looked through my body! The hedge was thorny;
I clawed it, eager for the sight of blood
As the thronging ghosts Odysseus drove with his sword
From the red pool. But I was an empty ghost
And no blood came. I had seen Death at last:
He had ridden past me, not on his pale horse,
But on a cycle with the *Sunday Times*.

It mattered little
The service was begun. The Ten Commandments
I could take as read – what were they to me now? –
Omit the Offertory – silver and gold,
Could I not say, with Peter, I had none?
Reaching the lych-gate, where at first I fainted,
I almost fainted again. As I stole a glance
At the white chrysanthemums that buried my grave,
The sun made rainbows on my wet eye-lashes.
Lift up your hearts, I heard; but my heart sank;
My ghostly hands had not strength enough to turn
The door's iron handle. I darted to a window;
But the priest was not in view. I outdid Zacchaeus;
Overflying the roof, I perched on an Irish yew,
That grew on the farther side against the chancel.
The priest was kneeling: like God or an eavesdropper
I knew the words he spoke. At the Consecration,
When he stood with hovering hands over the Birth,
I watched him like a young communicant,
Who through his fingers spies on the priest's action.
But when he raised the Host,
The Bread that feeds us as we feed the Bread,
He straightened upwards in a fearful elongation,
Tall as a seraph. I gazed at him aghast
As at the sight of something that could not happen.
My trembling shook the tree. Then all grew dim,
Cloudy, tumultuous, a swirling smoke.
'Fire! your church is on fire!' I almost cried
To the sleeping villagers, but I remembered
The prophet's words, *The house was filled with smoke*.
As the candle flames, indignant eyes, burned through it,
I slid down from the tree; not church, but churchyard,
Fitted a ghost. I was excommunicated.

7 *Mattins*

The fog had left the sun
A heavy dew to lift; Thomson, the farmer,
Trailed a dark track in the cow-pasture. But I,
A ghost, a little fog myself, trailed none
Through the churchyard grass. Shunning chrysanthemums,
I sat on a flat stone, alive with lichen.
It might have been a moonbeam the sun cast,
For I felt no warmth.

Locked out by St Peter's key!
And from the church that he and I had shared
As patron saint and priest! I was the more
Aggrieved, for churches were my love and study,
Not theology. I sat and wrapt myself
In their warm memory, from Norman naves,
Huge monsters standing on elephantine legs,
Tame at the altar, to the little churches
With scarcely room for God. Stone foliage
Showed me the spring in winter at West Walton,
Angels smiled down as they spread their wooden wings
To fly off with Knapton's roof. I thought of Gloucester,
Where under the swirling fan-vault of the cloister
I walked like a river-god; of Beverley's
Dense forest of choir stalls, where I unearthed
Strange creatures, salamanders, unicorns,
Peacocks and men whose faces were their bellies.
Lincoln's rose-window so hurt me with its beauty,
It was like broken glass; sun shining through,
Apollo was a Christian.

Was the church a well,
That filled from within? I had seen no people enter,
Yet voices sang to the organ. They sang *Venite*,
But I did not come; I sat, too, through the Psalms
Like an invalid. Gazing about the churchyard,
I saw it was autumn; berries on the hedge
Hung in bright bracelets; bryony, nightshade, how vain
To remember the names. A silence grew more than silence,
A vacuum, that drew me to a window.

One of my friends stood at the lectern eagle;
Jove's messenger, the brazen bird looked bored,
It had so often listened to the Lessons.
As I peered at the priest, the stranger in my stall,
The congregation rose, filling the church,
For the *Te Deum*. So they must have risen,
When I was shouldered out, smothered with flowers
To make my death the surer. The thought was bitter;
It turned the *Te Deum* to the *Nunc Dimittis*.
Two women stood at the other side of the window;
I could have touched the nearer but for the glass
And a lost world between. Turning her head,
She stared at me in wonder. Would she start the story
She had seen her late vicar's ghost? Though I told myself
I was only another window she looked through,
I stole from the church's shadow.

The white chrysanthemums
Seduced my feet. I stood over my grave
At the priest's end. It was my mother Eve,
Apple still in her mouth, who tempted me
To take the plunge into that foaming gulf.
I saw a wonder: the coffin-lid mere glass,
I gazed down at the gaunt philosopher.
I hardly knew myself; here was a change
From Epicurean to the Stoic school.
But the coffin was a trap; springing to life
He rose, a towering wave of lust, and gripped me;
I choked in his close embrace, cold awful kiss.

8 *World's End*

It was touch and go,
That I escaped the shaking of the sheet,
The breathless suction, being buried in my grave.
Corpses so amorous, earth was not safe
For wandering ghosts. The prison would be safer,
No fear of being murdered by a dead man.
But was I back in prison?
I gazed on nothing; even the floor had fled;
The prison, not the prisoner, had escaped!

All was so absent, I had the baffled sense
That in looking I did not look. It was like a sea
Without the water. Hung on a spacious point,
I feared to stretch a hand; I might overbalance,
Fall without end; it was dangerous as a dream.
I viewed myself with distaste. Emphatic Ego,
A speck of horrible conspicuousness,
I felt exposed. Shaming the one-eyed Cyclops,
I borrowed the whole universe for eye,
A gazing-stock to myself.

Flowing ectoplasm,
This body would not last, not even as long
As that other body lying in its sunk boat,
Shipwrecked on land. This was a replica,
That the original. I felt for its defeat
A self-pity: face that had hoisted the white flag
To the invaders; veins, once fruitful rivers,
Stagnant canals; the heart, that had kept good time,
Stopped; inner works, that had gone of their own accord,
While I, the engineer, had walked on deck,
Run down; the precious idol that all my life
I had fed with hecatombs of sheep and oxen,
Given rich libations, fallen. Though the Creed
Spoke of an exhumation and Coroner's inquest,
It lay in a world that itself had fallen to nothing.
I was further from that world than the nebulae,
Not space enough between us to drop a pin.
Trout in time's stream, nosing its solid wind,
Helped by a heavenly hook, I had leapt out
And landed on the bank.

9 *The Rainbow*

Was I near the Magnetic Mountain,
Climbed by those saints who, wounded by love's arrow,
Had sought for healing at their Hunter's wounds?
Rapt from themselves to a murmuring solitude,
A silent music, they were abroad in bliss,
A merry heat, and tasting marvellous honey,

They loved and burned and shone and in a tempest
Were overthrown. By comprehending not,
They comprehended and in a fathomless staring
Became the light they saw. Through an abyss
That in the Godhead's mountain-range disported,
Beyond activity, wayless and idle,
They passed to a wild estrangement, the Dark Silence
Where all lovers lose themselves.

Saints were the world's adventure.
I had explored their poor cells of self-knowledge,
Tasted their fasts; my faith leaned hard on theirs,
As substance of things hoped for, evidence
Of things not seen. Now, answering my faith,
The sudden rainbow!

At first it puzzled my eyes;
Red, orange, green, blue, violet, the names
Did not apply; I could not read the colours
I knew for colours only by their contrast.
It was a rainbow in a foreign language,
If rainbow it was, that overflowed with flowers,
Amorous, dangling in a gay rebellion
From their strict arch. I gazed in frightened joy;
What was to follow, the Book of Revelation
Having opened at this marker? I lay still,
Awed, crouching, tightly clutched by its wide arms,
Eyes drawn up to the supernatural magnet.
Time was not long or short enough to measure
My gazing. Then the strange fires melted.

My makeshift body, too,
Melted away. My substance was a thought,
That fell back on itself like a wave rising
White on a stream's current. Buoyant, open,
I expatiated in freedom. But not for long;
Too near to nothing, exposed, I craved for objects,
The body's mutual touch, the rough and hard,
A rock's resistance, the boundary of a thorn,
A limit to my false infinitude.

My thought dropped to the churchyard.
It gaped with an easy earthquake, the coffin-lid
Flying open of itself and the dead man –
Did I catch his action? – pulling back the sheet.
He had drawn his skin-coat tight against the cold
And, pale ascetic, crossed his hands in prayer.
'Brother,' I said, 'I need your blind statue eyes
To see the rainbow's overflowing flowers;
Your deaf ears, so intent, to hear what gospels
Hum round its whispering gallery; a thin hand
To shade me shyly from the Deity.'

Like the soul of Hermotimus,
Returned from the air to find his body burnt,
I was at a loss. I could have hailed a stone,
Made it an idol; squeezed into a rabbit's burrow
To crush myself to shape. All was so empty,
I was not even defined by what I was not;
I might have flown for ever and not found
A desert. If others like myself were here,
Each had arrived with his own universe.
Whatever it might be after the Judgment,
Our universes now could no more mingle
Than the imaginations of a man and woman
Lying in the same bed.

Where was my ground,
Support? Trembling, naked, I was an O,
A nothing and a cry of astonishment.
Where there is nothing there is God: the word
Came to my mind; it might have been a flower
Dropt from the rainbow. My sole support was God.
The thought was electric; at the toleration,
God as my unseen, contemplated ground,
My mind began to sparkle.

10 The New Body

It was a phantom,
Not the true Helen, who was rapt to Egypt,
Paris took to Troy. Phantasmal, too, the body

I lived in, loved on earth; for now the body
I saw, knew as my own, though not yet adopted,
Was real in excess.

Fantastic coffin,
The boat that bore it slowly sailed in sight,
Lit by St Elmo's fire; it might have come
From anchoring off the rainbow. Solomon's cargo,
The gold and silver, ivory, apes and peacocks,
Was not so precious as that solemn barge's.
Its cargo was its captain, but not dead;
In sleep surmounting sleep he lay in state
Distant, superior, unrecognising,
My new authentic body!
Holy, immortal, my eyes saw it so clearly
They stung me like jelly-fish, as I remembered
How I had profaned its earthly prototype,
Though only a phantom.

I saw it put to shame
The miracle of loaves and fishes. It stirred,
Sprouted with life, rose spreading, multiplying,
Changed to a Jesse-tree. The sleeping Adam
Had more ribs than a wreck: warm, fertile, breathing,
They stretched as boughs, laden with all the bodies
I had worn on earth, child, lover and man.

Gazing at the child,
In whom I saw myself, *O Hesperus,*
That bringest all things back the bright dawn scattered,
I sang with Sappho. Narcissus-like I eyed
The lover who aspired to climb love's ladder;
Petrarch had climbed it, led by Laura's eyes,
But he, who aimed at an eloping angel,
Climbed two or three steps, when beneath his weight
The ladder gave way. The man was multiple,
The one in many, the same, yet different.
I hailed the token! At the Resurrection
It was a changing Proteus who would rise,
Choosing, repeating variable ages,
His life a newel-stair, ascending, descending.

Caught up to heaven,
Or charmed away by an Orphean lyre,
The tree vanished; it did not even leave
The progenitor. Yet I was not alone;
I knew by the different silence there was an Other,
Invisible, hiding behind himself.
I waited, listened. There was no need to listen:
Silence interpreting itself, the words
Were reflected on my mind like flowers on water,
'Come, see the Bride'. They were as plain as speech,
But whose they were, I had no time to wonder;
As tiny as a thought at first, but growing
To hazel-nut, to apple, to balloon,
A world swam up, losing its shape in size.
If worlds could speak like maps, it would have said,
'The New Earth'.

Her beauty sparkled;
Though I knew her for the old earth, now renewed,
Reborn, she was so transfigured, so unearthly,
I felt I tarnished her even with looking.
All things were conscious, trees talking together,
Streams their own Sirens; mountains might have moved
Slow shoulders. Miraculously as in a dream
She drew close to my side. Distance so near,
Thin as a window-pane, I could have leapt
And landed on her lap, in a laughing ditch
Or cow-gate smiling with subliminal mud.
But I was stuck in space. Not for one lover,
A paralytic too, had this Venus risen.

If the Jesse-tree,
Laden with bodies, a Christmas-tree at Easter,
Had shamed the miracle of loaves and fishes,
What I now saw excelled. It came in glimpses,
As the Earth, a changing Proteus too, repeated
Her variable ages. It flung out
Wild liberty to move both ways in time,
Backward, forward. The moment in reverse,
Past following future, as future followed past,

Clio, playing Penelope's part, would unweave
Her historic web. What sights would be disclosed,
Time ebbing: cities would unbuild themselves,
Temples fly back to their quarries; fossils unfreezing
Would show toothed birds and five-toed horses; coal,
Mining itself, would rise as ferny forests,
Air feel again the weight of flying lizards.
One glimpse I had: it was a dead volcano,
That remembering its old anger, furiously
Stoked its cold fires; perhaps I saw it clearly,
I was so blinded by the frightening flames.

Time's two-way traffic
Would let the apelike man, a sinless satyr,
Loping into the future, view the Parthenon,
While Aristotle, hieing back to the past,
Watched fish that, coming to land, grew legs and lungs.
And myself? I should wander to and fro in time,
Historian of all – its present ages.
I should taste Eternity. Why had I said,
There was no future in this future life?
The New Earth opened out so bright a prospect,
I forgot about its sky!
I looked too late, that strange earth floating away;
But womanlike she tossed me a last word,
'Sun, moon and stars lay in that tomb with Christ'.

12 The New Heaven

Vanished to permanence,
She left a hollow in the emptiness,
That waited to be filled. Should I now hear,
'Come, see the Bridegroom'?
My Monitor – for so I named the Other –
Alarmed me by his stillness. Was he waiting
Prelude, star-signal? The silence grew peculiar,
Then self-assertive, till, swelling immense,
It rocked me as it rose to bursting-point,
To the explosion! I was lifted up,
Dead and alive at once, stunned by a rock,
Assaulted by the sight –

Plato died in his dream,
But I woke muttering 'The Terrible Crystal'.
What did my lips remember? For my mind
Held nothing real; it was an empty net
Drawn up at night from a phosphorescent sea.
I even felt the distant rainbow frowned
On the effort to remember. I clutched at symbols:
The sky a mirror, feet moving to and fro,
An albatross, a fountain rising in prayer,
One who bent over me, tall as a pillar,
Reflected faces, swaying like flowers, astonished.
Had I scared the angels by my conspicuousness?
Shattered the Crystal?

I knew with a blind man's feeling
My Monitor was there: I could have kissed
His faithful, invisible feet. He even read
My dumb question, 'Why the earthquake, heavenquake,
The evocation of those foolish symbols?'
The answer came as though written on my mind,
'You flew too high: come, see the saints in flight'.
He proved a Mercury. First his soft rod
Charmed my sick memory asleep; and then!
Argus had fewer eyes shut by that rod
Than I had opened, though in a steadfast sleep.

13 The Three Hierarchies

He rose in flamelike flight,
Singing to music dumb as a music-score
A song inaudible as a bursting rosebud's,
I following in straight ascent. We halted
Where a waterfall, cascade after cascade,
Made an endless thunder. Pools swirled with wondering bubbles
And overflowed in wide columns of water,
That in crashing down stood still. Salmon darkened
Its white tumbling extravagance, leaping out
To fall back, curved like bows, or straight as arrows
Shot through the current. I heard, close as a kiss,
'Look back; see her who sends to heaven these saints,
Missiles, love-letters'. Earth in an empty nadir
Shone like a star reflected in a pool.

The waterfall stopped,
Salmon hooked in mid-air, the spray a frozen silence;
All was a picture waiting to come alive.
My Monitor called from above, 'Look higher'.
To look was to ascend; I was on a peak,
Exhausted pinnacle. The air was filled
With flying gannets that – Was space upturned?
Why, when they plunged, they rose and fell into the sky,
Not down into a sea. It brought to my mind
How waterdrops fall *up* to a lake's surface
Reflecting drips from an oar. Sharing my thought,
He said, 'Some birds come back; they are not lucky
Like the false water-drops that falling up
Meet their true selves to perish in a kiss.'

'The Holy Trinity
Is celebrated in three hierarchies;
Come, see the third'. As though at my Monitor's word,
I flew up like a bubble from a stream,
Exploding, lost in air. Yet I gathered myself,
Grew sufficient, and to his mocking 'Look beyond',
I looked. My strained sight took so long to travel,
It might have been climbing an invisible mountain.
But I saw them, even to their gold and purple feathers,
The phoenixes. They struck at the Godhead,
One moment birds and the next moment ashes.
Though they flocked in thousands to their immortal deaths,
Each was God's only phoenix. My Monitor said,
'Yet an archangel's wing, darkening the sky,
Would frighten those small larks'.

The height relaxing,
I fell away so fast the waterfall
Passed in a flash; I could have overtaken
A stone or shooting star. But I was halted;
The New Earth swam in sight. Rapidly rising,
She burned with an intolerable beauty
That would have scorched my feet, yet seemed each moment
A new creation. She carried her own morning,
A sunny light, to which her heart kept humming.
'Bridegroom waits Bride; the saints will hail the Union,

Inherit both, descending or ascending,
As they see God in creatures or creatures in God',
My Monitor said, and put my dream to sleep.

14 *The Last Look*

If he was not myself,
The primal self who never had left heaven,
My Monitor was gone. A ghostly light
Hovered over an open door; it led to a stair,
That invited my downward steps. Though I had played
Ghost in the misty garden, through the window
Watched like a thief the Celebration, stared hard
At the amorous body in his wooden bed,
All had been timeless. The funeral was not finished;
Priest and people would stand by the open grave,
Till I descended the stair.

The light advanced as a torch,
Paving a pale way through my mind's recesses.
It illuminated notions, a knowledge lost
As I stumbled down the faulty, circular stair.
It paused at a window, where sparkling frost-ferns waved,
Commemorating summer. Touched by the torch,
A sudden repentance, they melted in tears. Outside
Floated a misty world I knew by instinct
Was the old earth. It was still in its ancient youth,
Volcanoes bending over it in level smoke,
Foundations settling. In a waste of waters
I discerned the Symbol, shadowy as a shark,
Foreseen, foreseeing, patient without pain,
Jealous and wrathful without perturbation.
The monster would rise, spreading ambitious arms,
Embracing the world, yet empty, Adam's tree,
Leafless, forlorn, clothed with a naked Man,
The Prodigal Son, who came to save the world.

A Traveller in Time

1 I Set Out

The light was on my face,
But my thoughts were cast behind into the Shadow
I had emerged from. Was the Last Judgment passed?
With nothing seen or heard but a sounding flash
Like the soft explosion when a photograph
Is taken in the dark, it had been enough;
The illumination had been interior,
And to all self-portraits I had said Good-bye,
Meeting that stranger, myself.
Timidly as a plant stretches pale leaves
From a dim cave to the sunlight, I had stolen
Out of the Shadow. I stood on the living world's
Momentous threshold. Was I free again to play
My garden part, the ghost?

So abrupt the border,
It was like the edge – of a flat precipice.
The way was open, but my heels still stuck.
The sun peeped over a hill, a half-closed eye
That made me restless. I moved a few slow steps.
I was in the world; it was the familiar earth,
But more familiar! Hill, meadow, trees and grass,
So like themselves, had an essential look.
Escaping ghost, dead man on holiday,
Where was I? What was I about to see?
Solvitur ambulando.

A path offered its company.
It led me up a hill; the ascent was sharp,
But I lost no breath; ghosts borrow from Vulcan's stithy
A pair of bellows for lungs! Looking back I saw
The Shadow had vanished. Or had it not turned to trees?
A group of witchlike birches was so weird,
Demoniac, for a moment I was startled.
But I smiled at myself; for a ghost who should frighten others
I was too nervous. But it was not long before

Again I was startled. Though the air hung breathless,
No breeze to alarm a leaf, I suddenly staggered
In a strong gust of wind. Lasting a moment,
It gave me the feeling of an invisible man
Walking through my body. For a long time I stood
Still as a stone; but I was not as patient
And thoughtfully I persisted up the path.
Yet not without bravado; the invisible man
Had scared me with the sense of solitude;
No other traffic on the empty path –
It was wider than a desert – shepherd, gamekeeper,
Would pass so lightly through my ghostly body;
I should stop it with my heart.

From a shoulder of the hill
The path fell to a wooded dale. But I hung back,
A third time startled. For, looking round for comfort,
The conscious smoke that rises from a chimney
Or dull intelligence of a ploughed field,
My eyes opened to a world I recognised
No longer in a mode of separation,
But intimate, reciprocal. Its substance
A thin device to retain the inner spirit,
It disclaimed the name of earth. It was transfigured,
Caught up beyond itself, remote from time,
Even outside space, hung in a holy trance.
I was daunted, frightened by the incarnate beauty,
The ecstatic landscape. Earth in love with heaven!
As I turned away, flowers followed me with eyes
Surprised, reproachful.

A stream ran down the dale
With stepping-stones. The earth so visionary,
Was the water real? Or did it appear to flow
As in a picture? Descending to the dale
I dipped my hand; the stream rose round my wrist
Resenting the question. On the stepping-stones
I scared a shoal of minnows; all of one mind
They darted off in one body. How thin the love
That bound that brotherhood in their watery convent;
Yet it was love, appropriate to the place.

Though I knew my shadow shivering on the current
Kept them from coming back, I almost fancied
It was love's shyness.

Still musing on the minnows
I was about to step from the last stone,
When I was halted. A man had crossed my path
Walking downstream. But was he a man and walking?
All I saw was a head and shoulders!

2 *The Dale*

Herod was not so startled
By the Baptist's head on a charger. He ordered that dish,
But the floating head and shoulders were unannounced.
They had the timeless air of a marble bust,
Yet eyes were alive and looking straight ahead,
Intent on the future. Near, but as though from a distance,
He slowly faded from sight. If I saw nothing,
It was too real a nothing not to follow.

Leaving the hill-path,
I took a grassy track along the bank.
At first I outpaced the stream, too lazy to flow,
Carried along by its weight. Then for no reason
My pace, too, grew slow; I laboured in my walk,
As though wading through water. Stranger still,
When the stream with gathering speed raced down a decline,
Showing white heels on the cobbles, the descent
Perplexed me like a hill. No wind was stirring;
Autumn leaves, brown as bronze, hung down as heavy;
Yet I laboured as in a gale. Foot followed foot,
Not marking time; I passed a tree, a rock,
More trees, more rocks, yet felt at every step
I was blown back a mile. Should I be carried
Out of the world? I caught hold of a branch,
But quickly let it go; it was in bud!
Autumn had changed to spring; loose hazel catkins
Dripped in a yellow rain, palm-willow wands
Stretched out gold paws. Time had moved with a jerk

Backward or forward; had I moved with time,
Not knowing I moved, the sense of motion felt
As an imaginary gale?

3 The Tiltyard

Head and shoulders again!
I saw him through the trees. Gone soon as seen,
I read the inviting sign. The air now calm,
I walked with ease. Like Amadis of Gaul
Forcing his way through the Firm Island enchantment
I had fought with the strange gale, but now my feet
Carried me smoothly, as though borne on a rhythm.
But was I not myself in an enchantment?
Nothing looked real; trees, bushes, rocks, the stream,
The small black swine routing up leaves, all seemed
A dream's decoration. Was I in the half-man's world?
And what was this new feeling? Leaving the track,
I stepped down to the stream, where water waited
In a patient pool, and gazed at my floating face.
No wonder what I saw had a startled look;
It was a young man's face. My mind went blank
As though struck by a black lightning.

Months blown away like clouds,
It was high summer, briars with Tudor roses,
The sedge with yellow fleur-de-lis, when, waking,
I took the track again and looked around.
It passed a heath-thatched hovel; a bent figure,
Hair dangling over what he read or wrote,
Sat by the door. Had it been the Middle Ages,
I might have wondered which, hermit or wizard,
The strange man was. He did not raise his head,
And I passed on, my eyes like the half-man's
Intent on the future.

The dale soon opened out
To a broad meadow with a line of willows
Hiding and showing the stream. On level ground
Before a castle people held a pageant,

Dressed to their parts. Had I visited the earth
To view a pageant? Travelled through time to see
Time's imitation? What I saw was phantasma;
People, if not the castle, would dissolve
At my approach. But castle stayed as stone;
And the people! Amazed I saw it was no pageant;
Those were real knights, plumes tossing in the air
Like birds-of-paradise. It was a passage of arms
In a tiltyard.

It was late evening;
A swollen sun hung over the purple hills,
Its gold changing to blood. It pushed out shadows
From tree and castle, but where it struck on armour
Steel turned to shining water, shields were wounds,
White, azure, vert. A long beflagged pavilion
Was gay with people; it was as though a rainbow
Had fallen and broken. Two knights with their squires
Waited on chamfered horses in the lists,
Their fork-tailed pennons fluttering like swallows
Caught on their lances. What was the argument?
By a flying Cupid hung in the pavilion
Shooting an arrow, each upheld his love
Against the other. Was it to the utterance?
Did he with the three gold lilies on a field
Vermilion, say to his squire, 'If I am killed,
Dig out my heart and carry it to my lady;
I would not have to give account to God
For keeping what is not mine'? Did he with the swan
On a field purple pray, 'As I have held
God on my right hand, my lady on my left,
So, Jesu, sweet knight, help me'?

Cannon fired roses,
And bending peak-nosed helms, setting at rest
Long staves like pens with which they meant to write,
Those clerkly knights flew on a trumpet's flourish
To fall in a confused tumble. Both rose dazed,
Avoiding their stallions. Taking to their swords,
They traced and traversed in a shower of sparks
As though the danger were less wounds than fire.

How strange to see these knights,
Who died too long ago to be called dead,
Now fighting for life. For the ancient castle was new,
The spectacle extant. In love with love
Were they not a counterpart to the lovesick earth,
Even the shoal of minnows? The fight stopping itself,
They froze to figures in a stained glass window.
Colours fluttered away; once again I was struck
By the black lightning.

4 *The Abbey*

Even in the dark I knew
It was a church. And soon a tall arched window,
Twin lancets balancing a quatrefoil,
Began to kindle. Dawn stoking its rich coals,
Rubies, emeralds, opals, two saints appeared,
Their dresses bright as the vestments that St Goar
Hung on a sunbeam. Between Lauds and Prime
I guessed the hour, the monks back in their dorter
Or walking the cloister.

How unlike this church
To that cathedral, grey ghost of itself,
Where I held my Canon's stall. Here clustered columns,
Sprouting gilt foliage from the capitals,
Blossomed like Aaron's rod, and in the choir-screen
Dead timber, coming alive, renewed rich summer
With leaf, flower, berry. On the painted walls
Abraham drove the birds from the sacrifice,
And ravens fed Elijah; Yebel and Salome,
The midwives, watched an ox feed from the manger,
Its mouth close to the Child. It was strange to think
In the great Doom over the chancel arch
That Child was the seated Judge; on either side
Were naked souls, some stepping up to heaven,
Glad hands pointed in prayer, others in chains
Slowly creeping to hell, a whale's gaping mouth,
No Jonahs to return. But the congregation!
Patriarchs, prophets, kings, apostles, martyrs,
Not waiting the resurrection, had put on

Spare flesh of glass and worshipped at the windows.
St Margaret and St George had brought their dragons,
St Lawrence his iron bed; St Sebastian
Bristled with arrows like a startled hedgehog.
But all were martyrs in those burning windows,
God's salamanders. Built more of flame than stone,
But most of spirit, reared on argument
Of thrust and counterthrust, Thomistic logic,
This adoring church wooed God.

The light of four candles,
Praying on prickets, drew me to the chancel,
Where gold stars glittering on an azure roof
Made a strange night. In front of the high altar,
Two candles at his head, two at his feet,
Sword, shield and armour peaceful by his side,
One of the knights, his three gold lilies cropt,
Lay under a white pall. Fantastic lover,
He, too, had been a religious, armour his habit,
A casque his cowl, and in the end love's martyr.

I was stooping down
To draw aside the cover from his face,
When something hurled me back. At the same moment
The abbey vanished. I saw only a man
Hastening away; he was hidden by a hedge,
All but the head and shoulders.

5 *I Travel Farther*

Had he grown arms and legs,
Like tadpole turned to frog? Body or not,
The determined shoulders carried off the head
As though a trophy. But what was the haste, the fear?
Should I recognise a face, a family likeness?
At the stepping-stones the face had floated past
As alien as a statue's. Had he dropped a mask?
Might I not know the man? His shoulders' shape,
Back of the head, woke in me a strange feeling
Instinctive, warm.

Gliding away so fast
Half-hidden by the hedge, he was like a centaur
Galloping on himself. I was no Achilles
To overtake that Cheiron. But the abbey?
It had slipped a hundred years behind my mind,
Was slipping still. I was travelling in time!
A strange wind had risen as in the dale,
But a softer wind, making my passage easy.
Backward or forward, which way was my journey?
Was I passing, too, through space? But I saw nothing,
All lost in a mist.

6 *The Nymph's Well*

So suddenly I saw
The mist was gone, it was as though I had waked,
And yet not slept. A low sun, swollen with sleep,
Lit up a land that rocks and rocklike plants
Seemed less to fill than empty. Slow black shadows
Moved on the hillsides, showing they were goats;
All else was still; no note dropped from bird's bill,
Grasshopper's wing. I was seated by a well;
Shaped like a shrine, it was sacred to a Nymph.
I felt her presence, and bending over the pool
I saw myself in her arms. But I was warned
The fancy was profane; a wild fig-tree
Leaned over the well as though a holy Watcher,
And on a ledge, a pious offering,
Lay three small loaves. The sand stirred with her breath,
And quicksilver bubbles rose like uttered words,
But soundless, empty.

My travelling in time
Had made me look no older. The young man's face,
That had so startled me in the windy dale,
This sacred well repeated. For its strange truth
I had the Nymph's own word! Yet I had lived
As long as Aeson. What Medea's herbs
Renewed my years? Was I in the Age of Gold
With Kronos ruling as in Plato's fable,
All in reverse, sun rising in the west,

Spring following summer, old men born in graves
And growing younger?

But I heard voices;
Two girls were slowly climbing up the slope,
Each with a basket. Raising a festive dress,
They picked a delicate way among the stones,
Great earrings jangling. Painted to the neck,
Eyes like blue mussel-shells, they approached the shrine.
Bowing with hand on knee, each added a loaf
From her straw basket; then, breaking into laughter,
They ran down to a road. They had not glanced my way!
I was wearing Perseus' cap, invisible.
I turned to where I lay drowned in the pool;
My floating face and I, exchanging looks,
Saw more than the laughing girls.

What on the road seemed people
Were gods and goddesses, olives and poplars,
Lining a Sacred Way. It left a city
I knew for Athens; in the pure Attic air
The Acropolis was plain, even, though minute,
The Parthenon, perched like a silver beetle
Newly alighted. Ground strewn with gossamer,
I guessed it was late autumn; but what year,
What century? Was Socrates alive?
Wrestling that morning in the Gymnasium
With argument or lover? Or setting out
To sit with Phaedrus in the plane-tree's shade,
Grasshoppers his holy Muses? Going to Athens,
What should I find? I was about to rise,
When behind a tree, laden with images,
Owls and small pigs, I caught sight of the half-man!
So I wildly thought for a moment; then I knew
That head and shoulders rested on a plinth,
A roadside Hermes. Would the god's stone eyes
Be sharper than the girls'? He drove off ghosts!
What else was I?

The fear was heathenish;
Ghost or no ghost, if there were comings and goings

Between the two worlds, why, what should I not see?
I should come in spring when red anemones
Burn up dead thistles, and in the river-beds
The oleanders make pink waterfalls.
Indifferent to space, ranging around,
I should see Dodona's oak, that talking tree,
Hear nightingales at Daulis. Choosing my moment,
I should fly in time like Merops, the Bee-eater,
Backward or forward; watch in the theatre
Theodorus play Antigone, or even,
Intruding on the Banquet, Socrates
Soaring in high discourse, while the other drinkers
Flapped feeble wings. I should witness famous battles
And truer than the Delphic pythoness
Foretell the issue. At Thermopylae
I should see the Spartans on the green sea-rocks
Combing their oily hair; young Sophocles,
A naked choir-boy, dancing with ivory lyre
After Salamis. I should go farther back,
To the Trojan war; if ghost could spare a penny
For a blind rhapsodist reciting verses,
Homer should have it. Greece for a beginning,
I should not find eternity itself
Hang heavy on my hands.

7 *The Procession*

On the eve of Salamis
Two men had seen on the Eleusis road
A cloud of dust, heard, too, a holy music
With Bacchic cries, but all had proved a phantom;
The procession I now saw approach was real,
Myself the ghost. The god in the farm-wagon,
Drawn by white oxen, was more alive than I;
He sprouted vine-leaves. By his spotted fawn-skin
Dionysos I should have named him, but the cries,
Iacche, *Iacche*, gave him another name,
Iacchos. Unlike that slant-eyed mystagogue,
Bearded, effeminate, this was a frightening god,
His mask with gaping mouth. Did a pine-cone hide
A spear-point on his staff? A throng of people,

As though goaded by his horns, waved fennel-stalks
And danced so wildly that the bearded goats
Looked philosophers. Men to the beat of drums
Stamping the ground, women to Phrygian flutes
Arching their bodies back like scorpions,
They danced the Holy Marriage. Let Heaven's rain
Impregnate Earth; then the long summer drought
Breaking, Korè will rise in her green veil,
The autumn grass and corn. It was to Eleusis,
The Mysteries, they bore the god. Iacchos,
Born of a bull's heart, would outface Hades
And bring back to her mother, virginity
Renewed like Aphrodite's, the tender Korè,
Whose spring is in the autumn.

Had Athens emptied itself
That morning? Purple-bordered sindon dresses
Mingling with woollen peplums, parasols
With crutches, the long procession slowly passed,
Dragging a tedious tail. Then all at once
It took to wings, was flying along the road
Like a frightened goose!

Another trick of time,
Not keeping time, I thought; time went so fast,
The slow procession was flying before my eyes.
And sure enough, already in the west
The sun, growing hot with haste, slid down the sky.
If it should strike the earth! But it slipped safely
Behind a mountain. First the air grew crimson,
Then violet; hill-slopes ran with purple,
Dionysos treading grapes; earth fell asleep
In a dream of her own beauty. A full moon rose,
And the empty road gleamed like a serpent's ghost,
A small owl moaning.

8 At Eleusis

If the flying goose was gone,
I had followed it, exchanging the Nymph's Well
For lights, cries, music. I was in Eleusis,

My journey's end the Mysteries. As I stood
Beside the wall of a tall enclosure, voices
Made me look up to two men in a tower
Leaning over the parapet in Corinthian helmets.
Were they watchers of a precinct, eyeing me,
Suspecting a temple thief? I moved away,
But came to a standstill. The moonlight showed
A yard strewn with black rocks; but the rocks breathed,
Heaps of small sleeping pigs that soon would redden
A priest's gold knife.

I shuddered as I turned
To heads outlined against a smoky glow.
A crowd was gathered round the god's ox-wagon,
That stood on a dancing-floor. The god was gone,
But wearing mask, fawn-skin and horns, a priest
Sat in his place. Their faces smeared with gypsum,
Kobolds ran in a ring, flame-flattened torches
Trailing a roof of smoke. Within the circle
A din of drums and flutes worked wild-haired women
To a dancing frenzy; they might have been the Maenads,
Who milked the lionesses on the mountains
And made great cheeses. But where was the god gone?
To the Hall of Mysteries, the tall enclosure?
My feet almost as fast as the thought they followed,
I reached the entrance. It was guarded by two soldiers,
Leaning on spears. For a moment I hung back;
Then remembering I wore my Perseus' cap,
I cut across the barrier of their talk
And was through an open gate.

A paved path in a garden,
Rows of white statues and dark cypresses,
The hall itself carved out of frozen moonlight,
These I remember, though vaguely as a dream,
But nothing else, not even how I entered,
Till I saw Demeter's eyes. The great jewels glowed
Through an incense-cloud, and, as it thinned and thickened,
Their flashes came and went. Was the goddess angry
My profane eyes saw her giving birth to children?
For from a fold of her black marble robe

Appeared a figure, like a dead man rising,
Naked but for a sheet. Were two old people,
Who, standing side by side, wept as they watched,
Seeing their new-born son? From the same birthplace
A woman rose; her eyes meeting a man's,
They shared one smile. So figure followed figure
From that strange womb, the goddess giving birth
To her adopted children.

Did Iacchos lead them out,
Twice-born himself, from lightning-stricken mother
And father's thigh? What was the Hierophant
Showing the mystics? Was it the little Korè,
A barley-corn? Was he placing in their hands
The sacred cup from which Demeter drank
Water and meal? And what did they repeat?
I could not pluck the heart of the mystery,
And tortured by half-truths I ranged around,
Defied by Demeter's eyes. But as I heard
The awed audience here and there break into sobs,
I grew ashamed. Retreating to a corner,
I stood by one, an old initiate,
Who viewed the scene with disillusioned eyes.
I felt he would have said, if he had spoken:
All is the effort to accomplish death,
The returning to the safety of the womb,
First and last love.

9 *I Travel Still Farther*

The Sphinx, her riddle read,
Died of heart-failure; did the hall collapse
Because I read its secret? For all went,
Demeter, Hierophant, the new-born mystics,
Wiped from a mirror, not even the mirror left.
But had I read it? There was no time to ask;
I was in motion, travelling again.
But where and when? I could not even guess
The continent, nor by a thousand years
The hour of my arrival.

The imaginary wind,
I faced in the dale, had veered round to my back,
Was taking me with itself. What of the half-man,
Was I leaving him behind? But how had I fancied
That wandering bust was real like the knights,
The girls, the mystics? If I smiled at the thought,
The smile faded from my face when I turned my head;
He was standing at my side!
The man himself, a fellow-traveller,
Complete as Adam. From my wondering gaze
He moved away; but his back was not forbidding;
Having seen the family likeness, I read 'Follow'.
He led me down a slope; the way was steep,
For it was on a narrow mountain ridge
We had landed from the air.

All others I had seen
Were living in their own time, though long since dead;
This timeless man I viewed with curious eyes.
Head and hands were distinct, but body and clothes
Confusingly one. He was neither clothed nor naked,
Or both at once; or was he like a statue
With flesh and drapery all of a piece?
Or was he a ghost? Stamped with the family likeness,
Why else was he silent? It might have been in answer
That, pointing to a mountain across a valley,
He said, 'Mount Gerizim'.

It took me time
To dig the name out of my memory.
'Mount Gerizim, sir, in Palestine?' I asked;
'And this is Mount Ebal', he replied. These twins
The Samaritan woman saw; this was her land;
A shoal of hills bare to the grey limestone,
Hoary and bald at once, a pallid wilderness,
Yet upheld by golden valleys. 'And that is Shechem',
He added, pointing downward. The small city lay
Beneath our feet, its streets narrow and crooked,
As though bent out of shape by the stone wall,
That bound it like a belt. A lazy smoke
Hung over it, but men, women and children

Knelt in fields, cutting the short corn with sickles.
I faintly heard their cries. On the terraced hill-slopes
Grew grape-vines; did they watch with small green eyes
That glad corn-killing, the warning of their own
Even merrier death? How strange to know the season
But not the century. But he said Shechem,
Not Neapolis or Nablus, later names;
I was in the time of the Old Testament,
But at which book? Was Dinah yet unravished?
Had Joseph's painted coffin come from Egypt
Or Joshua set up the listening stone?
For this was Samaria. But why was I here?
As though with 'Come and see', my guide moved on.

Black and tan goats
Lent us a track that crept down by the edge
Of a deep watercourse. Though sullen pools
Fed one another with a grudging trickle,
The tumbled rocks were echo and prophecy
Of winter torrents. Half-way down he stopped:
'You see that man'. Where a long scree of stones
Streamed down the mountain like a silent scream
And broadened at the base, a man stepped over
A vineyard wall. He climbed the slope obliquely
Towards a thrust-out shoulder of the mountain,
Itself a small round hill. To myself I said,
That man did something more than step over a wall,
He stepped out of the Bible.

Leaving the watercourse
We made our stony way along the slope
To the small round hill. Its green grass a surprise,
It was like the place where the multitude was fed
With the loaves and fishes; but how unlike was the feast
That tainted the air with a sweet holy smoke.
A fire greedily fed on the sizzling fat
And entrails of some beast heaped on an altar,
A priest throwing on incense. It burned before a Bull –
Made of gold it was even smaller than a calf –
Set on a pillar. Roofed by shaking trees,
It seemed in the interchange of light and shadow

A living creature. The Baal had his Baalath,
A green-painted Asherah. Husband and wife,
They feasted together on the savoury smoke,
While the worshippers were reclining at a banquet
In a great hall. Though open at one end,
Its other sides bulged out in small annexes,
A sinister spawn. Women glanced at their lovers
Like languid queens, but judged by a silver star
Tattooed on their foreheads, they were sacred slaves.
We had approached the entrance, even stood
Close to the couches, when a woman screamed
And, covering her breasts, ran from the hall.
She had seen him first, the man who climbed the hill.
'Hosea', whispered my guide.

Her lover staggered forward,
A wine-cup in his hand, and splashed the wine
Full in the prophet's face. Licking the drops
He spat them out, while the other feasters frowned,
Shaking their heads. His eyes were the first to speak;
Then he lifted up his voice in a wailing cry
As in a funeral dirge. Of his rhapsody
I made out nothing but a repeated word,
A fierce 'Yah-yah'. It was like a hyena's bark,
The 'Yah-yah'. The feasters spread protesting hands
And in the Hebrew gabble they answered back
I heard the same 'Yah-yah'. What was this word
They bandied about, he with accusing finger
Pointing to the Bull, the feasters in defence,
An edge of anger rising in their voices?
Was it their name for God?

Silence fell on the tables,
When a white-robed priest appeared, his piled-up turban
Flashing with angry jewels. But his look was mild,
As equable as the empty pair of scales
Held in his hand. As, stricken by the sight,
Hosea bent his head, I read their meaning:
He had come to buy her back, the screaming woman,
Gomer bath Diblaim, his children's mother,
The wife who had woven her way through paramours

To temple-slave. Slowly lifting his head,
He looked up to the sky with muttering lips,
As though his case were Heaven's. Were they not one,
God's painful case with His adulterous people
And his with Gomer?

It might have been her wedding,
Feasters the guests, the money the priest weighed
Her dowry. Slowly she came down the hall,
A smile carved on her face. He kissed the brow
Tattooed with the star, but with so cold an effort
I felt the prophet disappointed Heaven.

As he led Gomer away,
The feasters sprang to their feet, overturning tables,
And hubbub rose in the hall. The lover ran
And with upthrust thumb gave him the fig. Women laughed
And smiling men plucked kisses from their beards
And flung them after Gomer, as he, God's actor,
Passed on, playing his part in the charade.
But what of Gomer? Would that silver star
Be inauspicious? Was the ascent too sharp
From temple-slave to rigid wife? Not long
I wondered; as I watched them hand in hand
Descend the hill, the sun swooned in the sky,
Rocks thinned in a thickening mist.

10 At Nazareth

Had the light gone out
As in a theatre when scenes are shifted?
What should I witness next? I blindly turned
To my fellow-traveller; his face was radiant!
It shone with light, not sharp as a spot-light
Flung on a stage, but soft, self-evident
As a glow-worm's torch. 'Are you dead?' I breathed;
He nodded. 'Long dead?' But he shook his head,
Then, as though seeing I misunderstood,
'Here we take no account of time', he said,
'Nor – look around – of space'. Shadowy shapes
Looming through pallid air, nothing distinct,

Was all I saw, when he caught me in his arms,
Startled, half-frightened. 'I am that dead brother
'You never knew', he said, and added quickly,
Thrusting me off, 'We are in Nazareth;
Watch for a woman; she carries Christ in her womb'.

That he thrust me off
Impatiently, as though to free himself
From a forced embracement, so took me by surprise
I hardly heard the word about the woman
Till it echoed in my mind. Even then it needed
A sharper 'Look!' to drive away my gaze
From my new dead brother. The stage was being set,
A city building itself before my eyes
On a steep slope. A mist, halving the hills,
Made them look flat-roofed as the boxlike houses.
It was early morning. We stood by the city well,
A pool fed by a spring gushing from grey rocks
Like a special creation. No one came to draw;
Through the loud noises, tossing cypresses,
Scratching palm-leaves, the wind's own naked voice,
The city slept. One of its scavengers,
A tall gaunt hound, slouched down the muddy path,
But stopped; the hair left on its leprous hide
Bristled with fear. Then with a sidelong leap
It fled in a low-backed scamper up the slope.
I had frightened it, a ghost in Nazareth
Two thousand years ago!

Was it her amulets,
A magic blue, that blinded the old woman,
First at the pool? But I was empty air
To all the others as well, women and children,
Who followed fast. A child strayed picking flowers
Close to my feet; it was the ghost who stared!
I stared at her flowers, crocuses and narcissi.
Why, it was spring. Would Christ be born at Easter?
Or Pentecost?

But I remembered Korè,
Whose spring is in autumn. It was autumn now,

Thin grass already rising in a green tide
Round rocks, corn sprouting in untidy ranks;
The early rain had fallen, was now falling,
Scores of compasses drawing circles in the pool.
It might even be Advent – without the Advent collect.
The Birthday was approaching. Child or man,
How often had I thought of Christmas coming,
But not in this strange fashion.

As we watched the women,
Their figures taller for the water-jar
Held by arched arm, go swaying up the slope
With a reedlike motion, one, staggering, stopped,
And, hand clutching her side, leaned on a rock.
My brother bowed, and almost of itself
My head, too, bowed. Not different to the eye
From others, how unlike God's chosen vessel.
She made Christ's coming to the earth seem furtive,
Occult. By Son of Man, ambiguous name,
His nature would be veiled, but to arrive
As though He stole from the paternal shore
A stowaway!

Fingering the door-post,
She disappeared in the darkness of a house.
What had she touched? The 'Hear, O Israel,
The Lord thy God is one Lord'. These were words
Joseph, adopted father, would teach his Son.
The paradox! that He who came as light
Should learn of the darkness. All created things would help,
Birds would be happy omens, and the flowers
Would not stand idly by. For everywhere
He would see the scattered letters of the Word,
And each, a Delphic oracle, would call
Its '*Know thyself*'. Obedient to the call,
Christ would be the first Christian.

The thought grew in my mind,
All I had witnessed in my ghostly travels
Was of the Light, begotten and partaking,
Yet not the Light itself; it was as though,

Moving in time, I startled hues of a crystal,
Red, violet and gold. Instinct with spirit,
Stript almost naked, even of itself,
The amorous earth had an unearthly beauty;
Love, too, though dark and native, bound the minnows,
That darted like a shadow from the stones,
In their mute brotherhood. When the two knights
Fought in the tiltyard, flags and hearts a-flutter,
That summer evening, the sun of earthly love
Was at its meridian; and when I woke,
I saw a church, where pillars, arches, roof,
Had less been built than of themselves had risen,
Drawn up by heavenly love. It was by the Light
Illumined, the two Greek girls saw in the well
A divinity, a favourable Nymph,
And left their pious loaves; while at Eleusis,
Teaching the parable, the Seed of Corn,
It so inspired the mystics that in a symbol
They died to be reborn. If at Mount Ebal
Hosea, his shame so hot, laid a cold kiss
On Gomer's ill-starred brow, yet it prefigured
The kiss the father gave the prodigal son.
In Mary prophecy had reached its end;
The Light Itself was come.

11 The Cave

My brother nodded,
My sign to follow. The sun was in mid-sky,
As we climbed to Nazareth; in its noon sleep
The city made me feel even more a ghost
Stalking its empty streets. Climbing beyond,
We gazed from a hilltop on a low level land,
That did not need my silent guide to name
The Esdraelon Plain. For how could I mistake
That famous battlefield, flying cloud-shadows
The ghosts of passing armies? But my brother
Drew me with an intimate arm to where a cave
Gaped with wide mouth. Though by a bounding wall,
Heaped stones and thorns, I knew it for a sheepfold,
It was like a sepulchre for the pigmy bodies

Hung from the roof. But we woke memories,
Not sleeping bats.

That afternoon
Lasted a day. As though held by a hand
The sun hung stationary, filling the cave
With a warm light, while we sat and talked together,
That brother, dead before I was born, and I,
Sharing news of our two worlds. At last I pointed
To where a caravan had long been winding
About Mount Tabor, yet had never moved,
'Those camels, are they stuck in mud or time?'
'We are the Joshuas who halt the sun',
He said. His light words might have made the sun
Indignant, for time began to make up time;
Rocks grew long shadows; bats one by one awaking
Flew from the cave; the sun, too, its own Phaeton,
Fell into the sea, setting up a conflagration;
Darkness came quickly, sowing the stars broadcast.
He broke the silence softly: 'Though I led the way,
Your half-brother at the stepping-stones' – the half-man!
He was smiling at the jest – 'your heart was the helm
I followed'. 'And you still will follow!' I cried;
But I cried it because he was already gone.

The alarm I felt at first
Quickly gave way to wonder, out of nothing
A picture shaping itself. Was it a dream
Such as a ghost might dream? Then how did it come,
By the ivory gate or the horn? Or was it prophetic,
A foresight of the future? He was no shadow
Who stood, a pillar of light, in the sunbeam
That through the open door of a carpenter's shed
Thrust a bright shoulder, no, not Joseph, but
The carpenter's Son. I watched Him at His work,
The eternal Worker, the Word within the word,
'Let there be light'. What was He making now,
Cradle or bier or – ?

But could that be real
Which dreamlike came and went? For He now knelt,

A camel's skeleton for company,
In a land of fire-chewed rocks and gouty shrubs
That spat out spiteful thorns. Heaven had rained stones
On its defiance of the creative Word;
Was He being challenged to change them into bread?
He was near to hell in that weird Jordan gorge,
Where the flat Moab hills, underground mountains,
Rose to earth's surface, and the blue Dead Sea
Glittered beneath them like a fragment of heaven
Dragged down in Lucifer's fall. The pale winding river
Might have been the upturned body of that old Serpent;
But it was not dead; I almost saw the Darkness
With which He wrestled, clutching Himself in prayer.

Stones turned to water,
Not bread. The lake was sparkling in the sun,
A blue sky full of stars. Beside a creek,
Where a brook drowned itself, and a kingfisher
Hovered, I saw Him standing, still, erect,
Watching the brown-sailed boats. When on the road
A circus passed with girls and wrinkled dwarfs
Led by a fat man riding on an ass,
He did not turn; I thought the camels scowled,
Thrusting out the lower lip. The kingfisher flew
And lumps of mud changed to live tortoises,
As a boat raced in and ran aground. Two fishers,
Stepping ashore, busied themselves with their net.
'Two of the Twelve', I said, knowing the picture,
And added, when they beached their boat so high
It looked abandoned, 'The yeast works in the dough'.

But why did they stand still,
As though hanging back? And then I saw the picture
Was changing; with these two was a third,
St Peter. Shivering mountaineers, they stood
Beneath an immense snowy summit, Hermon.
With fear they shivered, aghast at the enigma,
The familiar Figure in a sphere of light,
A spirit in a crystal. His back was turned
As though He talked with Moses and Elijah.
Was Hermon, outshone, envious? A mist,

That had been agitating its snow-bound brow,
Thickened and, swooping down, darkened the picture.
Or was it by some heavenly jealousy
My sight became extinct?

12 Jerusalem

Would my brother come?
But to what could he return? All was dissolved;
The cave, gaping too wide, had swallowed itself,
The hill was its own mist. Alone and nowhere,
I might have been afraid; but I remembered
His parting jest. I jested with myself:
My loving brother had not so stolen my heart,
He had not left the helm. And the helm was set!
I saw in my mind's eye the little hill,
Where Adam's skull was buried, and Jeremiah
Had sung his Lamentations in a grotto,
Golgotha. No guide, not even the head and shoulders,
It would be my maiden voyage.

Alighting on a bridge,
I felt it was a symbol of my flight
Across a Limbo. But it spanned a deep hollow,
High over a watercourse, stony and dry,
Shrunk corpse of a stream. Sprinkled with olives, tombstones,
One slope rose to a ridge, where houses huddled
As though in fear to fall; a battlemented wall,
Blocking the sky, weighed down the other slope,
Climbed by a stair.

Though all else was clear,
Passers-by on the bridge were strangely blurred;
They might have walked in water. That no one stopped
To stare at the interloping ghost, alarmed me;
I felt I was not there! Was I superstitious
To see in myself a ghost? My apparent body
Mere memory, old clothes, might I not vanish
Like an image from a forgetful mirror, or slowly
Dissolve like a naked toadstool, melting in tears?
Perhaps he came in answer,

Not blurred in an aquatic atmosphere,
But clear as though he carried his own light,
My brother! Greeting and leavetaking one,
The moment might have been forbidden, snatched,
We clung in embrace so warm the passers-by
Looked cold fish in a tank.

I once saw an apparation,
A lady gliding across a lawn to vanish
Through a wall of Ludlow Castle; my brother gone,
It was with the same smooth motion without movement
I glided up the stair, a level road,
To the battlemented wall, built of huge blocks
As long as coffins; passed through a guarded gate
To flutter about in a maze of Corinthian columns,
Perplexed as a bat. That it was Caesar's Cloister
I knew, when through the building's open side
I saw the Temple, saw it with amazement,
Rise like a snowy mountain.

Not criss-cross like a bat,
But with the sure flight of migrating swallow,
I flew towards it. A Babylonian structure,
Less marble than solid light, hung with gold plates
Burning as though in snow, it rose from the rock,
Earth's navel, a place of pilgrimage for angels
Before the man was made without a navel,
Adam. Jews saw their tribes in the painted vine,
That with twelve purple bunches of grapes hung over
The brazen doors. Slowly I floated past
Its frontispiece. 'A lion, broad in front,
Narrow behind', the saying said; I added,
'A porcupine above', the gilded roof
Spiked against Herod's pigeons.

But the little hill, Golgotha!
I had hit the time of year; by the throng of people,
That filled the outer court, hiding the pavement,
And glitter of helmets showing Roman posts,
It was the inflammable Feast of the Passover.
I had even hit the hour; the sun still climbing,

The Shadow of Death crept closer to the Cross,
Though to its own defeat.

But I was fated,
A revenant on earth, an inquisitive ghost,
To miss the hour. For I had hardly passed
Beyond the outer court, when darkness fell
So suddenly, night killed, not followed, day.
Somewhere in the wide precinct I came aground
To grope among carcasses, oxen and sheep,
Laid out in rows. I saw them by a sky
Stars flooded with quicksilver.

What made the earth restless
Was the light of the hidden moon: but soon, a flat orange,
It floated up from the hills. It grew smaller, brighter,
Showing its geography. Objects became plain,
Though less substantial than their crouching shadows.
Safe instinct guiding me, I crossed the precinct
To a guarded gate. Daylight at the Cloister gate
Had blinded the sentry to the gliding ghost:
The sentry here saw nothing, even by moonlight.
Beyond were lanes with houses, shuttered shops,
Bare booths and buildings with carved pots of manna,
The synagogues. My instinct was too blind
To miss the way. Leaving the lanes behind,
I crossed an open space and 'City wall',
I said, 'and this must be the Damascus Gate'.
Three figures approached. The wind that rose with the darkness
Tossed their white mourning weeds: black funeral masks
Covered their faces to reveal their eyes.
One woman's tears were shining in the moonlight
So brightly, they repented they were tears;
'His mother, holy Mary', I breathed.

Outside the city
The moon was enamoured of the pale tombstones
That paved the level ground; but where the land
Sloped slowly to a valley, it blackened caves,
Rich sepulchres in orchards. Nothing showed
At which the women had wailed, but I knew by its shape

Golgotha, Hill of a Skull. One side declined
To the white Damascus road, but the other ended
Abruptly in a cliff, where I traced the skull,
The brow and broken nose, but how chap-fallen.
The three crosses were gone.

A traveller in time,
Backward, forward, I had but to set my heart!
Why, with Good Friday hardly yesterday
I could wake the sun, sleeping in its sea-bed,
Say it had missed a day. The regress was so short,
It was but a step to the miles of centuries
I had lately journeyed. What then held me back?
That sudden darkness, the night falling at noon,
Had warned me those three crucial hours were private,
Not for ghost-moths, perhaps not even for angels.
I pitied Him who so transcended time
His eternal eye could never escape the sight,
His Son hanging on a cross.

All other loves,
That in my trivial travels I had witnessed
Were thin outcroppings of the primal love
The creative Word imparted to the world
On its six birthdays. They were geologic;
This was Uranian; it fell vertical
Faster than Lucifer, the very Word,
God's Proper Name, creating a new earth,
A kingdom, holy church, all, alas, more veiled
Than the Word made flesh.

13 Back in The Dale

It was still a windy dale,
But not as when I set out from the Shadow.
Trees waved wild arms, grasses rose up like hair
Standing on end; yet I was no more shaken
Than beech-bole or, insubstantial as myself,
Shadow of a flat stone that caught my eye.
But at the stone I stared;
Why, it was there I had seen the strange man sit,

Hair dangling over his book. The hut was gone,
As though it had not been; but I remembered
The rill, a river in its petty rage,
Tugging at the grass. The time was different;
It had advanced, overleaping centuries,
As far as then it slipped back. I should find the castle
A ruin now, gaunt spectre of itself
Or its own tombstones. Had it been my aim?
Or the abbey? No need to follow the track farther:
Here was my journey's end.

Was the stone magnetic,
Drawing my steps? Its smooth surface said 'Sit',
But it might have been an ant-hill. I sprang up,
My body tingling. Yet the stone was bare.
Sitting again, I felt the prickly heat.
To what was I sensitive? Not ants, but bees;
They were swarming in my breast; they hung from my ribs
A honeycomb, my body effusing the fragrance.
Then I heard birds; was it in my head or heaven
Those sweet birds sang? I rose and looked around;
Heat, bees and birds were gone. Again I sat,
And they were back; they even grew in strength,
Fire, hornets, music. Strange words of themselves
Came to my mind: 'a merry and unknown heat';
'Ghostly electuary'; 'lovely burning';
'The bread of angels'; then, clear as though called out
In rapture, 'O my honey! O my harp!
O my psaltery and song! O my heart's rose!'
But these words I remembered;
The case was clear; here in his hermitage
I was sitting on the stone with Richard Rolle
Writing *The Fire of Love*; we shared the same stone,
Though centuries apart. Or had he risen,
Gone into the heath-thatched hut, no longer there,
For all suddenly ended?

The autumn dale
Gave a sad welcome to approaching night,
And an owl hooted. Still sitting on the stone,
I watched a small faint feather, blown sky-high,

Change to the moon. No wind stirred the tired trees,
Yet there might have been a hurricane in heaven,
For all at once it was covered by a cloud,
No flying island, but a continent,
Putting out the moon.

But could it be a cloud
That held my gaze? Its strangeness was familiar.
It had the troubled look of a black diamond,
Blinded by its own light. I knew its name
With a dream's credulity, *Cloud of Unknowing*.
Moses entered that cloud; Plotinus, too,
Flew through it with the flight of a homing pigeon.
Beyond it was the land with no horizon,
The murmuring Solitude and idle Quiet.
Its heat, honey and singing Richard Rolle
Foretasted on the holy stone; I, also,
At a remove. But all God's mystic children,
With sparkling stones, ladders of love, sharp clothing,
Rings of espousals, flaming darts, assaulted
That cloud, an obscure night of loving fire.
Singing with Caterina Serafina
'O love's sweet slavery that sets us free',
Or with God's Goldfinch 'I die because I cannot die',
They escaped the shipwreck of the world and pierced
The lightsome darkness, lost, annihilated,
Their nothing-at-all preserved in the All-in-all,
To a blind and lovely beholding of the Word,
The imperishable 'Is', without where or when,
God in a point.

Infused with grace,
Had their geologic love flown off at a tangent
And touched the Uranian? Was it appointed
I should follow those athletes, cry with Meister Eckhart,
'Up, valiant soul, put on thy jumping-shoes
Of love and understanding'? Soon I should learn;
The ghost must go; the cocoon spun by the worm,
The butterfly would burst. New eyes would see
The invisible world into which my brother vanished.

NOTES

The text of the short poems of Young's canon used in this book is that of *Collected Poems* (1950), with the correction of occasional misprints and the acceptance of modern conventions such as the omission of unnecessary hyphens. The origin of many of these poems is available to us in the early books which Young used as 'quarry'. The Notes specify this origin, giving dates, and quote many examples of early versions, enabling the reader to see the ways in which Young improved his poems and developed his personal style; these Notes do not refer to all minor alterations. Additional information on some of the poems is given; more detailed comments will be presented by the Editors in their forthcoming study of Young's life and work, and an extensive critical commentary, with details of variant versions, is available in Dr Sell's book.*

The following abbreviations are used:
rep. (reprinted); rev. (revised); BC (*The Bird-Cage*); CC (*The Cuckoo Clock*); CP 1936, 1950, 1960 (*Collected Poems* 1936, 1950, 1960); CP 1974 (*Complete Poems* 1974); GM (*The Green Man*); NS (*The New Shepherd*); QM (*Quiet as Moss*)†; SE (*Speak to the Earth*); WB (*The White Blackbird*); WH (*Winter Harvest*).

p. 3. *WINTER HARVEST* (Nonesuch Press, 1933) contains eighteen new poems and twenty-seven rep. or rev. from poems in earlier books. Some poems were rev. when the book was rep. in CP 1936.

p. 4. *The Green Woodpecker*: rep. from NS 1931.

p. 4. *Winter Morning*: rev. from NS 1931, where line 6 read 'Painted by Constable, Cotman and Crome'; otherwise unchanged.

p. 5. *The Old Tree*: rep. from CC 1928.

p. 6. *Loch Luichart*: rev. from CC 1928. There are minor changes in stanzas 1 and 2; the last stanza in CC read:

> If pulling from the shore
> I drifted (like that buzzard), I could climb
> Among those mountain-tops for miles and miles
> Breaking their hardest rocks to gentle smiles,
> As I, alas, many and many a time
> Have done before.

Slightly rev. in CP 1936 from WH 1933.

* *Trespassing Ghost: A Critical Study of Andrew Young*, by Roger D. Sell, Acta Academiae Aboensis, Ser A Humaniora, Vol 56 nr 1, Åbo Akademi, 20500 Åbo 50, Finland, 1978.

† *Quiet as Moss*: Thirty-six poems by Andrew Young . . . chosen by Leonard Clark (Hart-Davis, 1959).

p. 7. *March Hares*: rev. from NS 1931, where the first line read 'I made myself a tree'; otherwise unchanged.

p. 8. *The Beech*: rev. from BC 1926 where stanza 3 read:

Its long thin purple buds point to the sky;
Last year's leaves dry and brown
Lie under it, though a young beech hard by
Still wears its withered crown.

p. 9. *On the Pilgrims' Road*: rep. from NS 1931.

p. 9. *In Romsey Abbey*: rep. from CC 1928.

p. 10. *The Sheaf*: the form of this poem (see also *The Men*, p. 20) – a single paragraph in lines of irregular length and rhyme pattern – is one which Young often used in his later poems (e.g. his well-known poem *Idleness*, p. 79).

p. 10. *The Star*: rep. from NS 1931.

p. 11. *The Lane*: rev. from BC 1926, where stanza 2 line 2 read 'Saxon and sturdy Sussex yeoman', and line 7 read 'Seems to me walking in this place'.

p. 12. *Palmistry*: see also *The Rat* (p. 19). Young was interested in all psychic phenomena.

p. 13. *The Roman Wall*: slightly rev. from CC 1928.

p. 13. *The Spider*: rev. from BC 1926, where last line read 'O deadly symmetry!'; this revision is an example of Young's reaction against rhetorical gesture.

p. 14. *The Rain*: rev. from BC 1926, where first line read 'Alas, for broken vows!'. The insertion in WH of parentheses in stanza 3 lines 3 and 4 and of an exclamation mark in line 5 clarifies the syntax.

p. 15. *The Stars*: rep. in WH 1933 from *Thirty-One Poems* 1922; line 6 of stanza 2 rev. in CP 1936 from 'Flashed down like falling tear'. The earliest poem that Young admitted to his canon.

p. 16. *The Wood*: rev. from BC 1926 where stanza 2 lines 3–8 read:

And thin grass and slow-footed moss
And daisies, blue in shadow, creep across,
Till scarcely on the narrowed path
The ruffled sparrow finds a dusty bath;
I see, breasting the crowded leaves,
Green caterpillars arched on my coat-sleeves.

Stanza 3 lines 7 and 8 read:

Here two rust-breasted robins mate,
Hard winter held apart in a cold hate.

p. 17. *The Shadow*: rev. from NS 1931, where there was the following middle stanza:

A stranger,
That stalks across the hollow hanger
Crashing in silence or
Uprisen from its falling floor
To a tree-trunk will start,
So near but nearer to my heart;

In the last stanza lines 2–4 read:

Your arm is like a tossing bough
When you too stand
And wave back to my waving hand

In WH 1933 the middle stanza was retained, but line 2 read 'That stalks beneath me through the hanger', and line 6 read 'As though myself were from myself apart'.

p. 19. *The Feather*: slightly rev. from BC 1926.

p. 21. *Penelope*: slightly rev. from NS 1931. In NS, WH and CP 1936 the title is *Autumn*.

p. 22. *The Burnt Leaves*: 'blue-eyed one' refers to Young's mother who died in 1925 (see also *The Flood*, p. 28).

p. 23. *The Evening Star*: rev. from BC 1926 (*The Star*), where line 5 read 'Within the branches, not behind', and an additional stanza followed stanza 1:

A star of such bright amplitude,
It followed with me through the wood;
All other stars before its sphere
Pale as their own reflections were,
And Plough by pebbly fallow spurned
High in the sky lay overturned.

(In Young's Scottish accent 'wood' rhymed perfectly with 'amplitude').

p. 23. *Late Autumn*: rep. from BC 1926.

p. 24. *On White Down*: the line 'Wind chilling my premonitory blood' uses a favourite image that appears also in the early poem *Autumn* (p. 116); related images occur in *A Barrow on the Quantocks* (p. 18) and *Twilight* (p. 102).

p. 24. *Illic Jacet*: slightly rev. in WH 1933, and further rev. in CP 1936, from NS 1931, where it read:

Stanza 1, line 2: 'One moth-bright eye'

Stanza 2:

His door I never crossed
But still preferred
Some prehistoric ghost
Or even a bird.

Stanza 4, line 1: 'But still he often says'

In NS and WH 'Jacet' (he lies) was misprinted 'Jacit' (he throws). The poem is about a friend who had a country cottage and said 'Drop in on us'; it was written shortly after the friend's funeral. Young probably took the title from A. E. Housman's poem *Illic Jacet*.

p. 26. *The Yellow-Hammers*: rev. from BC 1926 where stanza 5 lines 2 and 3 read:

> I stood awhile, becalmed in a deep muse,
> Thinking how I had served so sweet a use,

p. 26. *Loch Brandy*: rev. from NS 1931, where line 2 read 'From rock to dripping rock'.

p. 28. *The Last Leaf*: rep. from BC 1926.

p. 28. *The Flood*: rep. from BC 1926; another reference to Young's mother, 'blue-eyed one' (see also *The Burnt Leaves*, p. 22).

p. 29. *The Pines*: rev. from NS 1931, where stanza 2 line 5 read 'Save for the still rustle of snow'; further rev. from WH 1933, where lines 2 and 3 read:

> Where a light falls in pallid lines,
> Were struck by the sunlight at noon,

The poem was inspired by the famous Ballochbuie Forest near Braemar.

p. 29. *The Signpost*: rep. from NS 1931.

p. 31. *THE WHITE BLACKBIRD* (Cape, 1935) contains thirty-one new poems and thirteen rep. or rev. from poems in earlier books. Rep. in CP 1936 with a few poems slightly rev.

p. 31. *The Dark Wood*: in WB 1935 and in CP 1936 called *The Wood*.

p. 33. *The Loddon*: rev. from BC 1926, where stanza 1 line 5 read 'Like buried eels have their roots sunk', and stanza 3 read:

> This way or that – But O let come
> May that on greening boughs lies dumb,
> This water drifting to the sea
> Shall keep of us no memory
> Who by these pollards on the flat
> Follow our whim this way or that.

p. 34. *Stay, Spring*: much rev. from NS 1931 *O Spring!* (p. 150).

p. 35. *Sea Wormwood*: rev. from NS 1931, where stanza 1 read:

> It grew about my feet
> Changing the bitter of the sea to sweet,
> The sea's scent that is bitter
> Though no flower could be sweeter;
> And when I turned inland
> Its loosened scent was hanging on my hand.

p. 36. *The Swans*: Of this poem, one of his best-known, Young said it was 'saved from being nothing but pleasant-sounding by the somewhat paradoxical idea of the last line' (BBC reading, 1961).

p. 36. *The Slow Race*: much rev. from NS 1931, *The Stour* (p. 150).

p. 37. *The Sunbeams*: rev. from CC 1928 where it had 3 stanzas; last stanza the same, but stanzas 1 and 2 read:

The tired road climbed the hill
To where green rolling clouds hung still
Nursing blue thunder in their bosoms;
But O the sunny-footed blossoms
That on the idle needles of the wood
Danced or in bright expectance stood.

Old wrinkled trees in umbered shades
Ogled each other with gay oeillades
And gold mouths on the ground parted and singled
And ran together again and met and mingled
Two, three or five or seven
No other way than souls that love in heaven.

In WB 1935 stanza 1 lines 1 and 2 read:

I climbed by the tired road
Where light-spots in the hanger flowed

p. 38. *The Dead Crab*: rev. in CP 1936 from WB 1935, where line 4 read 'The long black eyes staring about'.

p. 38. *An Evening Walk*; rev. from NS 1931 where there were 3 stanzas; stanza 1 the same; stanzas 2 and 3 read:

I know it is the sunlight paints
The faces of these travelling saints,
A dying flame across the sky
Gilding the tall-towered cumuli;
But shall I hold in cold misprision
The calm, the beauty of their heavenward vision?

The soft clouds from their journey cease
As though partaking of the peace
That God Himself on earth has breathed,
On earth so strangely now bereaved
Of the old sin and strife and sorrow
That makes to-day to-day, to-morrow to-morrow.

This poem, recalling Wordsworth's *Stepping Westward* and *An Evening Walk*, was written at a time when Wordsworth was Young's favourite poet.

p. 40. *Thistledown*: rev. from BC 1926, *Ghosts* (p. 136).
p. 41. *To the River Dove*: much rev. from NS 1931, *The River Dove* (p. 149).
p. 41. *The Cuckoo*: rev. from BC 1926, where there were 3 stanzas; stanza 1 read:

The air was hot under the trees;
Where pale-skinned flints fell in loose screes
I stood. 'Joy, joy', shrilled the bird-voices,
'Love, love', hummed the air's hidden noises;
Each flower of white, sulphur and blue
Looked in my eye with 'You, you, you'.
Then first of spring and early still
'Cuckoo' called cuckoo from the hill.

This stanza shows the type of writing Young was strenuously excluding from his new work. Stanza 3 line 3 read 'That call so faint and far-away'; line 7 read 'Was gone already. Sparrow hopped' – the omission of articles was frequent in Young's early poems, possibly through the influence of C. M. Doughty whom he read avidly at that time.

p. 42. *Gossip*: much rev. (and improved) from *The Gate* in BC 1926, which read:

The wind's hand shook the gate
Impatiently as though in haste and late,
Shook and shook it, making it rattle;
But still the gate kept up the tittle-tattle,
Asking of this and that,
Tidings of hill, coppice and river-flat;
And all the wind could tell,
Of how the last leaves from the beech-trees fell,
Though where the trees were young
Or pruned in hedges brown leaves clung
Delaying autumn till the spring,
Of how the rooks with heavy-flapping wing
Followed the plough, of how the gamekeeper
Set flags of paper here and there and there
To frighten pheasants back into the wood,
All that I heard and understood,
But not why when it might by flying over
Have clasped the whole world like a lover,
The wind stood rattling at the gate
Impatiently as though in haste and late.

p. 47. *The Secret Wood*: much rev. from NS 1931, *In the Spinney* (p. 157).
p. 48. *On Middleton Edge*: in WB 1935, lines 1–3 read:

If this life-saving rock I hold
(To me pure gold)
Should yield too much to my embrace

p. 50. *Last Snow*: cf. opening couplet with *The Hanger*, stanza 3 lines 3 and 4 (p. 146).

p. 51. *The Fallen Tree*: much rev. from NS 1931, where it read:

The subtle shade crept in and out
And round about,
Dim trunk and tangled boughs
Quietly obsequious
To the time-keeping sun;
Now, tree, you with that shade are one.

Though you should leave behind
Nothing but smoke that by the wind
Distracted is not smoke,
Yet it was here, O oak –
Time too to nothing flies –
I found and ate those white wild strawberries.

p. 52. *NEW POEMS*, in *COLLECTED POEMS* (Cape, 1936). Of these seventeen so-called 'new' poems, ten were rep. or rev. from poems in earlier books.

p. 52. *Cuckoo in May*: cf. *This Cuckoo still will talk* (p. 164).

p. 52. *Autumn Seeds*: rev. from BC 1926, *The Seeds* (p. 138).

p. 53. *The Ventriloquists*: rev. from BC 1926, where last two lines read:

On air and listening ear and in my blood
That still its 'Here and there' sighed and 'Nowhere'.

p. 54. *The Nest*: rep. from NS 1931.

p. 55. *The Chalk-Cliff*: rev. from BC 1926 (*Sea-Stock*), where stanza 1 line 3 read 'Reared the erect white chalk-cliff with flints lined', and stanza 3 read:

Like a soul strayed in Paradise
Dazed by deep light
I held my hand to shade my blinded eyes,
Till I saw how the white
Hardness of chalk
Was purpled by sea-stock.

p. 55. *The Chalk-Quarry*: rev. from NS 1931, where there was an additional opening stanza:

Through the wood's leafy lattice
The watery light-spots spill
On pale gold candelabra of wood-lettuce
And prickly stars of sanicle.

The picture was less clear in NS, stanza 3, where line 1 read 'The sun that darkens still', and line 4 read 'The sepulchre of the old chalk-quarry'.

p. 56. *Snow*: rep. from BC 1926.
p. 57. *South Downs*: rep. from NS 1931.
p. 57. *August*: rev. from BC 1926, where there were two extra stanzas (3 and 6), and a different reading of stanza 5 (stanza 4 in rev. version):

Stanza 3: Trees with the soot of August suns were black
Though splashed in places with a bright fire-light;
I praised the daemon of that dim wood-track
Where pepper moths were flittering by night.

Stanza 5: No leaf in the least breath of wind was turning
But foliage hung on trees like heavy wigs;
White sun, fringed with long rainbow hairs, was burning
Inflammable leaves and the light-blackened twigs.

Stanza 6: From that small sun patching the wood with light –
O strange to think! – hung all things that have breath,
Trees, insects, cows, even moths that fly by night
And men, and life in every form, and death.

p. 58. *February*: rev. from BC 1926, *January* (p. 125).
p. 59. *The Missel-Thrush*: rev. from CC 1928, where stanza 2 lines 3–6 read:

Incurious
To see far down under the boughs
A creature come
Aquatic, eel-like and so dumb.

p. 60. *Man and Cows*: Hathor (misprinted Hethor in earlier editions) was the cow-goddess of Egyptian mythology.

p. 62. *SPEAK TO THE EARTH* (Cape, 1939) contains a large proportion of new poems (thirty-five out of forty-three); the other eight poems are much rev. from earlier books. The title comes from the Book of Job: 'Speak to the earth and it shall teach thee'.

p. 64. *The Gramophone*: a re-working of a poem with the same title from NS 1931; the new version is an example of how Young condensed by omitting dead phrases, and sentimental and pietistic images. The earlier version read:

Now starlings roost thick in the trees
As culverkeys
And from that farm a yellow spark
Tells it grows dark,

I think how you would often say,
'What shall I play?'
And nightingales would trill to us
From moonlit boughs.

But those same nightingales were dead,
When all is said,
Though their clear voices lingered on
Your gramophone.

So as by this dark track I go
Through dissolute snow
Your voice in me lingers awhile –
Dear saint, you smile;

You smile like that white star that now
Lights the hill-brow,
That only a dead voice should be
Your immortality.

p. 64. *Culbin Sands*: near Young's birthplace, Elgin. In 1694 a catastrophic sand-storm overwhelmed fields and houses at Culbin, so that people fled for their lives; on returning they found their houses buried and the land a desert.

p. 66. *Nightfall on Sedgemoor*: line 3: 'reen' in SE 1939 is amended to 'rhine' in CP 1950.

p. 68. *The Archaeologist*: rev. from NS 1931 (*The Celandines*) which read:

Haply they might dig up
Bacchus holding a vine-wreathed cup
Or helmeted chryselephantine goddess;
Some Venus too, divine and godless,
Might rise, helped by a rope, out of the sea;
Greek music's perished from all memory.

Why do I think of that
When kingcups flash from river-flat
And primrose leaves unwrinkle,
Blue twisted stars of periwinkle
Crawl under cottage hedge
And celandines shine from the coppice-edge?

These glitter with gold light
And sharpen, as is said, the swallow's sight;
I am not like that twittering bird,
Too clear a memory my eyes has blurred;
Not this side heaven I'll see again
Celandines shine by an English lane.

p. 68. *Cuckoos*: Young said that to avoid writing about Nature in too sentimental a way he sometimes affected a certain whimsicality, as in speaking of the mocking call of cuckoos in this poem (BBC reading, 1961).

p. 69. *The Swallows*: in SE 1939 the title was *The House-Martins*, and stanza 2 line 1 read 'House-martins twisting here and there'.

p. 69. *Wiltshire Downs* uses material from two poems in CC 1928, *Cuckoo Bottom* (p. 139) and *Downland Shepherd* (p. 146).

p. 72. *Drought in the Fens*: lines 1–4 are taken from *Audley End* (CC 1928).

p. 73. *Passing the Graveyard*: rev. from BC 1926 *Findon* (p. 132); lines 1–3 are rev. from BC, (*On the Hillside*), where the last three lines read:

> I never went to my friend's funeral,
> Though crossing the churchyard to-day I shivered
> To see how fast on a fresh grave the flowers had withered.

p. 75. *The Thunderstorm*: rev. and condensed from BC 1926 (*Walna Pass*) where the last (4th) stanza read:

> Then when I came to Walna Pass
> With hail that hissed and hopped among the grass
> The thunder-storm exploded close beside me;
> Snatching the least shelter that would hide me
> Between two stones I laid my head
> And lay like one awaking from the dead.

p. 79. *Idleness*: some lines quarried from BC 1926, *Rooks* (p. 126). Young said of this poem: 'That I speak of a wall as being made of stones which were once shells and bones in the sea shows that it was written in a limestone country, actually the Mendips' (BBC reading, 1961). Walter de la Mare admired the poem, from which he unconsciously 'lifted' two lines; *The Owl*, the last poem in his last book, *O Lovely England*, refers to 'exquisite pregnant idleness', and ends:

> Hark, now! that owl a-snoring in his tree,
> Till it grow dark enough for him to see.

p. 80. *A Wet Day*: rev. and condensed from BC 1926 (*The Sign*), where stanza 3 read:

> Then turning on my steps, startled I stood
> To see a dead man hanging in that wood;
> Clear from the ground by two free feet of air
> By hat and coat I marked him swinging there.
> Who was that man? I lifted hasty eye;
> Heaven laughed to me from the blue-rifted sky.

p. 83. *Christmas Day*: rev. from CC 1928 (*Christmas Eve*), where there were five stanzas: first stanza almost the same; stanzas 2 and 3 read:

First came in the shepherds
  And snow-flakes on their hair
Seemed the white angels' feathers
  That fell through the dark air.

Next came in the Magi
  And the gold crowns they wore
They took off in deep silence
  And laid upon the floor.

Stanzas 4 and 5 in CC were similar to stanzas 2 and 3 in SE; the final stanza in SE is completely new. Young chose this poem as the last in CC, SE and CP 1950. It has been set to music by Neil Butterworth, Robin Milford and Mervyn Roberts.

p. 84. *THE GREEN MAN* (Cape, 1947) contains thirty-eight poems, twenty-seven of them new.

p. 84. *Hard Frost*: written during the winter of 1939, using war-time imagery ('ferny ambushes', 'fish interned'). Young said he thought this poem illustrated the two main things he aimed at in writing short Nature poems: 'a certain strangeness . . . a likeness in unlikeness', and 'to use as few words as possible . . . terseness' (BBC reading, 1961).

p. 85. *In Avebury Circle*: slightly rev. from NS 1931. In Young's personal copy of NS an improved version of stanza 1 is pencilled in his writing:

Whitened by clouds [that] blow
From cottages thick-thatched with snow
A ghost myself I meet
This great stone monster without head, wings, feet.

p. 85. *Field-Glasses*: lines 1–2, cf. NS 1931, *The Teasels* (p. 155). Another version called *The Field-Glass* was published in *Horizon*, Jan. 1941; the last stanza read:

Waking from winter sloth
Trees stretch themselves with magic growth,
And as I watch them shake
I see, but cannot hear, the sound they make.

p. 88. *A Shot Magpie*: an earlier version entitled *A Dead Magpie* appeared in *The Nineteenth Century*, Mar. 1939:

Bird, though on brightest morning
  And on your nuptial flight
You always wore half-mourning
  Of a staid black and white,

Of death you had no care,
   Not even when your own
Feathers fell through the air
   Surer than a stone.

p. 89. *In Moonlight*: rev. from *Thirty-One Poems* 1922 (*Full Moon*). Stanzas 1 and 2 the same, except for the first line ('The raindrops pattered on the trees;). In GM 1947 stanzas 3 and 4 replace stanza 3, which read:

So through the night walked three of us
   By earth and air and sky,
Dim shadow and moon luminous
   And in between them I.

p. 91. *The Blind Man*: this epigram is derived from a rather diffuse poem, *The Old Man*, in BC 1926, where the following lines occur:

But when he raised a listening finger
Each bird-note in the silence seemed to linger
Till to each one he gave a name;
Though he was blind he knew them all the same.

Cf. also *The Blind Man* (p. 170).

p. 92. *The Shepherd's Hut*: commenting on this poem, Young wrote 'There is something very affecting about a shepherd's hut situated at the far head of a lonely glen. Such a hut I came across in the wilds of Sutherland. But I had to write about it in a somewhat fanciful way so as to avoid being sentimental' (MS. undated). Another poem called *The Shepherd's Hut* appeared in SE 1939 (p. 65).

p. 94. *The Shower*: rev. from CC 1928, where there were two stanzas; the first as in GM 1947, the second as follows:

Now when the last shower-drops have ceased
And the smooth Medway lies uncreased
Fish raise round ripples like the first
Drops of a storm about to burst.

The poem in CC is dedicated to Miss V. Sackville-West, probably because Young had been influenced (lines 3 and 4) by these lines in her poem *The Land*, which had recently appeared:

A ghostly orchard standing all in white,
Aisles of white trees, white branches, in the green.

Young's short poems from WH 1933 onwards carry no dedications.

p. 94. *At Formby*: rev. from NS 1931, where it read:

How strange to walk that shore
No foot had ever trod before
Or since the sea drew back the tide;
It seemed so vast, lonely and wide
As though God were not there
To mitigate that empty sea and air.

Strange too on the coastland
Those pines no higher than my hand;
Though as I walked the trees grew taller
And I myself grew small and smaller,
Till in a high dark wood
I seemed to find again my lost childhood.

p. 95. *The Revenant*: much rev. and improved from CC 1928 (*The Birds*). In stanza 2 'double-ganger', more familiar in its German form '*Doppelgänger*', is an eye-rhyme (the ear-rhyme is with 'hanger'). In *A Prospect of Death* (p. 82) Young rhymes 'stranger' with 'anger', but eye-rhymes are relatively uncommon in his poetry.

p. 97. *The Blind Children*: much rev. from BC 1926 *The Children* (p. 134), where some of the imagery is clearer than it is in the rev. version. The image of 'hazels' mealy leaves' is borrowed from NS 1931 *The Hill-Wood* (p. 152).

p. 97. *On the Hillside*: rev. from BC 1926. The last line resembles line 3 of *Passing the Graveyard* (p. 73).

p. 99. *View from Mountain*: much rev. from *Thirty-One Poems* 1922 *At Owley* (p. 123). The mountain is Canisp in the Western Highlands. Young wrote that the atmosphere on this mountain seemed to belong 'less to a material world than to a spiritual' (MS undated).

p. 100. *The Day Ends*: a reworking of material from two poems in BC 1926, *Pasque-Flower* (p. 128) and *The Day Ends*. 'Chill dews' is a favourite image, appearing again in *Twilight* (p. 102).

p. 100. *By the Erme*: much rev. from NS 1931 *On Dartmoor* (p. 153).

p. 107. *SONGS OF NIGHT* (De la More Press, London, 1910). Written while Young was at the University of Edinburgh.

p. 109. *Bacchos Chthonios* (Bacchus under the Earth). The quotation from Heraclitus is translated 'But Hades is the same as Dionysus [i.e. Bacchus] in whose honour they go mad and keep the feast of the wine-vat'. In the original this sentence follows one which means 'For if it were not to Dionysus that they made a procession and sang the shameful phallic hymn, they would be acting most shamelessly.'

p. 112. *The Leaf*: the only poem from *Songs of Night* in CP 1960. Young expressed surprise and some amusement at its inclusion by the editor.

p. 113. *BOAZ AND RUTH AND OTHER POEMS* (J. G. Wilson, London, 1920). Published in the year when Young moved from Scotland to Sussex. Most of the poems were probably written before the move and could have been written at any time between 1910 and 1920.

p. 116. *THE DEATH OF ELI AND OTHER POEMS* (J. G. Wilson, London, 1921).

p. 116. *Autumn*: 'premonitory blood': cf. *On White Down* (p. 24) and *Twilight* (p. 102).

p. 119. *THIRTY-ONE POEMS* (J. G. Wilson, London, 1922).

p. 119. *Epitaph*: written for an eight-year-old girl whose funeral Young conducted in 1921.

p. 119. *Cuckoo*: Young asked the editor of QM 1959 to replace 'thy' with 'your' in stanzas 1, 2 and 4, a change retained here. Lines 2 and 3 recall Wordsworth's cuckoo; 'bubble-note' (stanza 4) cf. *Wiltshire Downs* (p. 69).

p. 123. *At Owley*: cf. *View from Mountain* (p. 99).

p. 124. *Islands*: in this, the final poem in *Thirty-One Poems* 1922, Young seems to be aware that he is at last finding his true voice.

p. 125. *THE BIRD-CAGE* (J. & E. Bumpus Ltd, London, 1926). The contents list is in three sections entitled Spring, Summer and Autumn.

p. 125. *Go now, my Song*: an introductory poem before the contents list of BC.

p. 125. *January*: cf. *February* (p. 58).

p. 126. *Rooks*: cf. *Idleness* (p. 79).

p. 128. *Pasque-Flower*: cf. *The Day Ends* (p. 100).

p. 129. *June*: To Alison, his daughter, on her fourth birthday.

p. 130. *July*: CP 1960 and CP 1974 omitted the last three lines of stanza 2 and the first three of stanza 3. The editor described this as a 'revised version', but the omission breaks the rhyme scheme. Young apparently did not notice this; in old age he was no longer deeply involved in his short poems.

p. 130. *The Young Martins*: lines 25–26 cf. *The Crow* (p. 168).

p. 132. *Findon*: cf. *Passing the Graveyard* (p. 73).

p. 134. *The Children*: cf. *The Blind Children* (p. 97).

p. 135. *Night-Flowering Campion*; stanzas 4 and 5 are a surprising reversion to the mode of *Songs of Night* 1910. Young was apparently aware of the uneven quality of this poem, for in *A Retrospect of Flowers* 1950 he quotes the first and last stanzas, but revises the content of the middle stanzas in racier prose.

p. 136. *Ghosts*; cf. *Thistledown* (p. 40).

p. 138. *The Seeds*: cf. *Autumn Seeds* (p. 52).

p. 139. *THE CUCKOO CLOCK* (J. &. E. Bumpus Ltd, London, 1928).

p. 139. *Cuckoo-Bottom*: cf. *Wiltshire Downs* (p. 69).

p. 140. *The Moon*: this poem and *Restalrig* (p. 157) are Young's only poems in Scottish dialect.

p. 141. *Kilnaughton Bay*: Young uses the image of winking in several poems; he was fond of communicating silently with children by poker-faced winking.

p. 142. *Osea Island*: dedicated (rather formally) 'to Mrs Debnam'. This was Young's sister Margaret, who lived at Chelmsford.

p. 146. *Downland Shepherd*: cf. *Wiltshire Downs* (p. 69).

p. 149. *THE NEW SHEPHERD* (J. & E. Bumpus Ltd, London, 1931). The image of the shepherd seems to have had a special significance for Young. While at Temple he was much attracted to the life of the farming community there.

p. 149. *The River Dove*: cf. *To the River Dove* (p. 41).

p. 150. *The Stour*: cf. *The Slow Race* (p. 36).

p. 150. *O Spring!* cf. *Stay, Spring* (p. 34).

p. 152. *The Hill-Wood*: stanza 3, lines 2–4 cf. *The Blind Children* (p. 97).

p. 153. *On Dartmoor*: cf. *By the Erme* (p. 100).

p. 154. *The Flint-Breaker*: dedicated to Miss Viola Meynell.

p. 155. *The Teasels*; cf. *Field-Glasses* (p. 85).

p. 156. *Grime's Graves*: cf. *At Grime's Graves* (p. 169).

p. 157. *In the Spinney*: cf. *The Secret Wood* (p. 47).

pp. 161, 161, 162. *Late Summer*, *Sea Birds* & *Friston Church*; from Janet Young's MS books. Probably written in early or mid twenties. First printed in CP 1974.

p. 163. *The Cobweb*: from the dust-jacket of BC 1926. It refers to several poems in the book, and might well have been intended as a kind of blurb.

p. 164. *This Cuckoo Still Will Talk*: from a letter to John Freeman, April 1927. Cf. *Cuckoo in May* (p. 52). Unpublished.

p. 164. *In the New Forest*: from a letter to John Freeman, August 1927. Unpublished.

p. 165. *At Newlands Corner*: from a letter to Gordon Bottomley, April 1929. Young quotes the first two lines of this poem in *A Prospect of Britain* and *The New Poly-Olbion*. Otherwise unpublished.

p. 165. *Drosera Anglica*: from a letter to J. W. Haines, 1935. Unpublished.

p. 165. *While Doubters Ask*; published (with title *He Dwelleth In –*) in *The Observer*, 2 June, 1940.

p. 165. *By a British Barrow in Wartime*: in *The Nineteenth Century*, July 1940, and CP 1960. Young did not consider it good enough for GM 1947, but it is rep. here because it contains one of Young's rare references to the war, which he links with his recurrent imagery of death and burial.

p. 166. *The Bleeding Nun*: MSS (unpublished) in National Library of Scotland and in Berg Collection, New York; the latter has the following introductory lines, with which Young was at one time intending to introduce the episode in *Into Hades*:

I stiffened; but a voice, Remember, read,
So probed the memory it grew inflamed;
I was again the trembling boy
Who, scarcely daring to put out the light,
Crept upstairs to the safety of my bed
To read the story.

Date of composition unknown. Young's fascination with the links between adventure, horror, blood, religion and the supernatural are concentrated in this poem.

p. 168. *The Crow*: in *The Nineteenth Century*, March 1945. Cf. *The Young Martins* (p. 130), lines 25–26.

p. 168. *Suilven*: from *A Retrospect of Flowers*, 1950.

p. 168. *Hymn*: written for the BBC Hymn Book, 1951; in CP 1960. Young was unhappy about its position at the end of that collection. He wrote to the editor, Leonard Clark: 'What I do repeat is that the Hymn should not come last. Can you not strain a point?' Presumably he felt the poem was not representative of his mature style. The Hymn has been set to music by Lennox Berkeley, Herbert Howells and Cyril Taylor.

p. 169. *In the Dingle*: in CP 1960, slightly rev. from *A Prospect of Britain*, 1956 (*A Radnorshire Dingle*).

p. 169. *At Grime's Graves*: from *A Prospect of Britain*, 1956. In CP 1960. Cf. NS 1931, *Grime's Graves* (p. 156), also the passage from *Into Hades* quoted on p. 332 of the Notes.

p. 170. *The Blind Man*: from QM 1959. Rev. from BC 1926 *The Old Man*. Cf. also GM, *The Blind Man* (p. 91).

p. 170. *Pevensey*: from *The New Poly-Olbion*, 1967. Rev. from NS 1931 (*The Sea*), where the last four lines read:

My footsteps keep so harsh a speech
With these loose miles and miles of beach
I think that it is still the sea
That follows me.

p. 171. *At Arley*: MS in National Library of Scotland. In CP 1974.

p. 171. *In Wingfield Manor*: MS in Berg Collection, New York. Unpublished.

p. 172. *Two Prose Poems*; from *The New Poly-Olbion*, 1967. Young referred to the short essays in the book as 'prose poems'.

p. 177. *MEMORIAL VERSES*, from *CECIL BARCLAY SIMPSON: A MEMORIAL BY TWO FRIENDS*, Edinburgh (privately printed) 1918. The other friend was D. M. Baillie, who wrote a prose tribute. Simpson was a fellow student at New College in Edinburgh; he was killed in October 1917 on active service in France.

p. 184. *THE ADVERSARY* (J. G. Wilson, London, 1923). Also contains *RIZPAH*. As late as 1932 Young was intending to revise *The Adversary*.

p. 227. *NICODEMUS: A Mystery*, with incidental music by Imogen Holst, (Cape, 1937; rep. in CP 1950).

p. 230. *I am not blind except I cannot see*: a paradox typical of Young and such mystics as St John of the Cross. As a child Young lay blind for a long time with erysipelas. The theme of blindness haunts many of his poems.

p. 263. *THE SIRENS*: unpublished; intended as a children's play for radio.

p. 266. *OUT OF THE WORLD AND BACK: INTO HADES AND A TRAVELLER IN TIME: TWO POEMS* (Hart-Davis, 1958). An earlier version of *INTO HADES* (Hart-Davis, 1952) was extensively revised for the 1958 edition, which we have used. It is beyond the scope of these notes to give a detailed account of the revisions, or of the numerous references in both poems to mythology and to mystical literature. Some information, however, is provided on a few recondite references and on matters related to Young's life. In an introductory note to the 1958 volume Young wrote: 'When the spring of short Nature poems ran dry, I was not altogether sorry; for while my interest in Nature was intense, it was not as deep as the underlying interest that prompted me to change my style and write *Into Hades*.'

p. 270. *Palmerin of England*: a romance written in the sixteenth century by a Spanish or Portuguese author. It was one of the tales of knight-errantry cherished by Don Quixote. Young enjoyed reading it in his youth.

p. 271. *Bernard de Morlaix* (also known as Bernard of Cluny, or Morval, or Morlass), a monk of Cluny in the twelfth century, wrote a long poem (*De Contemptu Mundi*) on the transitoriness of life on earth, in rhymed dactylic verse; it was the source of some well-known hymns, including *Jerusalem the Golden*.

p. 273. *In the twilight, in the evening*: a quotation from Proverbs (vii, 8–10) 'and he went the way to her house, in the twilight, in the evening, in the black and dark night: and, behold, there met him a woman with the attire of an harlot'. Young's account of his resistance to such temptations by the mediation of a mystical female presence is modified here from its statement in the first version of *Into Hades*, which was as follows:

> I found her most in Paris; in the unfamiliar,
> half out of the world already, I starved myself,
> a St John the Baptist in the Latin Quarter,
> to break out to the prospect, the fulfilment.
> I was immune by night;
> she cooled me *in the twilight, in the evening*
> more than the corpses set up in the Morgue

(In the 1958 edition Young reverts to his usual practice of starting each line with a capital letter).

p. 274. *The old boat*: there was a disused boat in the pond by which Young used to write in the garden of Stonegate Vicarage.

p. 275. *The house was filled with smoke*: Isaiah 6, iv.

p. 280. *Hermotimus* (of Clazomenae): Greek philosopher of the sixth century BC, probably the first to suggest that mind is the cause of all things. According to Lucian and Pliny he could detach his soul and send it on long journeys: during one of these, his enemies burned his body, leaving his soul homeless on its return.

p. 284. *The Terrible Crystal*: see Ezekiel 1. ii.

p. 286. In *Into Hades* (1952) the last section (*The Last Look*) opens with the following lines:

First thought was of that night
I came through moonwasht Breckland to Grime's Graves,
where prehistoric flint-flakes looking as fresh
as though the dead men were on holiday
glinted in moonlight with green snaky eye;
but the broken lights that welcomed me on waking
shone from themselves, peculiar, mother-of-pearl,
friendly. They even hinted their strange nature,
outlandish fragments, thin echoing reflections
of the Terrible Crystal. I stooped to one glow-worm,
but it darted away. Challenged to walk on space,
I was stumbling after the fire-fly, when my feet
struck stone. It danced down a dark broken stair
to hang itself, a lamp over a door.

I recognised the signal.
My Monitor, if he was not myself,
the primal self who never had left heaven,
was gone; my sleep, first broken at the lych-gate,
was inviting my downward step.

Some of the imagery of this passage, discarded in the version of 1958, was used again in the poem *Grime's Graves* (p. 156).

p. 289. *Herod was not so startled*: there is another reference to John the Baptist, whose history fascinated Young, in *Nicodemus* (p. 228), where Andrew raises the cover from a dish of eels, and says, 'See, they have lost their heads like John the Baptist.'

p. 292. *St Goar*: (misprinted *St Gear* in the 1958 edition and in CP 1974); a sixth-century hermit from S. Germany who was said to have hung his vestments on a beam, 'radius', later interpreted as a sunbeam.

p. 294. *I was no Achilles*: cf. Pindar, Nemean Odes No. 3, in which the six-year-old Achilles is seen, as a pupil of the centaur Cheiron, excelling in fleetness of foot and hunting down lion and wild boar.

p. 296. *Iacche, Iacche*: Iacchus was a demigod associated with the Eleusinian mysteries, sometimes identified with Dionysus (Bacchus). There is a link here with Young's early Swinburnian verses to Zagreus and Bacchus, and a link between the cults of intoxication and mysticism.

p. 297. *Korè*: another name for Persephone.

p. 300. *Mount Gerizim*; where Jotham pronounced the parable of the trees (Judges, 9)

p. 304. *I am that dead brother/You never knew*: Young told a correspondent that he had introduced his brother William, who died in infancy, 'to suggest that those who die young have a mature future'; he also said that he presented William as head and shoulders 'merely for dramatic effect'.

p. 314. *The Cloud of Unknowing*: the authorship of this fourteenth-century English mystical work is unknown.

p. 314. *Richard Rolle*; the English mystic (fourteenth century); in *The Fire of Love* he spoke of three spiritual moods, Heat, Sweetness and Song.

p. 314. *Caterina Serafina*; St Catherine of Genoa (1447–1510), whose biographers, Cattaneo Marabotto and Ettore Vernazza, referred to her as 'this glorious Seraphin'.

p. 314. *I die because I cannot die*: the refrain '*Que muero porque no muero*' of a poem by St John of the Cross (verses about the soul which suffers with impatience to see God).

p. 314. *Meister Eckhart*: German mystic and philosopher of the thirteenth to fourteenth century.

INDEX OF FIRST LINES

Heinemann A461.756 17/5/85.